CHURCHILL IN AMERICA

Robert H. Pilpel

CHURCHILL IN AMERICA

1895-1961

An Affectionate Portrait

HARCOURT BRACE JOVANOVICH

NEW YORK AND LONDON

Printed in the United States of America

Library of Congress Cataloging in Publication Data
Pilpel, Robert.
Churchill in America, 1895–1961.
Bibliography: p.
Includes index.
1. Churchill, Winston Leonard Spencer, Sir,
1894–1965. I. Title.
DA566.9.C5P54   941.082'092'4 [B]   76-21239
ISBN 0-15-117880-1

First edition

B C D E

To Judy Appelbaum and Julian Muller
for the gift of faith
and to
Lord Goodman of Westminster, C.H.,
for the gift of Anglophilia

Contents

Past and Prologue
By Way of Introduction

I WAS TWELVE YEARS OLD when Winston Churchill retired as Prime Minister in 1955 and twenty-one when he died. He was a gigantic figure, of course, but to me no more real and immediate than comparable titans such as Caesar, Napoleon, and Alexander. It was only after his death, paradoxically enough, that I came to know him.

I first encountered the man in his role as historian. I was a hopelessly dégagé law student casting about for mental sustenance, something or anything to distract me from accumulated precedents and split hairs. One day in the Yale bookstore I ran across a boxed paperback edition of his *Second World War* volumes, on sale at the memorably reasonable price of $6.95. I took the plunge, returned to my room, and cracked the binding of *The Gathering Storm*. Five thousand pages later I was hungry for more.

How can I describe this first encounter with Churchill and Churchill's style? First of all and most striking was the feeling of warm communion that enveloped me as I started to read, an almost immediate sensation of fraternal intimacy, of being taken into confidence as a fellow member of the English-speaking tribe. Then there was the wonderful Britishness of expression: the robust roast-beef-and-pewter phrases, rolling cadences, portentous Latinate locutions—alien yet eerily familiar, the echo of a racial memory. Before long I caught sparkles of irrepressible humor percolating through the majestic narrative façade, as though Puck had escaped from *A Midsummer Night's Dream* and infiltrated *Paradise Lost*. Long before I turned the last page of *Triumph and Tragedy* my impression of Churchill had crystallized: so forcefully had his personality come through in his writing that he emerged more alive to me than all contemporary statesmen put together. Whether this was due to the way I am or the way he was— or the way they are—is difficult to say; most probably all three factors are involved. Whatever the explanation, though, the fact remains: I felt I knew him. To be sure, I did not know him quite as well as I presumed, but that was unimportant. What really mattered was not how much I knew, but that all I knew I liked.

Not long after I finished *Triumph and Tragedy* Sir Winston died, and the spate of books, magazine articles, and newspaper features that followed hard upon his passing introduced me to the rough outlines of the adventure that had been his life. It seemed to me that his ninety years had been almost incredibly full and rich: wife, children, books, glory, power, worldwide adulation, and a peaceful old age—all the gifts that could be bestowed by a prodigal and beneficent fate. Had I been older I might have realized that such bounty is by no means proof against the rigors of the human condition, but my ignorance served me well at the time, for I felt compelled to learn more about this phenomenally perfect life, and more about the man who had lived it.

After an interval of five years, during which I became, by turns, an attorney, an Air Force officer, a Fulbright fellow, and a Rome-based writer, my unforgotten quest led me to pick up the first volume of Churchill's official biography, written by his only son, Randolph. This book, along with the diaries of Churchill's physician, which appeared contemporaneously in 1966, revealed to me for the first time an aspect of Sir Winston's existence that contrasted sharply with everything I had hitherto read about him. Here was not the brilliant comet of twentieth-century British politics, the freewheeling hero of cavalry, the scribe, wit, laugher, fighter, and sage; here instead was an emotionally mangled little boy who grew to a tortured manhood, a desperately ambitious naïf whose every accomplishment was but a futile exercise in the avoidance of self-contempt. The life had not been so august and untrammeled after all; there had been suffering, misfortune, defeat, bereavement, and despair—the agonies of a tormented soul who never dared confront the psychic demons that were pursuing him.

Looked at in this light, Churchill became a more flawed, more recognizable, more sympathetic, and, in the final analysis, more admirable person than the avuncular giant I had conjured up under the spell of his writings. I saw him now as the supreme sublimator, a man whose neurotic afflictions kept him enslaved to the dictates of achievement but whose genius turned his servitude to the benefit of mankind. I also saw a new dimension to his courage, a sort of blind, dogged resistance to capitulation: primitive, almost brutish. But also magnificent. There was something at the core of the man, beneath logic, beneath intellect, beneath emotion, something ferocious and elemental that kept him fighting long after heart, mind, and spirit had been bludgeoned past insensibility. It was not an edifying quality, nor necessarily a noble one, but it called forth in me a strong visceral surging of pride, a sense of exaltation. Battered, stumbling, hopeless—yet unquelled: this is what it meant to be a man.

There was another feature of Randolph Churchill's volume that fascinated me, and that was his account of the first trips his father made to the United States. I had not known that Winston visited America twice during Queen Victoria's reign, and there was something intriguing about the thought of his coming here as an unheralded young Englishman, a "Winston Churchill" in ordinary type, so to speak. To me, a child of World War II, he had always been "Winston Spencer Churchill," in headlines, and his comings and goings had always been momentous occasions of state. In the biography, however, I glimpsed an altogether different figure roaming around my native country. Here was the legend in its chrysalis, its true lineaments enshrouded in a cocoon of time. Here was the headline. Winston Churchill, immanent yet concealed in his small-type aspect, and free to travel anonymously all over his mother's homeland like any average visitor—free to travel and free to write letters home.

Think, had Bismarck or Napoleon or even Hitler come to

the United States in their younger days, how exciting it would
be to chance upon a written record of their impressions. Well,
Churchill was of comparable historical magnitude, and there,
in extenso, was the record before me. "What an extraordinary
people the Americans are!" he had written, and in letter after
letter he elaborated and enlarged upon this theme.

Numerous as the letters were, they were not nearly numerous enough to answer the questions they raised in my
mind or to satisfy my curiosity. What had *we* thought of *him*
back at the turn of the century? What changes did his feelings
toward us undergo as he grew in political stature, and how
did we react to the ebb and flux of his personal fortunes?
What did America mean to Winston Churchill over the years,
and what did Winston Churchill mean to us?

The answers to questions like these, it seemed to me, were
not to be found in official testimonials or trans-Atlantic pro-
testations of affection. The fact that Churchill and the United
States had been passionately fond of one another was obvious,
and all the bouquets thrown back and forth across the ocean
did little more than make it more so. In any case, what the
parties to a love affair say to or about each other conveys at
best a very limited idea of what their relationship is really
like. If one concentrates not on what they say, however, but
on how they behave when they are together, one can learn
a great deal about them, more even than they may care to
have one know.

Churchill and this country were "together" some fifteen
times over the course of sixty-five years, and this book is
about their encounters. Winston came here first as a boy of
twenty and again as a young politician of twenty-five. He
came twice in his fifties and four times during World War II.
At age seventy-one he warned of an iron curtain, and at age
eighty-six he said good-bye. Throughout this span of years his
attachment to the United States grew in intensity, and, by the
time of his final visit to America, our attachment to him was
indissoluble.

Churchill in America, then, is an affectionate portrait of an
affectionate couple. It is part biography, part chronicle, part
opinion and surmise. It is as accurate as I could make it and

as objective as my veneration would permit. It presents opinions of mine about people and events that are no more preposterous, I trust, than those expressed by men of far greater wisdom and erudition. It is neither definitive nor revelational. Its object is to convey some measure of the delight and inspiration I have derived from my association with a very great man, a man who is dead but who lived with such verve and exultancy that his memory has become my friend.

Part One

BOY AND MAN

CHAPTER ONE

First Encounter

ON SATURDAY, NOVEMBER 9, 1895, the Cunard Royal Mail steamship *Etruria* glided through the Narrows into New York Harbor bearing a sensitive, driven, opinionated young subaltern in Her Majesty's 4th Hussars. He was but three weeks shy of his twenty-first birthday and had borne the loss of his father, his maternal grandmother, and his adored nursemaid all in the space of the prior ten months. His psyche reeled under two decades of parental neglect and denigration, yet he was about to embark on seven decades of achievement and controversy that would render him unique in twentieth-century annals. He was to suffer greatly, endure many defeats, display unmatched courage, and utter imperishable words. Now he gazed for the first time on the nation and the city that had fostered his mother. A troubled childhood, an anguished adolescence, and an unenviable scholastic record lay behind him. His life, in a very real sense, was about to begin.

His name was Winston Churchill.

Back in the halcyon days of the Victorian era, cavalry officers were allowed five months' leave a year, and a good ten weeks of that could be taken in a lump. Junior officers were "encouraged" to pass their winter furloughs chasing foxes around Buckinghamshire, an activity that required them to spend quite a lot while accomplishing only a little and thus prepared them for greater military responsibilities. Churchill, however, along with a fellow second lieutenant, Reginald Barnes, made other plans. As he wrote thirty-five years later,

"When I joined the 4th Hussars in January, 1895, scarcely a captain, hardly even a subaltern, could be found throughout Her Majesty's forces who had seen even the smallest kind of war ... [and the] want of a sufficient supply of active service was therefore acutely felt.... The general peace in which mankind had for so many years languished was broken only in one quarter of the globe...."[1]

That quarter was Cuba.

"My dearest Mamma," Winston scribbled in October. "I daresay you will find the content of this letter somewhat startling." Thus ever have aspiring young soldiers of fortune begun their attempts to get around their formidable mothers. "I have decided to go with a great friend of mine ... to America and the West Indies.... We shall go to ... Havana where all the [Spanish] Government troops are collecting to go up country and suppress the revolt that is still simmering on...."[2]

"My dearest Winston," Jennie replied a week later. "You know I am always delighted if you can do anything which interests & amuses you—even if it be a sacrifice to me ... *but* ..." Thus ever have formidable mothers squelched the attempts of aspiring young soldiers of fortune to get around them. "Considering that I provide the funds," Jennie continued, "I think instead of saying 'I *have* decided to go' it may have been nicer & perhaps wiser—to have begun by consulting me. But I suppose experience of life will in time teach you that tact is a very essential ingredient in all things."[3]

Although experience of life was to teach Winston Churchill a great many lessons—despite his apparent penchant for learning the hard way—tact was not destined to be one of them. Whatever aptitude for it he may have been endowed with at birth had been quickly subordinated to the task of psychological survival, a task which, given his parents' indifference and disapproval, demanded a large proportion of his psychic resources.

In upper-class Victorian England, children were supposed to be seen and not heard, but not seen too much. They were treated somewhat like prize farm animals: well fed, well groomed, well trained and cared for, but not the sort of creatures one wanted in one's drawing room. Once or twice a day they were to be visited and inspected, and their handlers— nursemaids, governesses, tutors—given fresh instructions. But until they approached maturity their propensity to be "awkward," that is, to make noise or be openly affectionate (tantamount to soiling the rug), excluded them from that peculiarly English *ballo in maschera* called "polite society."

Winston was simply too high spirited and intelligent to acquiesce in this state of affairs, and his intransigence cost him dearly. Even his birth had been awkward. It came at Blenheim Palace in the middle of the St. Andrew's Day Ball— at 1:30 A.M., to be precise, on November 30, 1874, a date that succeeded the marriage of Miss Jennie Jerome of Brooklyn, New York, to the rising young politician Lord Randolph Churchill by only seven and a half months. "As the weight at birth does not seem to have been recorded," an eminent biographer has commented, "or if recorded has not been revealed... we must suspend judgment on whether this was simply the first instance of Winston's impetuosity or whether it also involved yet another example of Lord Randolph's."[4]

Randolph Spencer Churchill was the popeyed, brilliant, and erratic third son of the seventh Duke of Marlborough. Blenheim Palace was his ancestral home, "the gift of a grateful nation" to his illustrious ancestor John Churchill, the first Duke. Both he and his American wife were among the brightest of the glittering social fireflies that swarmed round the figure of Albert Edward, Prince of Wales (later King Edward VII), and neither was at all squeamish about extramarital adventures. This was just as well, given the Prince's habit of regularly exercising his unwritten *droit de seigneur*, but several years after the birth of Winston's brother, Jack, in 1880, one of Lord Randolph's adulterous excursions resulted in his contracting syphilis, and whatever scarce family feeling existed in the Churchill household up to that time now rapidly dwindled away with his sanity.

Winston's problems with his parents had begun long before his father's health started to deteriorate, however. In fact, they had begun almost as soon as his nascent personality began to manifest itself. His clamorous demands for attention, for stimulation, for love, were completely incompatible with Victorian notions of childhood propriety. He had too much energy, too much imagination, too much initiative, too much ingenuity. He was always being *awkward*, in other words, always refusing to sit docilely in the nursery and await the onset of a stolid adulthood. He had too large an appetite for life and because he was, withal, only a little boy, he endured some fearful buffeting at the hands of a family whose dedication to "appearances" and to rigid Establishment notions of correct behavior was almost total.

He had but one advocate, his nurse, Mrs. Everest. "My mother . . . shone for me like the evening star," he wrote. "I loved her dearly—but at a distance. My nurse was my confidante. . . . It was to her I poured out my many troubles."[5] Everest was a staunch friend, and she was not afraid to upbraid her mistress on her charge's behalf. "Everest has been bothering me about some clothes for [Winston]," Jennie wrote when he was four, "saying that it was quite a disgrace how few things he has & how shabby at that. . . ."[6]

But Everest could not accompany Winston to school, and at the age of seven he was sent to one of the bleakest houses of learning imaginable: St. George's at Ascot. St. George's was run by a sexually perverted, social-climbing Anglican clergyman, and it exemplified the rote-memory, blind-obedience approach to education that has stultified so many potentially creative spirits. Churchill's life-affirming instincts came into direct and violent conflict with the dead weight of St. George's institutionalized adult tyranny. A near contemporary wrote in his memoirs, "Dreadful legends were told about Winston Churchill. . . . His naughtiness appeared to have surpassed anything. He had been flogged for taking sugar from the pantry, and so far from being penitent, he had taken the Headmaster's straw hat from where it hung over the door and kicked it to pieces. His sojourn at this school had been one long feud with authority. . . ."[7]

Churchill himself wrote, "How I hated this school, and what a life of anxiety I lived there for two years. . . . My teachers saw me at once backward and precocious, reading books beyond my years and yet at the bottom of the Form. They were offended. They had large sources of compulsion at their disposal, but I was stubborn. Where my reason, imagination or interest were not engaged, I would not or I could not learn...."[8]

But he was learning—defiance!

Things at home were only slightly less bad. After the birth of his brother, his parents' indifference had begun to shade into hostility. "As to Winston's improvement," Jennie wrote frostily to Lord Randolph, "I am sorry to say I see none... the first two days he came home he was terribly slangy and loud. Altogether I am disappointed. But Everest was told down there that next term they mean to be more strict with him. ... I shall take him in hand. It appears that he is afraid of me...."[9]

The promise of an increase in strictness was kept, kept to such an extent that Everest soon discovered livid scars on Winston's buttocks. Those scars along with a general physical collapse led to his finally being withdrawn from St. George's and placed under the more benign supervision of two spinsters who ran a small school in Brighton. He found this more congenial, but his improved conditions did not soften the sting of his parents' lack of interest in him. "My dear Papa," he scribbled shortly before his twelfth birthday, "I hope you are quite well. The weather is very wet today. You never came to see me on Sunday when you were in Brighton. . . ."[10] And several months later, "I wish you could come to the distribution of prizes at the end of this term, but I suppose it is impossible."[11]

From Brighton Churchill passed into Harrow, and Lord Randolph took a moment to decide upon his career. Having come upon Winston and Jack playing with their collection of nearly fifteen hundred tin soldiers, he asked the former, aged thirteen, if he would like to go into the army. "I thought it would be splendid to command an Army, so I said 'Yes' at once: and immediately I was taken at my word. ... I thought my father ... had discerned in me the qualities of military genius. But I was told later that he had only come to the conclusion that I was not clever enough to go to the Bar."[12]

Winston passed his first eighteen months at Harrow without
so much as a single visit from his father. He begged Lord
Randolph to come down for Speech-day during the summer
of 1889. "P.S.," he concluded a long letter of entreaty, "I shall
be awfully disappointed if you don't come."[13] And to his
mother he added, "Do try to get Papa to come. He has never
been."[14]

Harrow is close enough to London almost to be a part of
it, but Lord Randolph did not come.

⚹ As much as Churchill's parents neglected him, they rarely
missed an opportunity to berate him or compare him un-
favorably with his brother. Sometimes the neglect and the
scolding were combined. "Dearest Winston," Jennie wrote
after learning that he had been judged unready to take the
preliminary examination for the military academy at Sandhurst, "I am sending this by Everest who is going to see how
you are getting on. I would go down to you—but I have so
many things to arrange about the Ascot party next week that
I can't manage it. . . . Your report which I enclose is as you
can see a *very* bad one. You work in such a fitful inharmo-
nious way that you are bound to come out last. . . . I must say
I think you repay . . . kindness to you very badly. There is
Jack on the other hand—who comes out at the head of his
class every week—despite his bad eye."[15]

And when, after twice falling short, Churchill at last succeeded in gaining admission to the Royal Military College,
Lord Randolph rounded on him with one of the most with-
eringly scornful denunciations ever to pass from a father to
a son:

My dear Winston,
I am rather surprised at your tone of exultation over your inclusion in the Sandhurst list. There are two ways of winning an examination, one creditable the other the reverse. You have unfortunately chosen the latter method, and appear to be much pleased
with your success.
The first extremely discreditable feature of your performance was
missing the infantry [Churchill's score was only high enough for a
cavalry cadetship], for in that failure is demonstrated beyond refutation your slovenly happy-go-lucky harum scarum style of work

for which you have always been distinguished at your different schools. . . .

With all the advantages you had, with all the abilities which you foolishly think yourself to possess . . . this is the grand result that you come up among the 2nd rate & 3rd rate class who are only good for commissions in a cavalry regiment.

. . . Do not think I am going to take the trouble of writing to you long letters after every folly & failure you commit & undergo. I shall not write again on these matters & you need not trouble to write any answer to this part of my letter, because I no longer attach the slightest weight to anything you may say about your own acquirements & exploits. . . .

. . . I am certain that if you cannot prevent yourself from leading the idle useless unprofitable life you have had during your schooldays & later months, you will become a mere social wastrel one of the hundreds of public school failures, and you will degenerate into a shabby unhappy & futile existence. If that is so you will have to bear all the blame for such misfortunes yourself. Your own conscience will enable you to recall and enumerate all the efforts that have been made to give you the best of chances which you were entitled to by your position & how you have practically neglected them all. . . .[16]

There it was; he was hated. All the anxious suspicions that had tormented him throughout his youth were confirmed. All the rebuffs he had suffered in his desperate attempts to call forth some sign that he was loved had culminated in this squalid result. And the fault was most decidedly not in those shining evening stars, his mother and father, whom he loved so dearly but from such a great distance. The fault was in himself, that he was an underling, one of "the 2nd rate & 3rd rate class."

He had hit bottom. He had lost everything. He had nothing more to lose.

He was hated. So be it. He was hated because he was hateful. So be it also. Now, in the depths of the abyss, he had two choices. He could hate back, wreak unnamable vengeances on those who despised him, or he could prove that they were wrong, that, judged even by their own professed standards, he was fit to walk in dignity among them.

Hating back was out of the question. Too many years of

adoration and yearning had passed to allow that option. As
far as his mother was concerned, he might in later decades
have written, with George Bernard Shaw, "Her almost complete neglect of me had the advantage that I could idolize
her to the utmost pitch of my imagination and had no sordid
disillusioning contacts with her."[17] And in later decades he
did in fact write, "My mother always seemed to me a fairy
princess: a radiant being possessed of limitless riches and
powers."[18] As to his father, "The greatest and most profound
influence in my early life . . . I conceived an intense admiration and affection for him. . . ."[19] ". . . to me he seemed to own
the key to everything or almost everything worth having."[20]

Thus his only feasible alternative was to prove himself, and
while he had to observe certain ground rules in order to accomplish this objective, he also had a number of special resources he could draw on in the pursuit of it. First of all,
there was his despair over being unloved and his visceral
conviction that exclusion from the charmed circle wherein his
parents moved was the worst possible thing in the universe—
inclusion being the best (he never struck his own children
when they behaved badly; he simply banished them from his
presence). Second of all, there was his grimly fixed determination to win his way back into that charmed circle. Third of
all, the direct consequence of his anguish and resolution, there
was his extraordinary courage, the courage vouchsafed to the
despairing and the adamant, to those who have survived the
worst. Last of all, there was his mind, that deep well of crea-
tiveness fed by still deeper springs of mental energy which
had made his progress through the molding institutions of
British society so tempestuous and unsure.

The ground rules for proving his worthiness were equally
straightforward. First, he had to acknowledge his essential
inadequacy, as evidenced by his parents' disdain; second, he
had to believe that he could work his way into, or back into,
a state of grace; third, he had to idealize his images of his
mother and father and make them the models for his aspiration. In other words, he had to take his childhood visions of
two dimly comprehended figures at the summit of the Victorian
world and incorporate everything his child's mind believed

they and their milieu stood for into a rock-hard, time-resistant code of morality and honor. "Mr. Churchill looks within," said Isaiah Berlin in 1948, "and his strongest sense is the sense of the past . . . he does not reflect a contemporary social or moral world . . . rather he creates one of such power and coherence that it becomes a reality and alters the external world by being imposed on it with irresistible force."[21]

The final ground rule was perhaps the most important: he must never ever look too closely at the people around him, for if he did he would see overwhelming evidence to the effect that his parents (like other human beings) were not and could not have been as he believed them to be, that they were more complicated, more infirm, more *imperfect*, that the heavens where he had placed their thrones were suddenly empty. Professor Berlin: "Mr. Churchill is preoccupied by his own vivid world, and it is doubtful how far he has ever been aware of what actually goes on in the heads and hearts of others."[22] On no account must the Holy Grail stand revealed as base metal, for then the quest for absolution becomes a travesty, and the whole of life a pointless charade. Thus Churchill was always able to keep the fact of his father's illness (which he learned of in 1894) separate from its implications. Thus he was to be markedly insensitive throughout his adult life, even to the feelings of those who were closest to him

Thus, also, in 1895 he was extremely clumsy in broaching his plans for an American journey to his mother. But even though Jennie had grievous shortcomings in her maternal capacity, she was accomplished, intelligent, and more than usually adept in terms of *savoir-faire*. As Winston was now rounding into adulthood and showing signs of readiness to make his way in the great world, she began to take an interest in him, and she concluded the letter in which she had reminded him of the importance of tact with a friendly postscript: "Would you like me as a birthday pres to pay yr ticket??"[23] She also wrote to the man with whom she had most recently concluded an affair and asked him to look after Winston when he got to New York. This was the famous Tammany Hall orator Bourke Cockran, whom she had met in Paris in March, some two months after Lord Randolph had finally succumbed. Bourke, along with Jennie's numerous American relations, constituted a strong guarantee that Winston would receive a warm welcome on the far side of the Atlantic.

Churchill meanwhile was making preparations of his own. From Sir Henry Drummond Wolff, who was the British Ambassador to Spain and an old friend of his father's, he secured letters of introduction to the Commander of the Spanish forces in Cuba, Marshal Martinez Campos. From the Commander-in-Chief of the British Army, Lord Wolseley, he secured permission to visit the scene of hostilities, although his Lordship "rather hinted that it would have been better to go without asking leave at all."[24] From the Director of British Military Intelligence he secured an informal assignment to collect information on a new bullet the Spaniards were using. "This," he wrote his mother, "invests our mission with almost an official character & cannot fail to help one in the future."[25] Finally, and most significantly, from the *Daily Graphic* he secured a commission to write occasional dispatches from "the seat of war," for which he was to be paid five guineas each—roughly twenty-five dollars at then existing rates of exchange. This commission was particularly opportune, offering as it did the potential for both public recognition and financial sustenance. Being a cavalry officer was expensive, and Churchill accordingly faced the necessity of supplementing his purely nominal salary through personal initiatives. True, Jennie, as she herself had pointedly observed, provided the funds, but that was only for the moment. Given the extremely modest proportions of Lord Randolph's estate and the commensurately immodest sweep of her own self-confessed extravagance, the likelihood was that, before long, it would be Winston who was providing the funds for her. And so it came to be.

Churchill and Barnes sailed in clear weather from Liverpool on November 2. By the third, however, the *Etruria* found herself enveloped by typical late-autumn North Atlantic conditions, and she stayed enveloped clear across the ocean. "I do not contemplate ever taking a sea voyage for pleasure," a decidedly bilious (and uncharacteristically counter-prophetic) Winston wrote on November 8. His sour disposition extended to his fellow passengers and revealed a rough-edged snobbishness ("There are no nice people on board to speak of—certainly none to write of"), which was to dissipate with maturity, and an equally rough-edged intolerance of human inanity ("There is to be a concert on board tonight at which all the stupid people among the passengers intend to perform and the stupider ones to applaud"), which was not.[26] He was impatient to get to Cuba, moreover, and apparently regarded the United States as little more than an irksome obstruction impending his way thither. ". . . It is possible we may cut down our stay in N. York to a day and a half instead of three," he noted.[27] All in all, he was in an unreceptive frame of mind for his first encounter with his mother's homeland and fully in readiness to give it the shortest of possible shrifts. Had not Jennie herself cautioned him: "N.Y. is *fearfully* expensive & you will be bored to death there—all men are"?[28]

The *Etruria* steamed into New York Harbor shortly after noon on November 9. Bourke Cockran was waiting on the quay, and a scant few minutes after meeting him, Churchill's outlook on the United States began to undergo a change. "I must record the strong impression which this remarkable man made upon my untutored mind," he later recollected. "I have never seen his like, or in some respects his equal."[29] Cockran was forty-one years old at that time, a recently widowed attorney and a Democratic member of Congress. He whisked Churchill and Barnes off to his apartment on Fifth Avenue and Fifty-eighth Street, and that evening gave a dinner party in their honor at which leading members of the local judiciary were among the guests. "Very interesting men—" Winston reported to Jennie, "one particularly—a [New York State] Supreme Court Judge—is trying a *'cause célèbre'* here now."[30] After dinner the husband of Jennie's cousin Eva Purdy showed the two young subalterns a bit of New York's night life, winding up the tour with a postmidnight meal at the old Waldorf-Astoria.

Not surprisingly, all thoughts of cutting the New York stay short had been abandoned by the next morning. ". . . We have engagements for every meal for the next few days about three deep," Winston wrote his mother on November 10. "They really make rather a fuss over us here and extend the most lavish hospitality . . . one person seems to vie with another in trying to make our time pleasant."[31]

Far and away, Cockran was the person who vied most successfully. Literally overnight Churchill's relationship with him had ripened into friendship. "Mr. Cockran is one of the most charming hosts and interesting men I have met. . . . I have great discussions with [him] on every conceivable subject from Economics to yacht racing."[32]

⚡Churchill had been in America barely twenty-four hours, but already he had had dinner with members of the judiciary, a night on the town, and "great discussions . . . on every conceivable subject." His second twenty-four hours promised to be even more crowded, for at 1:00 P.M. on Sunday he was to have lunch with Eva Purdy, at three he was to call on the socially prominent Hitt family, at five he was to meet Cornelius Vanderbilt, and at eight he was to dine with another of his mother's cousins and her husband, an iron magnate. His jaundiced shipboard demeanor was a thing of the past. Whereas in England he had known little except disparagement and disapproval, here in the United States (where live male specimens of British nobility were considered the *summum bonum* by every hostess and every wealthy mother of an unmarried daughter) he was cosseted and praised without interruption. Small wonder that he conceived a profound affection for this unexpected New World Elysium and was moved to write: "This is a very great country my dear Jack. . . . What an extraordinary people the Americans are! Their hospitality is a revelation to me and they make you feel at home and at ease in a way that I have never before experienced."[33]

On Monday, the eleventh, his experience of this "extraordinary people" was further broadened. Cockran, bearing in mind that Winston was a member of Her Majesty's armed forces, took him around to all the forts and barracks constituting the Headquarters of the Atlantic Military District and then treated him to a tugboat tour of the city's harbor which culminated in a visit to the ironclad battle cruiser *New York.* "I was much struck by the sailors," he wrote his aunt, "their intelligence, their good looks and civility and their generally businesslike appearance." In fact, the ship's crew interested him more than the ship itself, for, as he sententiously explained, "while any nation can build a battleship—it is the monopoly of the Anglo-Saxon race to breed good seamen."[34] Coming from someone who had written "I do not contemplate ever taking a sea voyage for pleasure" barely three days earlier, this was a singularly bold assertion, but as there were no Phoenicians or Vikings around to take him to task for it, he went off unmolested to round out his second full day in America at the opening of the New York Horse Show.

On Tuesday the Supreme Court judge whom Winston had met at Cockran's dinner party invited him to have a firsthand look at the American judicial process. The jurist, Judge Ingraham, was presiding over the murder trial that Churchill had termed a *cause célèbre.* It concerned a certain David Hannigan, who was accused of having shot one Solomon Mann, Mann having been guilty of impregnating, and then procuring a fatal abortion for, Hannigan's sister Lettie. The defendant was eventually acquitted on the grounds of insanity, but when Churchill visited Ingraham's courtroom the trial had a full week yet to run. "I went and sat on the bench by his side," he reported to his brother, Jack. "Quite a strange experience and one which would be impossible in England. The Judge discussing the evidence as it was given with me and generally making himself socially agreeable—& all the while a pale miserable man was fighting for his life."[35] (Perhaps Judge Ingraham had an unmarried daughter of his own; it is difficult to think of any other explanation for such a flagrant abuse of judicial propriety.)

The next day, Wednesday, Churchill paid a visit to West Point, or "the American Sandhurst," as he called it. He was not favorably impressed by its Spartan traditions. "I am sure you will be horrified by some of the Regulations," he told Jack. "The cadets . . . are most of them 24 years of age. They are not allowed to smoke or have any money in their possession nor are they given any leave except 2 months after the

1st two years. In fact they have far less liberty than any
private school boys." As a veteran of "one long feud" with
scholastic authority, young Winston was incensed by the sub-
missiveness of America's future generals, and in this as in
other matters he was not reluctant about expressing himself.
"I think such a state of things is positively disgraceful," he
expostulated, "and young men of 24 or 25 who would resign
their personal liberty to such an extent can never make good
citizens or fine soldiers. A child who rebels against that sort
of control should be whipped—so should a man who does
not rebel."[36]

Despite his disapproval of what he saw, Churchill was still
extremely grateful for the kindness which the West Point
authorities showed him. "I was . . . only a Second Lieutenant,"
he told a friend fully sixty years later, "but I was . . . treated as
if I had been a General."[37] He must have had to keep his
mother's admonition about tact very much in mind.

On their return to New York City in the evening, Winston
and Barnes found that their host had another treat in store
for them. It seemed that the Fire Commissioner was an old
political crony of Cockran's and had agreed to alarm several
fire stations for the visiting subalterns' edification. Churchill
found the spectacle absorbing.

The social and sightseeing whirl continued for the rest of
the week. Churchill saw a great deal of his cousin Sunny, the
recently invested ninth Duke of Marlborough, and an equally
great deal of his cousin's new relations, acquired by the Duke
in virtue of his marriage on November 6 (while Winston was
grumbling his way across the Atlantic) to Consuelo Vanderbilt, great-granddaughter of the fabled Commodore. Churchill
and Barnes enjoyed themselves enormously, so much so that
on the sixth day of what was to have been a one-and-a-half-to
three-day visit, Winston wrote his brother, "We have postponed our departure from New York for three days [until
Sunday, the seventeenth] as there was lots to see and do."[38]
And lots to digest and evaluate as well.

Thanks to Cockran, when Churchill and his brother officer
finally embarked on their train journey Sunday morning, they

did so in the comfort and luxury of a private stateroom. Looking out the window as the eastern seaboard rushed by, Winston at last had some leisure in which to put his first American experiences into perspective. His overall impression had been favorable—overwhelmingly favorable, in fact—especially with respect to American technological know-how and entrepreneurial initiative. "So far I think the means of communication in New York have struck me the most. The comfort and convenience of elevated railways—tramways—cable cars & ferries harmoniously fitted into a perfect system accessible alike to the richest and the poorest—is extraordinary. And when one reflects that such benefits have been secured to the people . . . simply by business enterprise—out of which the promoters themselves have made colossal fortunes, one cannot fail to be impressed with the excellence of the active system."[39] On the other hand, he had serious reservations about other features of the American scene, the newspapers, for example: ". . . the essence of American journalism is vulgarity divested of truth. Their best papers write for a class of snotty housemaids and footmen. . . ."[40] And "the abominable currency": "I paid my fare across Brooklyn Bridge with a paper dollar, I should think the most disreputable 'coin' the world has ever seen."[41]

All in all, he visualized America as a nation pulsating with a raucous, infectious vitality, a vitality completely at variance with the indolent sophistication of his native Britain. His vision of the country bore a truly striking resemblance to his unconscious vision of himself as a child and adolescent. "A great, crude, strong, young people are the Americans—like a boisterous healthy boy among enervated but well bred ladies and gentlemen . . . a great lusty youth who treads on all your sensibilities perpetrates every possible horror of ill manners— whom neither age nor just tradition inspire with reverence— but who moves about his affairs with a good-natured freshness which may well be the envy of older nations of the earth."[42]

Without really being aware of it, Churchill had identified with America very strongly, and out of this identification was to come his lifelong dedication to the impossible dream of Anglo-American union. He had been a boisterous, healthy boy among enervated but oh so well-bred ladies and gentlemen;

he had been repeatedly condemned for treading on sensibilities and perpetrating horrors of ill manners; his ambition and
drive were to yield not a jot to age or just tradition. America
—especially in its coarser aspects—symbolized what he felt
he was; England symbolized what he aspired to be. No wonder the prospect of their union was to absorb his energies
increasingly as he grew older. If the sedate, somewhat effete,
parent country would only accept the child, and if the potent,
vigorous child country could only show the parent the essential
value concealed beneath its roughness, why then both nations
might dwell together in blissful harmony and walk in majesty
among the other peoples of the earth for decades and centuries
and, yes, even millennia to come.

Philadelphia passed by, and Washington. The train bearing
the sensitive, driven, opinionated young subaltern steamed on
into the night. America had unquestionably touched Churchill,
touched him more deeply than he was ever likely to suspect.
It had stirred long-repressed emotions and left him wistful for
the warmth and familial intimacy he had hardly known. He
thought of his little brother. "Some day Jack," he wrote, "when
you are older you must come out here and I think you will
feel as I feel—and think as I think today."[43]

On the evening of November 18 the train arrived in Tampa,
and on the nineteenth Barnes and Churchill transferred to the
steamer *Olivette* for the crossing to Havana. The next day, the
long journey complete, a grateful Winston wrote Cockran
from the Gran Hotel Inglaterra: "I can never repay you for
your kindness. . . ."[44] On Thursday, the twenty-first, he headed
for the interior.

The revolt that was still "simmering on" in Cuba had been
regularly flaring up and subsiding since 1868. It had erupted
most recently with the return from exile of two rebel leaders,
Gomez and Marti, some ten months before Churchill's arrival.
Initially Marshal Martinez Campos had come from Spain to
put down the insurrection with only seven thousand soldiers,
but the guerrilla fighting soon obliged him to call for more
and more in the way of reinforcements. Meanwhile, sympathy
for the insurgents built up around the world, not least of all

in England, and most particularly in the United States. As a political matter, therefore, Churchill and Barnes as "guests" of the Spanish Army could participate actively in hostilities only in their own defense. Presumably they could participate passively—that is, get shot at, without restriction.

Martinez Campos received the two subalterns at his temporary headquarters in Santa Clara, some one hundred miles east of Havana, and seconded them to his Chief of Staff, General Valdez, at Sancti Spiritus, forty miles farther on. Owing to the disruptions caused by the fighting in the area, it took three days to get to Sancti Spiritus, but when Churchill and Barnes finally arrived there, General Valdez proved to be a gracious host. "He explained, through an interpreter, what an honour it was for him to have two distinguished representatives of a great and friendly power attached to his column, and how highly he valued the moral support which this gesture of Great Britain implied."⁴⁵ Great Britain had not made any gesture, of course, and any moral support for the Spaniards was purely inferred, but Churchill and Barnes nevertheless managed a diplomatic, if not particularly eloquent, response: "We said, back through the interpreter, that it was awfully kind of him, and that we were sure it would be awfully jolly."⁴⁶

The next morning, November 26, General Valdez's column with its two British outriders set off to the northeast into rebel territory. For four days the march proceeded without incident, Churchill feeling increasingly ambivalent about his position as a war correspondent. He secretly sympathized with the rebels—with their objectives at any rate, if not their methods —but he was loathe to be outspoken in the face of the generous hospitality shown him by the Spanish forces. He therefore tried to keep his dispatches neutral, though he could not forbear acknowledging the obvious fact that the insurgents had "the sympathy of the entire population."⁴⁷

On November 30, the date of his twenty-first birthday, the issue of impartiality was abruptly supplanted in his thinking by the issue of survival. For the first time in his life, he came under hostile fire.

Valdez's column had stopped for breakfast in a small clearing, and as Winston stood gnawing on the remains of "a skinny chicken," a contingent of rebels opened fire from behind the surrounding trees. They were driven off in a matter of minutes, but not before one of their bullets passed close enough to Churchill's head to generate a healthy breeze. That close was too close for the tastes of the *Daily Graphic*'s special correspondent, and "I began to take a more thoughtful view of our enterprise than I had hitherto done."[48]

During the next week the thoughtful Winston came under fire several more times and even participated in an extended skirmish that came to be known as the Battle of La Reforma. He got back to Havana in one piece on December 6, however, and on the eighth Martinez Campos informed him that he and Barnes were to receive the military decoration of the Red Cross for their gallantry in that action. This award occasioned an outburst of criticism against the two lieutenants in both Britain and America, and when they returned to Tampa on December 10 Churchill had to tell the press, "I have not even fired a revolver. I am a member of General Valdez's staff by courtesy only, and I am decorated with the Red Cross only by courtesy."[49]

Cockran had sailed for England while Winston and Barnes were dodging bullets, but before departing, he arranged a stateroom for their return journey to New York. They got back to the city on the evening of the eleventh and checked into the Hotel Savoy. When they ordered dinner at 9:05, though, and were told that, pursuant to the by-laws of the hotel, no dinners were served after 9:00, they checked right out again and, amid a great deal of harrumphing, made their way to Cockran's flat, where the staff accorded them a more satisfactory welcome.

As the *Etruria* was due to sail on Saturday, the fourteenth, they had only two days to renew their recently made friendships, and the forty-eight hours passed quickly. Soon they found themselves back at the Cunard pier where Cockran had first greeted them just five weeks before. Their last task before leaving the United States was to answer the questions of the dozen or so reporters who had gathered to cover their embarkation.

Considering Churchill's feelings about American newspapers, this press conference was remarkably cordial. On two occasions, however, it became a little stormy. The first squall came when Winston was asked about the alleged political significance of his trip to Cuba. The New York *World* gave the following account of his reply: " 'Rot!' exclaimed Mr. Churchill, with a look that showed how tired the question made him feel."[50] The second spell of turbulence was more protracted. It occurred when a reporter from an unidentified morning tabloid raised a point. "I have nothing to say for publication in the paper you represent," Churchill snapped, and he then proceeded to explain to the other reporters that the newspaper in question had faked a cablegram over his signature, "attacked me editorially upon the very expressions it fraudulently attributed to me," and ignored his letter demanding a retraction.[51] One assumes that the reporter experienced suitable remorse on his editor's behalf.

Now it was time to sail. Apart from a souvenir bullet that had killed a Spanish soldier standing next to him at La Reforma, Churchill took away from the Western Hemisphere little more than he had brought in—as far as tangible items are concerned. On the intangible level he took away a great deal, but, more important, he left his boyhood behind. It was not simply that he had turned twenty-one or that he had been under fire; it was that the United States and the possibilities it represented had given him the necessary psychic breathing room in which to shed his uncongenial adolescent skin. Here he learned that he could be valued as a human being, that his sense of worthlessness was not wholly justified, that his struggle to achieve respect in the circles where his family moved might possibly succeed. Here he learned that his horizons were broader than he had suspected and that he had personal assets which he could employ in exploring them.

Taken as a whole, his visit had catalyzed his enormous capacity for achievement and launched him irreversibly on the road toward his and his country's Finest Hour. True, it was only the first step of what was to be a long and anguishing journey, but first steps make all the difference between moving and standing still.

CHAPTER TWO

The Sunlit Years

"... THE YEARS 1895 TO 1900 ... exceed in vividness, variety and exertion anything I have known.... When I look back upon them I cannot but return my sincere thanks to the high gods for the gift of existence. All the days were good and each day better than the other. Ups and downs, risks and journeys, but always the sense of motion, and the illusion of hope... Twenty to twenty-five! These are the years...."[1]

Indeed they are, or were, if Winston Spencer Churchill was one's name. This was the sunlit era of his life, the era bracketed—not coincidentally—by his first two visits to America. Literal sunlight shone on him in the tropical lands he traversed, Cuba first and then India, the Middle East, and South Africa. Figurative sunlight shone as he has described it above: a life at once vivid, various, vibrant, and propulsive, "the sense of motion, and the illusion of hope."

A fugitive from darkness, Churchill was to revel all his life in the light. "In my hot youth I demanded sunshine," he wrote in his 1921 essay on painting,[2] and some thirty years later Professor Berlin said of him: "... he thinks it a brave thing to ride in triumph through Persepolis; he knows with an unshakable certainty what he considers to be big, handsome, noble, and worthy of pursuit ... and what, on the contrary, he abhors as being dim, grey, likely to lower or destroy the play of colour and movement in the universe."[3]

"Abhors" was not too strong a word; even at his most tolerant, dimness and greyness were unwelcome: "I cannot pretend to feel impartial about the colours. I rejoice with the brilliant

ones and am genuinely sorry for the poor browns."[4] Again
and again in his writings and speeches it was "the broad sunlit uplands" that recurred as the ultimate destination of human
striving.

From 1895 to 1900 the youthful Winston traveled the globe
in search of fame, fortune, and adventure—and found them
all. All the pent-up energies that had accumulated over twenty
years of childhood servitude burst forth in an exuberant flood
of action, creativity, and learning. Even if it was not fully as
joyous and carefree as he recollected, even if hope was to
prove on many occasions to be no more than an illusion, nevertheless this half-decade stands out uncontrovertibly as the
brightest epoch in his life, at least until the Epiphany of 1940
and '41.

Winston arrived back in England from America shortly
before Christmas in 1895 with a nine-month period of virtual
limbo confronting him. The departure of the 4th Hussars for
India was scheduled for early autumn 1896, and as the regiment was to be away for some twelve to fourteen years the
men were allotted the preceding spring and summer to put
their domestic affairs in order. In April, moreover, they were
to demobilize themselves by yielding their horses to a returning regiment, and, as the winter season of leave extended into
March, the surrender of their mounts would be little more
than the official acknowledgment of a *de facto* demobilization
that had already taken place. As a result, Churchill oscillated
between partial and total idleness from January to October.
He played polo, he visited the great houses of the nobility, he
hobnobbed with political leaders and ladies of fashion, he
went to the races, he ran up debts. Had he been content to
dribble his time away in such aristocratic pursuits, Lord Randolph's prospective indictment of him as "a mere social wastrel" might very well have been confirmed. But he chafed. For
one thing, he had been granted access to the inner circles of
society only because of his pedigree, and he wanted to prove
that he *belonged* there. For another thing, there were all sorts
of exciting disturbances erupting all over the world in which
he might prove precisely that, but from which he was ex-

cluded by his military and, more particularly, his monetary circumstances. Crete was in turmoil; Kitchener was preparing to march against the Dervishes; the natives in Rhodesia were in rebellion. But Lieutenant Winston Churchill was marked for southern India, for Bangalore in Mysore State, where Raj and damned tranquility prevailed. ". . . You cannot think how I would like to sail in a few days to scenes of adventure and excitement—" he wrote his mother in August, "to places where I could gain experience and derive advantage—rather than to the tedious land of India—where I shall be equally out of the pleasures of peace and the chances of war."[5] It made him almost desperate with frustration; like the young Caesar contemplating Alexander's tomb, he was stung by how little he had accomplished in his two decades of existence. To be twenty-one and to have made no progress to speak of toward immortality was bad enough, but to be hobbled as well, left tethered in the starting gate while opportunity went aglimmering and contemporaries went galloping away—that was very agony. "It is useless to preach the gospel of patience to me. Others as young are making the running now and what chance have I of ever catching up."[6]

Eight months after his arrival in India he got his chance, or, more accurately, he made it. Pulling every string he could lay his hands on—and despite his army status—he got himself attached as a correspondent of the *Daily Telegraph* to the British-Indian forces engaged in putting down a revolt of the Pathan tribesmen on the Northwest Frontier. Out of this expedition came his first campaign medal, his first mention in dispatches, his first fame, his first notoriety, his first book, and his first "vice."

The campaign medal and the mention in dispatches derived from the almost reckless courage under fire he displayed whenever the occasion presented itself. "I was shot at from 7:30 [A.M.] till 8 [P.M.] on this day," he noted in mid-September 1897, "and now begin to consider myself a veteran. . . . I rode my grey pony all along the skirmish line where everyone else was lying down. Foolish perhaps but I play for high stakes and given an audience there is no act too daring or too noble."[7]

The fame and the notoriety derived from the outspoken accounts of battle which he first sent to the *Telegraph* and the Indian newspaper *Pioneer* and then expanded into book form as *The Story of the Malakand Field Force*. Both the articles and the book were well and widely received, but both provoked criticism. What was a mere subaltern doing participating in a campaign two thousand miles away from the rest of his regiment? More to the point, what was he doing making comments about the way that campaign was being conducted? The "vice," which was destined to become a lifelong amenity as well as a famous, though apocryphal (see pages 234–35), excess, was a taste for alcoholic spirits, a taste, Churchill tells us, that was necessitated by the rigors of "active service."

Winston returned to Bangalore in November 1897 and resumed a process of self-education that he had begun the previous year. He tackled the muscular gothic prose of Gibbon and Macaulay, the essays of Chatham and Clive, the theories of Malthus and Darwin, and, on a year-by-year basis beginning with 1870, the detailed chronicles of British political life as set out in the *Annual Register*. He also resumed his guerrilla skirmishes with his mother over questions of money, skirmishes that reached a new peak of intensity in January 1898: "Speaking quite frankly on the subject—there is no doubt that we are both you & I equally thoughtless—spendthrift and extravagant.... In three years from my father's death you have spent a quarter of our entire fortune in the world. I also have been extravagant, but my extravagances are a very small matter beside yours."[8] Fortunately mother and son were able to conclude a truce and then refinance themselves sufficiently to ward off immediate distress. It was to their mutual advantage to co-operate; Jennie needed Winston's support if she was to secure new sources of credit, and Winston needed Jennie's support if he was to accomplish the next step in his campaign to make a name for himself. "It is a pushing age," he wrote her, "and we must shove with the best."[9]

The object of Churchill's aspiration was the army that the Sirdar of Egypt, General Sir Herbert Kitchener, was methodically leading up the Nile Valley toward the eventual reconquest of Khartoum. Winston enlisted no less a personage than the Prime Minister and Foreign Secretary, Lord Salisbury, to aid him in his quest, but even with such pre-eminent authority supporting him, he still did not have enough leverage to counteract the Sirdar's jealous preservation of command prerogatives within the Egyptian theater of operations. Kitchener was a sort of nineteenth-century De Gaulle: he and he alone would decide who was to take part in his campaigns, and a cheeky subaltern with a mind—and a pen—of his own was the last thing he wanted in his vicinity. Luckily for Winston, however, the Sirdar's *hauteur* aroused the ire of Sir Evelyn Wood, the War Office's Adjutant General, and Sir Evelyn attached Churchill as a supernumerary lieutenant to the cavalry regiment called the 21st Lancers, which, along with an infantry division and an artillery brigade, constituted the British contingent of Kitchener's Anglo-Egyptian army. As far as the War Office—in the person of Sir Evelyn—was concerned, the Sirdar could propose all he liked in re: the assignment of Lieutenant Winston Churchill, but it was Whitehall and not Cairo that would dispose of the matter.

Although elated over his success, Winston gave no time to celebration. He could not serve with the Lancers unless he had leave from the Hussars, and since his request for leave might be turned down, he decided to start for the Middle East right away on his own initiative. He decided to go AWOL, in other words, reasoning that if he got as far as Egypt without being officially notified that his leave request had been denied, if it had, he would at least be in a position to present the army with a *fait accompli.* "Foolish perhaps but I play for high stakes . . ."

In the event, his temporary transfer went uncontested, and he joined Kitchener's forces (unbeknownst to Kitchener) in plenty of time to participate in the Battle of Omdurman and to ride in the last great cavalry charge in the history of organized warfare. Then, after the British emerged victorious— as was more or less mandatory in the Victorian era—he had reams of exciting copy to send to his newest employer, the *Morning Post.* He also had a wealth of material for his next book, which was to be a comprehensive history of the entire Sudan crusade.

Winston's adventures along the River Nile marked a fulcrum point in his life. Given all the troubles he had had and was likely to have again with General Kitchener, whom he had openly criticized in his dispatches, it seemed clear to him that his continued presence in the army could only hamper his further progress in the world at large. He therefore resolved to resign his commission and take up the life of a journalistic freebooter. On the boat back to England he made friends with a prescient young reporter for the *Daily Mail* named George Warrington Steevens, who divined in him the qualities —and the defects—that were henceforth to guide his star. Steevens set down his observations in a profile entitled "The Youngest Man in Europe":

Mr. Winston Spencer Churchill . . . is the youngest man in Europe. A gallery of young men's pictures could not possibly be complete without him, for there is no younger.

In years he is a boy; in temperament he is also a boy; but in intention, in deliberate plan, purpose, adaptation of means to end, he is already a man. . . .

Inheritance alone would not give him his grip and facility at twenty-three; with us, hereditary statesmen and party leaders ripen later. Perhaps it is his American strain, to which he adds a keenness, a shrewdness, a half-cynical personal ambition, a natural aptitude for advertisement, and happily, a sense of humour.

. . . He may and he may not possess the qualities which make a great general, but . . . if they exist they are overshadowed by qualities which might make him, almost at will, a great popular leader, a great journalist, or the founder of a great advertising business. . . .

He is ambitious and he is calculating, yet he is not cold, and that saves him. His ambition is sanguine, runs in a torrent, and the calculation is hardly more than the rock or the stump which the torrent strikes for a second, yet which suffices to direct its course. . . .

The master strain in his character is the rhetorician. Platform speeches and leading articles flow from him almost against his will. At dinner he talks and talks, and you can hardly tell when he leaves off quoting his one idol, Macaulay, and begins his other, Winston Churchill. . . .

What he will become, who shall say? At the rate he goes, there will hardly be room for him in Parliament at thirty or in England at forty. It is a pace that cannot last, yet already he holds a vast lead of his contemporaries. . . .[10]

And barely two years before, it had been: "what chance have I of ever catching up."

✕ Back in England, Churchill resumed two old undertakings with a new perspective, undertakings he had begun in India. One was a novel and the other was a courtship. Both were indicative of his emotional constitution. The novel was entitled *Savrola* and, like many first and only works of fiction, it was essentially an unintentional portrait of its author as its author secretly wished to be, a melodramatic fantasy in which the hero lives out the dreams of his creator on a suitably epic scale. Savrola is a brooding Byronic aristocrat and revolutionary in an imaginary West African (but Caucasian) dictatorship called Laurania. He seeks to do great things ("Ambition was the motive force and he was powerless to resist it"[11]) but the dictator, Molara, sensing that he is a threat to the regime, seeks to bring about his downfall. Molara enlists his beautiful and unscrupulous wife, Lucile, to act as his Delilah, but she of course falls hopelessly in love with her intended victim. After many momentous crises and disturbances, Molara comes to a bad end, and Savrola, with Lucile at his side, returns from a temporary exile to reign righteously over Laurania and live broodingly ever after.

Set to music, the novel would rival Gilbert and Sullivan's most satirical exercises,* but it does serve to show the fairytale cast of Churchill's imagination. While the hero exemplifies all the chivalric and aristocratic virtues that Winston attributed to his father and sought to cultivate in himself, there is also a genuine somberness in the character, a fatalistic cynicism, even a sense of futility, which suggests that on a certain level Churchill knew it would be impossible for him ever to regain the citadel of his parents' affection, even in a purely make-believe context. And if the hero contained elements of his fantasy father, it was only to be expected that the heroine would betray some features of his mother's image, which, with her beauty, wantonness, and ultimate conversion to Savrola's cause, she did. The Freudian elements in this scenario are too

* Churchill's opinion of the book may be surmised from this sentence in *My Early Life*: "I have consistently urged my friends to abstain from reading it" (p. 154).

obvious to warrant further elaboration. The weakness of Lucile's characterization, however, compared to the male figures in the book, is significant with respect to Winston's attitude toward women generally. "... Lucile is a weak and uninteresting personality," his grandmother the Duchess Fanny told him. "It is clear you have not yet attained a knowledge of Women—and it is evident you have (I am thankful to see) no experience of love!"[12]

⅄The Duchess was only half right; Churchill had not attained a knowledge of women, but he had had some experience of love, or at least of a facsimile. Despite the fact that women for him were either on a pedestal with his mother—radiant beings and fairy princesses shining like the evening star—or in the nursery with Mrs. Everest—compassionate beings and fairy godmothers radiating kindness like a blazing hearth—he had for more than two years been carrying on the Victorian equivalent of an affair. In October of 1896 he had written his mother from Bangalore, "I was introduced yesterday to Miss Pamela Plowden.... I must say that she is the most beautiful girl I have ever seen...."[13] In November of 1898 he was sending love letters to the young lady herself: "I met a [girl] the other day who is ... nearly as clever & wise as you.... I wonder if I arouse your curiosity.... Were I wise I would not allay it—by telling you that she is less beautiful."[14]

It is no slur on the sincerity of Churchill's affections to say that such gallantry was 99 percent convention. It is likely that, naïve as Winston seems to have been, he was not so much "in love" with Miss Plowden as he was fashionably enamored. She was by no means the first in a succession of uniformly beautiful actresses and débutantes for whom he conceived a "passion" that was almost as intense as it was chaste, almost as torrid as it was unconsummated. Mabel Love, Ethel Barrymore, Muriel Wilson, Molly Hackett, had all felt the heat of his adoration, but he would have been taken aback if any one of them had climbed off her pedestal and offered to play Guinevere to his Lancelot—and each one of them seems to have realized it. Pamela Plowden seems to have realized it too, but she also perceived the honest, almost canine hunger for affection that underlay Churchill's operatic declarations of desire, and she grew in time to be genuinely fond of him. Although his emotional immaturity—and limited finances— eventually rendered marriage out of the question as far as she was concerned, she still appreciated the potential underneath his lack of polish. "The first time you meet Winston you see all his faults," was how she summed him up many years after their romance, "and the rest of your life you spend in discovering his virtues."[15]

Churchill went back to India for the last time as an army officer shortly before Christmas in 1898. The following year promised to be very full: "... I planned the sequence of the year ... as follows: To return to India and win the [Inter-Regimental] Polo Tournament; to send in my papers and leave the army ... to write my new book [on the reconquest of the Sudan, to be called *The River War*] ... and to look out for a chance of entering Parliament."[16] The first objective was accomplished on February 24 at Meerut, just north of Delhi, when the foursome from the Hussars, Number 1 being Churchill and Number 4 being his old Cuban cohort, Barnes, defeated the challenge of the 4th Dragoon Guards by a single goal.

The second objective was accomplished less than a month later when Winston resigned his commission. "Had the army been a source of income to me instead of a channel of expenditure," he explained to the Duchess Fanny, "I might have felt compelled to stick to it. But I can live cheaper & earn more as a writer, special correspondent or journalist: and this work is moreover more congenial and more likely to assist me in pursuing the larger ends of life."[17]

Much of objective number three was accomplished on the long journey home from Bangalore. Not only was *The River War* brought a good way toward completion, but word arrived that the still unpublished *Savrola* had been purchased for a hundred pounds for serialization in *Macmillan's Magazine*.

Thus, with barely a third of the year consumed, all that remained for Churchill to accomplish was to get himself elected to the House of Commons. Here, however, though all went well at first, he eventually came a cropper. "Pamela," he wrote

on June 20, "I have just returned from Oldham [outside Man-
chester] tonight. The whole thing is in my hands as far as the
Tory Party there go. I fight the seat & am trying to find a
second candidate."*[18] Two weeks later he wrote again: "Well
we are nearing the end now. I don't think anyone has the
vaguest idea how it will turn out. . . . But whatever the result
may be it has been a strange experience and I shall never
forget the succession of great halls packed with excited people
until there was not room for one single person more—speech
after speech, meeting after meeting—three even four in one
night—intermittent flashes of Heat & Light & enthusiasm—
with cold air and the rattle of a carriage in between: a great
experience."[19]

The votes were counted on July 6; Churchill lost. He had
made a good showing, though, and Arthur Balfour, Leader of
the House of Commons, consoled him: "Never mind, it will
all come right; and this small reverse will have no permanent
ill effect upon your political fortunes."[20] It was a safe estimate,
that, and a prophetic one, as it proved fifteen months later.
Within three months, though, with *The River War* at last completed and at the printer's, Winston was off to South Africa.

He arrived in Capetown on Halloween. By the fifteenth of
November he was a prisoner of the Boers. In his capacity as an
accredited correspondent of the *Morning Post*, he had accompanied an armored train from Estcourt in Natal on a recon-
naissance sortie into enemy territory. Some fifteen miles into
the journey the train had been ambushed and derailed, but
thanks largely to Churchill's highly unjournalistic exertions in
the midst of constant rifle and artillery fire, the engine and
tender carrying some forty wounded soldiers had escaped
toward the British lines. He himself was on his way back to collect the remainder of the ambushed forces when "two figures
in plain clothes appeared upon the line. 'Plate-layers!' I said
to myself, and then with a surge of realization, 'Boers!' . . ."[21]
He spun round and sprinted down the tracks with bullets
whistling to his right and left. A few more seconds on the
narrow right-of-way and the *Morning Post* would be short one

---

* Oldham was a two-seat constituency.

war correspondent. But two hundred yards to Winston's right
the Blue Krantz River afforded protection—if he could reach
it. He clambered up the side of the railway cutting and made
ready to dash for the river. Before he could take a step, however, he saw a furiously galloping horse and rider bearing
down on him from the north. In seconds he found himself
staring down the barrel of the horseman's rifle, and, left with
no practical alternative, he raised his hands high and surrendered.

Along with the rest of the armored train survivors, Churchill
was sent to the Boer capital, Pretoria, and imprisoned, but on
the night of December 12 he escaped. After numerous brushes
with fate—and despite a twenty-five-pound price on his head
—he succeeded in making his way across three hundred miles
of Boer territory to Portuguese East Africa and freedom.

On his return to British lines, he found that he had become
not merely a hero but a household word. His capture and
escape were in all the newspapers. The Commander of Her
Majesty's forces, General Sir Redvers Buller, proudly offered
him a temporary commission as a lieutenant in the South African Light Horse. In a sweat of patriotic fervor, Winston accepted, meanwhile telegraphing the *Morning Post* that England
would have to be a good deal more active in its prosecution of
the war if it were to get anything more out of it than a bloody
nose. Some of his London acquaintances regarded this dispatch as presumptuous and telegraphed him in return: "Best
friends here hope you won't go on making further ass of
yourself."[22] But the overwhelming reaction to his exploits was
favorable, and Whitehall soon corroborated Winston's judgment by sending out reinforcements and generally stepping
up its military operations to a very marked degree. Among
the first of the new recruits to arrive was Churchill's brother,
Jack, who apparently did not share his sibling's luck; in his
very first battle he was wounded in the leg. Fortunately Jennie
—who may have foreseen just such an eventuality—had organized a hospital ship, the *Maine*, and she was even on board
when the time came to tend her youngest's needs.

Winston, meanwhile, was now beginning to reap the harvest
of his busy half-decade's activity. *The River War* was pub-

lished to great—and enduring—acclaim in November 1899. *Savrola* was published to indulgent forbearance three months later. In May and October 1900 were to come two more books, *London to Ladysmith via Pretoria* and *Ian Hamilton's March*, both based on his South African experiences and both commercially successful.

His name celebrated, his reputation established, Churchill returned to Oldham in September 1900 to contest the seat that had eluded him five hundred days before. On October 1 his victory was announced. All that now remained for him was to accumulate sufficient capital to see him through the next few years, a crucial matter since Members of Parliament did not then receive any salaries. Winston decided that the best strategy would be to undertake a lecture tour, and during October and November he spoke on his Boer War experiences all across the United Kingdom. There were audiences outside of England too, however, and on December 1 he embarked for the United States.

CHAPTER THREE

Twain, Pond, and Baths

"...I PURSUE PROFIT not pleasure in the States this time"[1] was how Churchill put it to Bourke Cockran in a letter sent from London a week before his departure. Given the fact that he had just completed five weeks of campaign speeches and a month and a half of lectures in Britain, it is understandable that the prospect of two more months of traveling and talking in North America was not an entirely pleasing one. But his Parliamentary career beckoned, and pleasure had to be subordinated to expediency.

Major James B. Pond of the famous Lyceum Lecture Bureau had contacted Winston in March 1900 with a proposal for an American tour; Winston in turn had requested his mother to check on the Major's reputation and undertake the necessary groundwork: "I beg of you to take the best advice on these matters. I have so much need of money and we cannot afford to throw away a single shilling."[2] Jennie's inquiries revealed that Pond was eminently respectable, having organized the speaking engagements of such luminaries as Arthur Conan Doyle and Mark Twain among others, so on July 30 Churchill cabled him directly: CONSIDERING GENERAL ELECTION HERE PROBABLY AND PRESIDENTIAL STATES CERTAIN IN OCTOBER [*sic*], PROPOSE COMING TO AMERICA DEC. JAN. & FEBRUARY, AND USE NOVEMBER IN ENGLAND.[3] He spelled out his requirements in a following letter: "I shall leave the whole arrangements of the Tour to you, but at the same time, you must not drag me about too much and I don't want to wear myself out by talking to two-penny–half-penny meetings in out of the way places.

In all my social engagements I shall exercise my entire discretion. . . . I don't want to be dragged about to any social functions of any kind nor shall I think of talking about my experiences to anybody except when I am paid for so doing."[4]

This, apparently, was going to be a business trip with a vengeance.

Before long all was satisfactorily arranged. The only difficulty was that a considerable segment of public opinion in the United States was rather aggressively pro-Boer, and a lecture by a noted Boer adversary, which was being advertised variously as "How I Escaped from the Boers," "The War in South Africa as I Saw It," and "The British Campaign in the Transvaal," did little to arouse friendly sentiment. Feeling ran so high that Pond felt obliged to warn Churchill against staying with Cockran, who was one of the foremost American critics of British policy; and while neither Winston nor Bourke believed in allowing politics to interfere with friendship, the former was sufficiently unsettled by Pond's letter to write his prospective host, "I am looking forward very much to seeing you again, although I feel no small trepidation at embarking upon the stormy ocean of American thought & discussion."[5]

In his anxiety over public relations Pond might profitably have paid more attention to his own utterances and less to his client's lodgings. It was bad enough, from Churchill's point of view, that, in advertisements he considered "vulgar and offensive,"[6] his manager had heralded him as "the hero of five wars" (when he had participated in only four), "the author of six books" (when he had written only five), and "the future Prime Minister of England" (when he had yet to attend his first session of Parliament).[7] What was even worse, however, was that Pond, in his role as the Barnum of the lecture circuit, had put together a "Reception Committee" for Winston's New York appearance that not only included such stout Dutch names as Van Ness, Van Dyke, Van Brunt, and (Mayor) Van Wyck, but did so without their knowledge in some cases, without their consent in others—William Dean Howells being the most prominent in this category—and in direct conflict with their expressed wishes in others besides. "While this was no fault of Churchill's," commented the celebrated American

writer and correspondent Richard Harding Davis (who had
refused to serve on the Reception Committee because of his
pro-Boer sympathies, even though he and Winston had become friends in South Africa), "it was neither for him nor
for the success of his tour the best kind of advance work."[8]

But the show must go on, and on December 8 Winston arrived in America aboard the Cunard steamer *Lucania*. He was
met at Quarantine by a crowd of reporters. "I am not here to
marry anybody," he told them in a humorous reference to the
ongoing proliferation of alliances between American wealth
and British nobility. "I am not going to get married and I
would like to have that stated positively."[9] This disposed of
his matrimonial intentions, but his love life was still to be
explored. "It has been said that a Dutch maiden fell in love
with you and assisted you to flee," a reporter observed. "You
yourself have said that it was the hand of Providence. Which
it true?" Ever the discreet cavalier, Churchill replied, "It is
sometimes the same thing."[10] (A somewhat more candid,
though still inconclusive, response came two weeks later in
Springfield, Massachusetts, when he volunteered the information that "the Boer women are notoriously unattractive."[11])
He answered several more questions and then excused himself
until that evening, when he was to be the dinner guest of the
New York Press Club. There he revealed for the first time a
rather obsessional aspect of his personality.

"After seeing many nations," he said amidst the postprandial
brandy and cigars, "after travelling through Europe, and after
having been a prisoner of the Boers, I have come to see that,
after all, the chief characteristic of the English-speaking people as compared with other 'white' people is that they wash,
and wash at regular periods. England and America are divided
by a great ocean of salt water, but united by an eternal bathtub of soap and water."[12] Although the momentous psychological inferences to be drawn from such a declaration are
best left to those qualified to elaborate them, one still cannot
escape the impression that Winston's preoccupation with bathing, at least as manifested on this visit to the United States,
was rather more pronounced than accords with standard concepts of normality. Three nights after the Press Club function,

for example, he spoke at a dinner of the Pennsylvania Society thus: "... There are two points that I want to tell about that are not often mentioned in which Britain and America are alike. We have a prejudice against attacking a man except in front.... Then we like cold water; we want our daily plunge. I've not known that in any other nation, but though the salt ocean separates us, we are united by soap and fresh water."[13]

This second decretal was too much for the refined sensibilities of the New York *Times*, and Mr. Ochs's hierarchs delivered themselves of the following baroque rebuke:

That very far from preponderating fraction of all Englishmen which has recently acquired the habit of bathing as frequently and as thoroughly as the primitive facilities that still content it will permit continues to be so vastly astonished at its own emergence from grimy barbarism that for some time to come we must expect to hear, every now and then, talk of the kind in which Lieut WINSTON SPENCER CHURCHILL indulged at the dinner of the Pennsylvania Society. Without the slightest apparent suspicion as to the good taste of his remarks, the amiable Lieutenant ran on at great length about the superior cleanliness of Englishmen and Americans as compared with all the rest of the world, and pictured them as advancing hand in hand from land to land, introducing the bath tub wherever they go and so elevating reluctant nations to unwonted heights of civilization. . . . Fortunately all this was very funny, for it was also rather outrageous and just a little disgusting. . . . There are probably twenty real bath tubs in America for every one on equal areas in England, and yet that fact is utterly ignored as a topic of polite conversation in this country. Why can't the Britishers be similarly reserved with respect to the intimate secrets of the toilet?[14]

But Lieutenant Churchill, as he was to do frequently and to good effect in later life, stuck to his guns on this occasion; at any rate, if he felt the least bit of contrition about the stand he had taken, he was careful to betray no sign of it.

٭ Winston spent Sunday, December 9, in relaxing conversation with Cockran, and on Monday he journeyed up to Albany to meet the Vice President-elect, Governor Theodore Roosevelt. TR had gone charging up San Juan Hill just two months before Churchill had ridden into the teeth of the Dervishes at Omdurman, and in their vitality, their enegry, their lust for adventure, the two men had other things in common as well.

It was a case of likes repelling.

"I saw the Englishman, Winston Churchill here, and . . . he is not an attractive fellow," Roosevelt confided to a friend several months after the meeting,[15] and this negative impression proved as enduring as the parallelism of careers—both Churchill and Roosevelt were to shift their political allegiances from the parties of their youth; both were to achieve the highest political office in their countries on two occasions; and both were to be awarded a Nobel Prize.

On Tuesday, in Philadelphia, Winston began his lecture tour officially—and began it well. "A large and intensely interested audience greeted the speaker," according to one newspaper dispatch,[16] and Churchill's fair-minded approach to the issues surrounding the hostilities in South Africa won him the audience's respect. The Boer War was still in progress at this time, and, as has been mentioned, it was a matter of heated public discussion in the United States. Churchill's attitude was that the British had been justified in intervening, but that the war was one involving two essentially right-minded adversaries unhappily compelled by circumstances to resort to the use of arms. Thus, though he was adamant for British victory, which by December 1900 was virtually an accomplished fact, he was eager to bring the Boers into the Commonwealth with full dignity and without recriminations as soon as that victory had been won. "In victory: Magnanimity" described his outlook then, just as it did almost half a century later when he came to write *The Second World War*. Also, he was generous in his praise of the enemy. When the Philadelphia audience defiantly applauded the magic-lantern picture of a Boer cavalryman that Churchill was using to illustrate his talk, he said to them, "You are quite right to applaud him; he is the most formidable fighting man in the world."[17] (After another visit to the United States, in 1942, he was to say of another adversary, Erwin Rommel: he is "a very daring and skillful opponent . . . and, may I say across the havoc of war a great general."[18]) The overall image he projected at his Philadelphia meeting was one of "gallant personality, tact and manliness," according to an appreciative reporter. "His accent is pronounced, his mannerism ultra-British, and his stage presence rather awkward, owing, principally, to inexperience [*sic!*]. But he spoke readily, without notes, and produced a decidedly favorable impression."[19] It was a good beginning.

Now came the New York début. The scene was the Grand Ballroom of the Waldorf-Astoria. The date was December 12, 1900, the anniversary of Churchill's escape from Pretoria. The time was 8:30 P.M., the conclusion of a large dinner party that Cockran had organized on Winston's behalf. A venerable white-haired gentleman, the author and raconteur who had introduced Tom Sawyer and Huckleberry Finn to the world some thirty years before, now rose to prepare the way for yet another memorable young man, and an audience that "was crowded to the doors"[20] hushed itself to hear him:

I shall presently have the pleasure of introducing to you an honored friend of mine, Winston Churchill, member of Parliament, and although he and I do not agree as to the righteousness of the South African war, that's not of the least consequence, for people who are worth anything never do agree. For years I have been a self-appointed missionary for the joining of America and the motherland in friendship and esteem. (Applause.) Wherever I have been and whenever I have stood before a gathering of Englishmen or Americans, I have urged my mission and have warmed it up with compliments to both countries. Mr. Churchill will tell you about the South African war, and he is competent to tell you about it. He was there and fought through it and wrote through it, and he will tell you his personal experiences. I have an inkling of what they are like, and they are very interesting to those who like that kind of thing. I don't like that kind of thing myself. (Laughter.) I saw a battlefield—once. It was raining, and you know they won't let you carry an umbrella, and when shells are added to the rain it becomes uncomfortable. I think that England sinned when she got herself into a war in South Africa which she could have avoided, just as we have sinned by getting into a similar war in the Philippines. Mr. Churchill by his father is an Englishman, by his mother he is an American, no doubt a blend that makes the perfect man. England and America; we are kin. And now that we are also kin in sin, there is nothing more to be desired. The harmony is perfect—like Mr. Churchill himself, whom I now have the honor to present to you.[21]

Samuel Langhorne Clemens sat down amidst cheers and chuckles; a man who might reasonably be described as "a tough act to follow." In his place appeared Churchill, "a very fair man of the purely English type," according to the New York *Times*. "His face denotes a highly strung temperament and the broad brow considerable mental capacity."[22] "He showed nervousness at first, but soon forgot himself in his subject, and held the attention of his listeners. . . . A touch of humor, introduced half unconsciously, lightened up the lecture considerably."[23] He took his audience from the armored train near Estcourt to the POW compound in Pretoria, from the railroad line at Resana Garcia to the hero's welcome at Durban. He took them and he held them. At the end of the talk Mark Twain rose again. "I take it for granted that I have the permission of this audience to thank the lecturer for his discourse, and to thank him heartily that, while he has extolled British valor, he has not withheld praise from Boer valor."[24] A flushed and happy Winston replied with becoming humility: "It is my chief duty to thank the chairman for coming here to give my lecture an importance and a dignity which it could not have otherwise obtained."[25]

This was not merely a *pro forma* genuflection by Churchill to Clemens. Writing over thirty years later in *My Early Life*, he said, "I was thrilled by this famous companion of my youth. He was now very old [he was 65] and snow-white, and combined with a noble air a most delightful style of conversation. Of course we argued about the war. After some interchanges I found myself beaten back to the citadel of 'My country right or wrong.' 'Ah,' said the old gentleman, 'When the country is fighting for its life, I agree. But this was not your case.' I think however that I did not displease him, for he was good enough at my request to sign every one of the thirty volumes of his works for my benefit; and in the first volume he inscribed the following maxim intended, I daresay, to convey a gentle admonition: 'To do good is noble; to teach others to do good is nobler, and no trouble.' "*[26]

---

* Actually, the edition of the *Writings of Mark Twain* in which the inscription appears contains twenty-five volumes rather than thirty, and what Clemens actually wrote is: "To be good is noble; to teach others how to be good is nobler & no trouble."[27] With regard to the respect and affection he and Clemens conceived for each other, however, Churchill's memory is perfectly accurate.

Fortified by his success, Winston went across the hall from the Grand Ballroom to the aforementioned dinner of the Pennsylvania Society and dilated on the intricacies of personal hygiene. It had begun to snow quite heavily outside, and it was not until after two in the morning that the still buoyant and by now slightly inebriate Churchill stumbled out into the darkness. Before leaving London he had been commissioned by twenty British officers who had fought with him in South Africa to shoot Richard Harding Davis on sight in retribution for his anti-English dispatches from the front. But Winston had taken a liking to Davis in the Transvaal; he was even using photographs Davis had taken of the scene of his escape in his lectures. And so, rather than shoot him, he decided in the end simply to wake him up. "... Three hours after midnight he came, in a blizzard, pounding at our door for food and drink," Davis recalled. Needless to say, he was provided with both, for, as the American reflected at the time, "What is a little thing like a war between friends?"[28]

Given this background of nocturnal carryings-on, it will come as no surprise that the *Evening Register* of New Haven, where Churchill was to speak next, reported the following afternoon that: "The distinguished young Englishman was expected in New Haven at noon, but shortly after that hour telephone and telegraph messages were received from New York stating that Mr. Churchill had been unavoidably delayed...."[29] In the event, he arrived somewhat the worse for wear around four o'clock and was met by a contingent of Yale undergraduates, who immediately took him on an open-carriage tour of the campus. After a reception at New Haven House, he proceeded to the Hyperion Theater for his lecture. He was introduced by Dean Francis Wayland of the Yale Law School, who said, "Young America has won for itself quite a reputation for precocious development. It is with great pleasure that I introduce to you a gentleman representative of England. At an age when Yale men are but just receiving their degrees, Mr. Churchill has already made a name for himself in two hemispheres, on the battlefield and in the department of letters. Mr. Churchill, descended as he is from the best blood of England and America, is at least one beneficial result of Anglo-American matrimony. I take pleasure in presenting our English cousin, Winston Spencer Churchill, M.P."[30]

While this introduction was not up to Mark Twain standards it was most decidedly cordial, and Churchill responded to it in kind. Then, still glowing from the previous evening's success, he permitted himself some humorous embellishments *extempore* on the subject of his imprisonment and escape. "I remained a prisoner for a little less than a month. Cooped up on a place a hundred yards square, for a month, with bad food—the service was shocking—constantly receiving the most discouraging bad news of the operations of my countrymen, you may imagine that the experience was not easy. I frequently asked the Boers to let me go. I knew no reason why they should let me go, nevertheless I tried many ways to persuade them. They were perfectly reasonable, and were not persuaded. So I finally made the attempt to go without their permission.... This experience I have already embodied in a book which I have written, and while I ought not to advertise this book here I hope everyone here will make it their business to procure it...."[31]

This lecture too was successful. The *Evening Register* described his speaking style as "graceful and easy and his drolleries immensely taking...the whole effect of the evening was decidedly agreeable."[32] After his talk he was the guest of honor at a reception of the Graduates' Club, and at ten minutes before midnight he left New Haven on the sleeper train for Washington, D.C., long overdue for a good night's rest. He must have felt considerable satisfaction though, along with the overpowering fatigue, for, as a local newspaper put it, his visit to the home of Yale University had been "a success in every detail."[33]

But now the hours he had been keeping and the pace he had been setting caught up with him. He arrived in Washington feeling distinctly unwell. Senator Chauncey Depew of New York served as his host, showed him around the Capitol, introduced him to President McKinley, with whom Churchill professed himself "considerably impressed,"[34] and presented him with profuse compliments to a fashionable afternoon audience at the National Theater. His health hampered his delivery, however, and the Washington *Post* reported: "He appeared embarrassed when he began, and throughout his lecture his words came in a jerky hesitating way."[35] It was understandable; as he wrote his mother a week later, "I was not at all well in Washington. A certain amount of nervousness in starting my tour and the hard work attendant on it, together with a chill I think I must have got travelling in these stuffy trains alternately too drafty to sit in and too hot to live in, brought on an attack of fever and my temperature ran up to 102, in which condition I had to give my lecture...."[36]

Thus afflicted, but undaunted, Winston journeyed to Baltimore, where, disappointingly, "only a few hundred assembled in a hall which would have held 5,000."[37] He bore up under his multiplying adversities, however, and the Baltimore *Sun* reported that he "made a pleasant impression."[38] He returned immediately to Washington and the shelter of Depew's home. "I found a good doctor who gave me some medicine which had the effect of driving my temperature down,"[39] he wrote, and on the evening of December 16, reasonably convalescent, he boarded the night train for the trip to Boston.

"In the Spring of 1899," Winston related in *My Early Life*, "I became conscious of the fact that there was another Winston Churchill who also wrote books; apparently he wrote novels, and very good novels too, which achieved an enormous circulation in the United States. I received from many quarters congratulations on my skill as a writer of fiction. I thought at first that those were due to a belated appreciation of the merits of *Savrola*. Gradually I realized that there was 'another Richmond in the field,' luckily on the other side of the Atlantic...."[40]

He proceeded to write to him:

London, June 7, 1899

Mr. Winston Churchill presents his compliments to Mr. Winston Churchill, and begs to draw his attention to a matter which concerns them both. He has learnt from the Press notices that Mr. Winston Churchill proposes to bring out another novel, entitled *Richard Carvel*, which is certain to have a considerable sale both in England and America. Mr. Winston Churchill is also the author of a novel now being published in serial form in *Macmillan's Magazine*, and for which he anticipates some sale both in England and America. He also proposes to publish on the 1st of October another military chronicle of the Soudan War. He has no doubt that Mr. Winston Churchill will recognize from this letter—if indeed by no other means—that there is a grave danger of his works being mistaken for those of Mr. Winston Churchill. He feels sure that Mr. Winston Churchill desires this as little as he does himself. In future to avoid mistakes as far as possible, Mr. Winston Churchill has decided to sign all published articles, stories, or other works, "Winston Spencer Churchill," and not "Winston Churchill" as formerly. He trusts that this arrangement will commend itself to Mr. Winston Churchill, and he ventures to suggest, with a view to preventing further confusion which may arise out of this extraordinary coincidence, that both Mr. Winston Churchill and Mr. Winston Churchill should insert a short note in their respective publications explaining to the public which are the works of Mr. Winston Churchill and which those of Mr. Winston Churchill. The text of this note might form a subject for future discussion if Mr. Winston Churchill agrees with Mr. Winston Churchill's proposition. He takes this occasion of complimenting Mr. Winston Churchill upon the style and success of his works which are always brought to his notice whether in magazine or book form, and he trusts that Mr. Winston Churchill has derived equal pleasure from any work of his that may have attracted his attention.

Winston Churchill hastened to reply:

Windsor, Vermont, June 21, 1899
Mr. Winston Churchill is extremely grateful to Mr. Winston Churchill for bringing forward a subject which has given Mr. Winston Churchill much anxiety. Mr. Winston Churchill appreciates the courtesy of Mr. Winston Churchill in adopting the name of "Winston Spencer Churchill" in his books, articles, etc. Mr. Winston Churchill makes haste to add that, had he possessed any other names, he would certainly have adopted one of them. The writings of Mr. Winston Spencer Churchill (henceforth so called) have been brought to Mr. Winston Churchill's notice since the publication of his first story in the "Century."* It did not seem then to Mr. Winston Churchill that the works of Mr. Winston Spencer Churchill would conflict in any way with his own attempts at fiction.

* Probably a reference to a short story titled "Man Overboard—An Episode of the Red Sea," first published in England in *Harmsworth Magazine.*

The proposal of Mr. Winston Spencer Churchill to affix a note to the separate writings of Mr. Winston Spencer Churchill and Mr. Winston Churchill, the text of which is to be agreed upon between them—is quite acceptable to Mr. Winston Churchill. If Mr. Winston Spencer Churchill will do him the favour of drawing up this note, there is little doubt that Mr. Winston Churchill will acquiesce in its particulars.

Mr. Winston Churchill moreover, is about to ask the opinion of his friends and of his publishers as to the advisability of inserting the words "The American" after his name on the title-page of his books. Should this seem wise to them, he will request his publishers to make the change in future editions.

Mr. Winston Churchill will take the liberty of sending Mr. Winston Spencer Churchill copies of the two novels he has written. He has a high admiration for the works of Mr. Winston Spencer Churchill and is looking forward with pleasure to reading *Savrola*.[41]

The next act in this real-life drama of interchangeable identities was now to be played out. "When . . . I visited Boston Mr. Winston Churchill was the first to welcome me," Mr. Winston Spencer Churchill wrote. Some people regarded the first encounter as being little short of momentous; large headlines on the front page of the Boston *Herald* announced it to the world: "Namesakes Meet. Winston Churchills Fast Friends."[42]

Winston Churchill—the British model—had arrived in Boston on Monday morning, December 17. First he went to the post office in search of a packet of letters that was supposed to have been redirected to him from Baltimore. It turned out, however, that the packet had been forwarded to the American Churchill's house on Beacon Street. Still weak from his illness, the British Winston went directly to the Hotel Touraine in order to resume his convalescence while Pond went to the American Winston's address in search of his client's mail. Of course, it had not yet been delivered, so Pond, not wishing to return to the hotel empty-handed, brought the American Churchill back with him. When he arrived at the British Churchill's room with the American Churchill in tow, words quite understandably failed him. At last, being no less a hand at introductions than, say, Henry Morton Stanley, Pond simply said, "Mr. Churchill. Mr. Churchill."[43]

Boston was the highlight of Churchill's 1900–1901 lecture tour, as evidenced by this front page from the Boston *Herald* for December 18, 1900. Churchill did not receive such prominent attention in the United States until he came here during World War II.

NAMESAKES MEET.

Winston Churchills Fast Friends.

NOT RELATIVES, HOWEVER.

Neither Can Think of Family
Ties Binding Them.

AS TO ONE MATTER THEY AGREE.

Discuss Richard Harding Davis in
a Very Sympathetic Way.

MEETING OF THE TWO WINSTON CHURCHILLS.

The two Winstons chatted amiably for a while and agreed to meet for lunch in the Touraine's Dutch [*sic*] Room shortly after one. The Englishman was somewhat less than sanguine about this particular portion of his American odyssey, given the direction in which it seemed to be moving thus far. Not only had his mail gone astray, but the Boston barber who had shaved him that morning had cut a liberal slice out of his upper lip in the process. The meeting with his American homonym had been a first indication that the trend might be starting to turn, and now a doctor that Pond had called for checked him over and pronounced him reasonably fit. Thus, when the time came for him to go down to lunch he was feeling distinctly more mellow. He and the U.S. Churchill talked at length and discovered that they had much in common besides their names. They were both under thirty (the American had been born in 1871), both interested in public affairs, both "fast starters." They did not appear to be related, however. Even given the British Churchill's extensive American background (which, among other things, linked him to an eighteen-year-old Hyde Park native—Franklin D. Roosevelt—as a seventh cousin once removed), neither he nor his American counterpart was ever able to come up with the name of a common ancestor.

After lunch the two nonrelatives took a walk across the Boston Common to the Charles. Midway along one of the bridges spanning the river they paused to look down at the water, and Winston Spencer said to Winston, "Why don't you go into politics? I mean to be Prime Minister of England: it would be a great lark if you were President of the United States at the same time."[44] Winston's response to this suggestion is unrecorded, but he did get elected to the New Hampshire legislature two years later, so we may assume that he was listening.

Dusk had fallen by the time they arrived back at the hotel, and they took temporary leave of each other until after Winston Spencer's lecture that evening at the Tremont Temple, a lecture that proved to be something of a high point in his North American tour: ". . . an enormous pro-British demonstration was staged, and even the approaches to Tremont Hall were thronged. The platform here was composed of 300 Americans in red uniforms belonging to an Anglo-American Society, and the aspect of the meeting was magnificent."[45] According to the *Herald* his lecture "drew to Tremont Temple one of the largest audiences ever seen within that edifice."[46] And according to the *Globe*, "The audience was dressy, largely of British sympathies, and thoroughly enthusiastic."[47] After a flattering introduction by Professor F. C. de Sumichrast of Harvard, Churchill rose and strode to the rostrum. British and American flags in draping folds hung intertwined from the choir gallery behind him. Apparently inspired by the magnitude of his welcome, he gave one of his best performances, and a reporter for the *Herald* set down a detailed account of his style and bearing at age 26:

He is very youthful in appearance, and, in complete harmony with this, has a quiet, modest manner which is most engaging. Hesitating occasionally as he goes, as if picking his words, or as if uncertain of what he wants to say, he puts his audience in a slightly apprehensive mood. You think, when you have heard him for a while, with those simple and perfectly unstudied gestures of his, in which the whole body moves in alternation with movements of the hands and arms, that he is going to commit some gaucherie for which you would not care to be responsible; but, as he proceeds, and you get accustomed to him, the simplicity takes on the appearance of the most subtle art, the gestures are seen to be perfectly appropriate to the situations described, while the hesitating delivery becomes a means to effects which even veteran lecturers would be glad if they could imitate.

In a quarter of an hour you find the address throbbing with the mingled humor and pathos of all battle experiences worthy of the name; in half an hour he gives you the impression, boy as he seems, of a keen and resourceful intelligence, not only familiar with the ways of the world, but also able to hold his own in it, and then you want to hear him to the end.

It is a cleverly managed narrative throughout, for the lecturer's problem is to weave his own personal experiences into a narrative of the South African campaign in such a way as to keep his audience interested. That he did this last night was abundantly shown by the running fire of laughter and applause which divided his story up into sections—like so many audible punctuation marks.[48]

At the close Churchill spoke passionately of Anglo-American friendship, and in reply to a formal expression of thanks from Professor de Sumichrast he gestured toward the American flag and said, "There is no one in this room who has a greater respect for that flag than the humble individual to whom you, of the city which gave birth to the idea of a 'tea party,' have so kindly listened. I am proud that I am the natural product of an Anglo-American alliance; not political, but stronger and more sacred, an alliance of heart to heart."[49] It would not be a complete exaggeration to say that this little effusion brought the house down.

Joyful and triumphant—even though Christmas was still a week off—the British Churchill was entertained to dinner by the American one at the Somerset Club, just down the road, at 42 Beacon Street, from the latter's home at number 181 (where the former's mail was still expected at any moment). It was "a merry party," to use the *Globe*'s description,[50] and only one minor mishap resulted from the revelry: whereas Winston Spencer's mail seemed determined to find its way invariably to Winston, the bill for the evening's festivities sped unerringly into Winston Spencer's hands despite the fact that it was Winston who was supposed to pay it. After a couple of hours, however, the entanglements were finally straightened out, and Winston Spencer got his letters while Winston kept his credit rating.

From Boston the British Churchill went to New Bedford for a lecture, and from New Bedford he traveled to Hartford. Although he not only interested his audience there, but also "amused and instructed it"[51] (according to the Hartford *Courant*), he was very unhappy that his net fee for the lecture was only fifty dollars. The house was somewhat better in Springfield, where he again made a very favorable impression: "Mr. Churchill is young and manly in appearance, with an active physique, a bright face and a pleasant smile. His mannerisms are many, and he is thoroughly English, but his personality is pleasant and genial, and the sense of oddity inspired by his address is soon lost in the interest of his subject, which he treats in a fine literary as well as graphic style, and in the quaint humor with which his speech abounds."[52]

Springfield offered Churchill the opportunity, always welcome, to have a look at an aspect of military technology, in this case the famous Armory. Arriving in town at around 3:15 P.M., he was conducted directly to the works, where he spent a good ninety minutes inspecting, examining, and asking questions. The next day he lectured in Fall River and then started on the first leg of a journey to Ottawa, where he was scheduled to spend Christmas with the Governor-General, Lord Minto. Although his trip had definitely had its high spots thus far, it had also been strenuous and financially disappointing. "I shall be glad to get back again onto British territory," he wrote Jennie from Boston en route, "and I am looking forward to finding out a great deal about the political situation there."[53]

When he arrived in Ottawa, he found that the political situation was less interesting than the emotional one, for by either "good fortune or good management" Miss Pamela Plowden was there awaiting him. Like most love affairs, true or otherwise, the course of Winston's and Pamela's had not been smooth. While he had been campaigning in South Africa he had written letters to her which indicated that his feelings remained intense, and Jennie had gotten the impression from Pamela that she, in turn, was considering matrimony very seriously. This impression may have been correct, or it may have been simply the product of wishful thinking; in either case the end result was a conclusion on Pamela's part that marriage with Winston would not be advisable. She does not appear to have discussed this conclusion with anyone, and her presence in Ottawa that Christmas was probably attributable to both a desire on her part to confirm her judgment and a desire on everybody else's part to play Cupid. Lord Minto had been alerted to be on the lookout for some sign of which way the wind was blowing, but all he could report to Jennie was that "everything seemed to me very tolerably Platonic."[54] From Winston, however, who was feeling rather like a wounded stag, came more explicit news about the Ottawa encounter. "Pamela was there—" he wrote, "very pretty and apparently quite happy. We had no painful discussions, but there is no doubt in my mind that she is the only woman I could ever live happily with."[55] (Of course, this prognosis, like most hyperbole, proved to be more histrionic than prophetic. Indeed, when Churchill at fifty-five looked back on his marriage at thirty-three to Clementine Hozier—some seven years after this virtual vow of

celibacy—he felt sufficiently genial about the whole arrangement to write, "I married and lived happily ever afterwards."[56]
Winston had other problems besides those of the heart. Pond,
it seemed, in addition to taking 30 percent of all fees coming
in, had subcontracted many of the Canadian lectures to local
agents and accepted from them a fixed guarantee that bore no
relation to the gross receipts. Thus, in Toronto for example,
Churchill ended up with less than 20 percent of the total ticket
sales money for his lecture—about $350 out of $2,250—and this
anomaly prompted him to put his foot down with a thud loud
enough to be heard five hundred miles away in New York City.
MR. CHURCHILL AND MAJOR POND, the *Times* headline trum-
peted on December 29. "Disagreement Leads to the Correspondent Refusing to Lecture at Brandford, Ontario, Last
Night."[57] Three days later, though, during the first hours of the
twentieth century, Winston was able to report to his mother:
"Peace has . . . been patched up on my terms, and I propose
to go through with the tour."[58] He did not expect to enjoy it,
however. ". . . last week I arrived to lecture in an American
town & found Pond had not arranged any public lecture but
that I was hired out for £40 to perform at an evening party in
a private home—like a conjurer. Several times I have ha-
rangued in local theatres to almost empty benches. I have been
horribly vulgarised by the odious advertisements Pond and
Myrmidons think it necessary to circulate—and only my cyni-
cal vein has helped me to go on."[59] A week later, still in Canada, his mood was no sunnier: ". . . I have only eighteen more
lectures so that the worst is over. I have got to hate the tour
very much indeed, and if it were much longer I do not think I
would be able to go through with it."[60]
    On January 9, 1901, Churchill returned to the United States
and began the western swing of his travels. His first stop was
the University of Michigan at Ann Arbor, where he was greeted
with boos and hisses when he declared that "when we have
won this war—as we surely shall . . ."[61] the Transvaal and the
Orange Free State would be incorporated into the British
Commonwealth. Pro-Boer, or at least anti-imperialist, feeling
ran very high at Michigan. During the Presidential campaign
the Democratic candidate, William Jennings Bryan, had made a

typically spellbinding speech there on the evils of colonialism, or colonialism as practiced by the McKinley administration, and he had pointed to the fighting in South Africa as another instance of a great power "waging an unjust war to crush out the liberties . . . of freedom-loving people. . . ." The speech, delivered only three months before Churchill's visit, had left a strong impression, on top of which Winston, fresh from two weeks of ardently sympathetic Canadian audiences, apparently failed to take his return to less indulgent American crowds into account. He got through his lecture more or less intact, though, and afterwards was approached by a young law student named Ohlinger, who asked him for an interview.

In Ohlinger's eyes, Churchill was "the handsomest young man I had ever seen, the scion of the house of Marlborough, the descendant of the great John Churchill, the victor of Blenheim, Ramillies, Oudenarde, and Malplaquet."[62] Even someone as oblivious of others as Winston must have been struck by unsolicited adulation of such intensity, and finding it neither unwelcome nor routine he settled down to a long night of private oratory which left his interlocutor even more transfixed with admiration than he had been to begin with. "I believe that as civilized nations become more powerful they will get more ruthless," he said. And: "I think the press affords a ladder which is available to everyone in a way afforded by no other profession; put out good stuff and in time people will say, 'We must have this.'" And: "You ask my advice to the young correspondent? It is: verify your quotations and avoid split infinitives." And: "The tendency of language nowadays is to diverge into dialect." And: "It is an enormous commercial advantage for the United States and Great Britain to speak the same language."[63] Et cetera, et cetera, and so forth. At four o'clock in the morning a thoroughly dazzled Ohlinger staggered back to his dormitory. Several hours later a thoroughly exhausted Churchill boarded a train for Chicago.

He called it "this strange place of pigs"[64] (referring to the packing plants, not the population) in a letter to his new—as of July 28—stepfather, George Cornwallis-West, who was only sixteen days his senior. His visit there went well, though, once he had surmounted a rather bellicose reception at his first lec-

ture. As he remembered it, "I encountered vociferous opposition. However, when I made a few jokes against myself, and
paid a sincere tribute to the courage and humanity of the
Boers, they were pleased."[65] The details of the incident were
that when Winston flashed his first stereopticon picture on the
screen and described the man shown as "a typical Boer soldier," a man in the balcony rose and shouted "Hurrah for the
Boers!" Most of the audience joined in, but several people
hissed, and Churchill seized the opportunity: "Don't hiss," he
shouted. "There is one of the heroes of history. The man in the
gallery is right."[66] From then on it was clear sailing; although
the audience continued to applaud pictures of the Boers, they
also applauded the young man who was speaking so fair-
mindedly about them.

After the lecture there was an informal get-together at the
University Club. The Chicagoans, all unsuspecting, called on
Winston to say a few words. Given his downtrodden childhood and his exalted ambitions, Churchill never quite got over
the thrill of being called upon to speak—and then actually listened to. It was opium to him, and he launched into the subject
of Anglo-American amity with great gusto, capping his declama-
tion with the inevitable: "... the greatest common trait by
which I lay most store is the fact that Englishmen and Americans wash. It remains after all is said and done that the sym-
bol of Anglo-Saxon unity is the bathtub and the toothbrush."[67]
Fortunately, no representative of the New York *Times* was in
the room.

Winston lectured again in Chicago on January 12, this time
before an even rowdier crowd than the one he had confronted
two days before. The Central Music Hall was packed with
Irishmen, who fueled their sympathy for the Boers with their
animosity toward the English—and with whisky. Churchill was
having a difficult time making himself heard and decided, in
recounting the progress of one particular battle, to alter history slightly in the service of more immediately pressing needs.
It seemed that in this encounter, as Churchill told it, the British
were in the direst straits imaginable. All seemed lost. Brave
men prepared to die. What could save them? "In this desperate
situation the Dublin Fusiliers arrived! Trumpeters sounded the

charge and the enemy were swept from the field."[68] The audience sat stunned for a second, torn between blood loyalties and political convictions. Eventually the blood won, and cheers rang out for the immensely gratified Lieutenant Churchill.

After Chicago Winston resumed the western swing of his tour. January 21 found him lecturing in Winnipeg ("a magnificent audience of men in evening dress & ladies half out of it"[69]). On January 22, the nineteenth-century world officially came to an end with the death in England of Queen Victoria. "So the Queen is dead," Churchill wrote his mother. "The news reached us at Winnipeg and this city far away among the snows—fourteen hundred miles from any British town of importance began to hang its head and hoist half-masted flags. A great and solemn event . . ."[70] Many Americans felt that Victoria's demise presaged the disintegration of the entire British Empire. One such was James C. Young of Minneapolis, where Winston lectured on January 23. Of course Churchill was staunch for the Empire, and he proceeded to back up his faith by betting Young one hundred pounds against the proposition "that within ten years from this date the British Empire will be substantially reduced by loss in Australia or Canada or India . . . in other words that the British Crown will lose one-quarter of India or of Canada or of Australia, before ten years are gone."[71] By January 23, 1911, Winston was Home Secretary and very very busy. It is not known whether he remembered to collect his hundred pounds.

The tour wound down. Churchill went on to St. Louis and then started working his way east. He arrived back in New York on January 31 for his final lecture, to be given at Carnegie Hall. He had earned slightly more than six thousand dollars for his labors in North America, but his trip had been arduous, and he was worn out. "I was exhausted," he wrote. "For more than five months I had spoken for an hour or more every night except Sundays, and often twice a day, and had travelled without ceasing, usually by night, rarely sleeping twice in the same bed. And this had followed a year of marching and fighting with rarely a roof or a bed at all."[72]

With his final lecture out of the way, Winston had Friday,

February 1, to spend in blessed idleness with Bourke Cockran.
Saturday was Queen Victoria's funeral and an official day of
mourning all over the world. Escorted by Cockran, Churchill
went down to the Hudson River docks and boarded the *Etruria*, which was due to sail shortly after noon. He was leaving
America on the same ship that had first brought him there five
years before.

With his five books and three months of lectures he had accumulated a capital base of better than sixty thousand dollars.
This money was to serve as the foundation for an unprecedented political career, leaving Churchill free to devote his
gargantuan energies to affairs of state. He was launched. Almost thirty years were to pass before he visited the United
States again.

CHAPTER FOUR

The First Career

FOR MOST PEOPLE the figure of Winston Churchill emerges from the ocean of history in the 1930s like a full-grown leviathan, a sudden prescient colossus rising from the depths of British politics to warn against the impending typhoon of Hitlerite aggression. His career during the first three decades of the twentieth century, if it is spoken of at all, is usually skimmed over as a mere prelude to his apocalyptic statesmanship during the second three. Yet that career was in many ways as remarkable in its particulars as the one that succeeded it. During the period 1901 through 1929, Churchill married one wife; quit two parties; sired five children; wrote ten books; fought twelve elections (winning eight), and served successively as Under-Secretary of State for the Colonies, President of the Board of Trade, Home Secretary, First Lord of the Admiralty, Minister of Munitions, Secretary of State for War and Air, Secretary of State for the Colonies, and Chancellor of the Exchequer. Given so much activity, it is not surprising that he did not come to the United States in these years, but, to begin with at least, such a visit was not often far from his thoughts.

One tie to America that continued strong was Bourke Cockran, who, like Winston, was an adamant Free-Trader. The tariff issue was a vital one in the early 1900s on both sides of the Atlantic, and Churchill, caught up in a dispute with the dominant protectionist elements in his own party, was eager to see how the struggle against high import duties was going in the United States. "My dear Bourke," he wrote in December 1903.

"If all is quiet in this country, I shall certainly come over to see
the Presidential Election next autumn. . . . It is rather an inspiring reflection to think that so many of us . . . are fighting
in a common cause—you to attack protection, we to defend
Free Trade. I think what the double victory would mean for
the wealth and welfare of the world."[1]

Churchill's differences with his fellow Conservatives were
not limited to questions of tariff. Indeed, he had been regularly
at odds with his party's leadership since his maiden speech in
Parliament in February 1901. On that occasion he had argued
against a punitive approach to the all but utterly defeated
Boers, prompting his Liberal opponent Lloyd George to remark to him, "Judging from your sentiments, you are standing
against the Light."[2]

Wherever Winston was standing, there were fewer and
fewer Tories standing with him over the course of the next
three years, and on May 31, 1904, he made the breach with his
ancestral party official and crossed the floor of the House of
Commons. As a consequence, "all" was most decidedly not
"quiet" for him in Great Britain as autumn approached, and
the condition precedent to another visit to America did not
exist. Things were so far from being quiet, in fact, that Churchill showed some definite signs of strain, the most notable of
which was his inability to finish a speech on a proposed labor-
relations law because of a lapse of memory. As he explained
the incident to Cockran, his practice had been to memorize his
speeches verbatim, but on this occasion, on approaching his
peroration, he had simply come up empty. Henceforth (and
for the rest of his life) he would fortify himself for a speech
with ample written notes. But regardless of his future fortunes
in Parliamentary debate, the pace of British politics was now
far too intense to permit a voyage to observe American politics
in action.

Cockran was disappointed. On July 1, 1904, the eve of the
Democratic Convention, he wrote, "My dear Winston, Before
leaving for St. Louis, I want to tell you how deeply I regret the
change of plans which prevents you from being my guest at the
Convention and for the remainder of the summer. . . ."[3] He
went on to invite Churchill over to watch the election cam-

paign and to plead with him to take several months' rest in the United States before jumping back into the melee in the United Kingdom. "Think over this," he concluded, "and let me have a line saying that I may expect you immediately after the adjournment of Parliament."[4]

It was not to be. Churchill, as the newest Liberal, had to solidify his position in his adopted party. More important, he had to find another constituency. Oldham had elected him as a Conservative, and while the local party organization was not prepared to force a by-election—which it might lose—in an effort to expel him from Parliament, it was clear that at the next general election it would do everything in its power to deny him a seat. Only a few miles from Oldham, however, was the staunchly Free-Trade district of North-West Manchester with its prominent Jewish community led by such men as Chaim Weizmann, Israel Zangwill, and Nathan Laski. As an underdog in life—at least by his own perceptions—Churchill had an instinctive sympathy for the Jews, and he had played an important part in defeating a Conservative bill that would have interfered with the immigration into Britain of refugees from the Russian pogroms. Thus he was ideally suited to North-West Manchester's specifications, and North-West Manchester promised to be equally well suited to his. In December 1905, Conservative Prime Minister Arthur Balfour resigned and the Liberal Campbell-Bannerman was called upon by King Edward to form a new government. The following month a newly appointed Under-Secretary of State for the Colonies proceeded to his new constituency to fight his first campaign for his new party.

The general election of 1906 was an unmitigated Conservative rout. The Liberals won an outright majority in the House of Commons, 377 out of 670, and together with their allies, Labour and the Irish Nationalists, they accounted for 513 votes as against only 157 for the former party in power. Churchill's determination to stand firm on his Free-Trade principles had saved him from a political wreck, and his onetime colleagues lost no time in likening him to the proverbial rat-leaving-the-ship. But Winston had acted out of motives of conscience

throughout; any advantage he derived from his conduct was
the consequence of chance, not calculation. Perhaps it was because chance favored him so lavishly that the word "oppor-
tunist" came to be associated with his name. With his superior
in the Colonial Office, Lord Elgin, sitting in the House of
Lords, it was Winston Spencer Churchill, barely out of his
third decade of life, who suddenly stood forth as the new government's primary spokesman on matters affecting His Majesty's Empire overseas.

⁂ January 1906 was auspicious for Winston not only politically,
but financially and literarily as well. For nearly four years he
had been working on a Life of his father, and on January 7 the
New York *Times* reported: "The rumor is current in London
that Macmillan & Co. paid Winston Churchill $40,000 for his
'Life of Lord Randolph Churchill,' and guaranteed him besides
one-half of the profits after $60,000 has been realized from its
sale. . . . America may share Great Britain's pride in this literary success, for Winston Churchill's mother was a member
of a New York family."[5] The rumor was correct; in 1905 Winston had empowered Frank Harris to act as his literary agent
(long before that gentleman published *My Life and Loves*),
and Harris had negotiated a handsome advance on his behalf
—a handsomer one, the *Times* noted, than either Charles Dick-
ens or Lord Byron ever received.

The two-volume Life was widely praised and only occasionally damned on publication. It can best be described as a
political biography, in the sense that its overwhelming concern
is with Lord Randolph's public life—there is no mention of
syphilis. Of course, Churchill was by no means impartial on the
subject of his father, but he made as valiant an attempt at objectivity as was possible given his psychological orientation.
The work is not hagiographic, in other words, even if it often
reads somewhat like an apologia.

In the United States the reception accorded *Lord Randolph
Churchill* was friendly and its sales were good; only the incumbent President, still dwelling on what must have been a truly
disastrous first encounter more than five years earlier, regis-
tered a disapproving vote. "I have been over Winston Church-

ill's life of his father," TR told Henry Cabot Lodge. "I dislike the father and dislike the son, so I may be prejudiced. Still,
I feel that, while the biographer and his subject possess some
real far-sightedness . . . yet they both possess or possest such
levity, lack of sobriety, lack of permanent principle, and an
inordinate thirst for that cheap form of admiration which is
given to notoriety, as to make them poor public servants."[6] To
historian George Otto Trevelyan, Roosevelt wrote, "Rosebery
[British Prime Minister, 1894–95] has a slight tendency . . . to
overemphasis; as witness the way in which he speaks of Winston Churchill's clever, forceful, rather cheap and vulgar life
of that clever, forceful, rather cheap and vulgar egoist, his
father, as if it was one of the very greatest biographies in the
world; instead of being one of the smart, bright, amusing
books of a given season."[7] Finally, to TR, Jr.: "Yes, that is an
interesting book of Winston Churchill's about his father, but I
can't help feeling about both of them that the older one *was* a
rather cheap character, and the younger one *is* a rather cheap
character."[*8]

Admired or despised, Churchill certainly seemed to have arrived, and the contemporaneous progress of his American
counterpart prompted the London *Sketch* to advise its read-
ers to "Watch the Winstons": "Two of the men most conspicuous in the foreground of public life at the present moment are the Winston Churchills. Ours has set the Empire
ringing with his speech on the Transvaal Constitution [deliv-
ered July 31, 1906, and calling for universal white male suff-
rage]. America's is the cynosure of 80,000,000 pairs of eyes in
the States. . . . He has just published a new novel. . . . Moreover, he fills the eyes of politicians, because he is a candidate
for Governor of New Hampshire [an unsuccessful one, it
proved]. Here is Lord Randolph Churchill's son at one and
thirty the most striking and picturesque figure in the Liberal

---

* Elting Morison, who edited Roosevelt's correspondence, offers an alternative explanation for this virulent antipathy—that is, one unrelated to
the unfortunate meeting of December 1900: "Possessing the Churchillian
talents, although perhaps in lesser degree, and the Churchillian defects,
although perhaps to a greater extent, Roosevelt may . . . have come . . .
naturally by his skepticism of the Churchillian personality. . . ."[9]

Party—a potential Premier. Across the water is his cogno-
menal double, a man of 34, whose goal is the Presidency.
Moral: Watch the Winstons."[10]

What was the British Winston like at this the dawn of his
political maturity? The best portrait of him at this period of his
life comes from Violet Bonham-Carter, *née* Asquith, who met
him for the first time at a dinner party:

> I found myself sitting next to this young man who seemed to me
> quite different from any other young man I had ever met. For a
> long time he remained sunk in abstraction. Then he appeared to
> become suddenly aware of my existence. He turned on me a lower-
> ing gaze and asked me abruptly how old I was. I replied that I was
> nineteen. "And I," he said almost despairingly, "am thirty-two al-
> ready. Younger than anyone else who *counts* though," he added, as
> if to comfort himself. Then savagely: "Curse ruthless time! Curse
> our mortality. How cruelly short is our allotted span for all we must
> cram into it!" And he burst forth into an eloquent diatribe on the
> shortness of human life, the immensity of possible human accom-
> plishment—a theme so well exploited by the poets, prophets and
> philosophers of all ages that it might seem difficult to invest it with
> a new and startling significance. Yet for me he did so, in a torrent
> of magnificent language which appeared to be both effortless and
> inexhaustible and ended up with the words I shall always remem-
> ber: "We are all worms. But I do believe that I am a glowworm.
> . . ."
> Until the end of the dinner I listened to him spellbound. I can
> remember thinking: *This* is what people mean when they talk of
> seeing stars. That is what I am doing now. I do not to this day
> know who was on my other side. Good manners, social obligation,
> duty—all had gone with the wind. I was transfixed, transported
> into a new element. I knew only that I had seen a great light. I
> recognized it as the light of genius.[11]

In 1907 Churchill's considerable responsibilities as Under-
Secretary of State for the Colonies impelled him to undertake a
grand tour of His Majesty's African possessions; at any rate,
they didn't impel him not to undertake such a journey. In
September, accordingly, he set off for Kenya and the Upper
Nile, and for four months he toured, inspected, hunted, and
wrote, bringing himself thoroughly up to date on Colonial affairs. He returned to England in January 1908. In March he

published a book called *My African Journey*. In April Camp-
bell-Bannerman died and Violet Asquith's father, Herbert
Henry Asquith, became Prime Minister. One of his first acts
was to promote Under-Secretary of State Churchill out of the
Colonial Office and into the cabinet as President of the Board of
Trade.

In Washington, D.C., meanwhile, Theodore Roosevelt was
planning an African journey of his own, to commence as soon
as he was relieved of his constitutional responsibilities by William Howard Taft. "I have just finished reading Winston
Churchill's account of his white rhinoceros hunt," he wrote
Whitelaw Reid, the U.S. Ambassador to the Court of St. James's.
"... I should consider my entire African trip a success if I
could . . . find the game as Churchill describes it. . . . In the
same mail with your letter came a very nice letter from the
Sirdar . . . saying that he would do everything in his power to
get me a white rhinoceros; but it will do no harm for you to
have Lord Crewe [Elgin's successor as Colonial Secretary]
write the Uganda people anyhow. . . ."¹² Churchill must have
heard of TR's interest in his trip, because six weeks later the
President was in touch with the Ambassador again: "I do not
like Winston Churchill but I supposed I ought to write him.
Will you send him the enclosed letter if it is all right?"¹³ The
enclosure read:

My dear Mr. Churchill: Thru Mr. Reid I have just received the
beautiful copy of your book, and I wish to thank you for it. I had
read all the chapters as they came out, with a great deal of interest;
not only the chapters upon the very important and difficult problems of the Government itself, but also the hunting chapters and
especially the one describing how you got that rare and valuable
trophy, a white rhinoceros head. Everyone has been most kind to
me about my proposed trip to Africa. I trust I shall have as good
luck as you had.

Again thanking you, believe me, Sincerely yours,

Theodore Roosevelt.¹⁴

Churchill's reply to this singularly restrained encomium, if he
wrote one, has not been preserved.

The year 1908 was an exciting turning point in Churchill's
life; it marked not only his accession to the cabinet, but his

relinquishment of bachelorhood—and his brother's relinquishment of bachelorhood as well. The first steps toward both the
cabinet room and the matrimonial altar did not go smoothly,
however. He had met Miss Clementine Hozier for the first time
in 1904 at a dance given by Lady Crewe. At his own request,
Jennie had introduced him to her, but once left alone with the
young lady—almost ten years his junior—his eloquence seems
to have failed him utterly. "Winston just stared," Clementine
Churchill recalled many decades later. "He never uttered one
word and was very gauche—he never asked me for a dance,
he never asked me to have supper with him . . . he just stood
and stared."[15] The next meeting in this dubious courtship occurred four years later at a dinner party given by Lady St.
Helier, who had helped Winston get into the 21st Lancers in
1898. On this occasion, apparently, Churchill was not struck
dumb, for he asked Clementine if she had read his biography
of his father. She admitted she had not, whereupon he asked,
"If I send you the book tomorrow, will you read it?" She said
she certainly would and did not hear from Churchill again for
a month. "That made a bad impression," she acknowledged.[16]
On their third meeting, despite the book incident, the young
couple finally managed to make some sort of contact, and as
Churchill prepared to take office at the Board of Trade in April
he wrote Clementine, ". . . what a comfort & pleasure it was to
me to meet a girl with so much intellectual quality & such
strong reserves of noble sentiment. I hope we shall meet again
and come to know each other better and like each other more.
. . ."[17]

When a member of Parliament was appointed to the cabinet
in pre–World War I Britain, the law dictated that he once
again had to place himself before his constituents. Winston
was thus obliged to return to North-West Manchester and
campaign for the seat he could have retained at leisure had he
remained an Under-Secretary. The Conservatives, free to concentrate their wrath on one by-election, went after the party
turncoat in a venomous mass. Churchill polled 651 votes fewer
than in 1906; his opponent polled 1,019 more. Churchill was
defeated. His correspondence with Miss Hozier took on a
slightly mournful tone: "Write to me again," he pleaded on

April 27, four days after his defeat. "I am a solitary figure in the midst of crowds. Be kind to me."[18]

All was by no means lost, of course. Two days after his letter to Clementine he accepted an invitation from the Liberal Association in Dundee, Scotland, to contest the seat which had become available there, and on May 9 he was returned with a plurality of over 2,500 votes out of some 16,000 cast. On August 4 Jack married Gwendeline Bertie. On August 10 Clementine came to visit Winston at Blenheim Palace. On August 11 they set off for a walk around the grounds, took shelter from a sudden rainstorm in an ornamental gazebo overlooking the lake, talked quietly to each other for several minutes, and became engaged. On August 12 Winston wrote to the beautiful young wife of the Earl of Lytton, "Pamela, I am to marry Clementine & I say to you as you said to me when you married Victor—you must always be our best friend."[19] The marriage took place exactly one month after this letter was written, in St. Margaret's, Westminster, the parish church of the House of Commons; it was to be till death did them part.

Nowadays we tend to think of Winston Churchill as having been an unreconstructed hard-line Tory, and even a reactionary in some respects. It may come as a surprise, therefore, to discover that, with his accession to the Board of Trade, he became one of the most militant and dedicated social reformers of his day. "Winston . . . is full of the poor who he has just discovered," wrote fellow Liberal Charles Masterman, with heavy condescension and indifferent grammar. "He thinks he is called by Providence to do something for them. 'Why have I always been kept safe within a hair's breadth of death,' he added, 'except to do something like this? I'm not going to live long,' was also his refrain."[20]

The Board of Trade was responsible for overseeing matters of employment and labor relations and was thus a good launching pad for reform. Here Churchill first made manifest those qualities of energy and intellect which rendered him so remarkable an administrator and political leader. To a certain extent his extraordinary capacity for work was a product of his noticeable preoccupation with mortality, his belief (or hope?)

that he would die young like his father. But to a much greater extent his productivity was the simple outgrowth of a prodigious natural endowment. In the context of day-to-day politics, however, his astounding talents were coupled with his equally astounding want of personal empathy; he still had absolutely no understanding of his impact on others and only a very limited understanding of human motivation. "He was as impervious to atmosphere as a diver in his bell," wrote Violet Asquith; ". . . for those outside it often seemed to be an impenetrable shell. . . ."²¹ On top of this obliviousness, he was essentially guileless; he was one of those innocent souls who are genuinely incapable of conceiving of the possibility that decent and respectable people might not share all of their fundamental convictions. He always argued and acted from principle, and assumed that everybody else did. He always dedicated himself to his causes without reservation, and assumed that everybody else did. He always fought ferociously for what he believed to be the right solutions to political problems, and assumed that everybody else did. Petty connivance, rancor, duplicity, and corruption were all incomprehensible to him; honor, loyalty, chivalry, and good faith were moral absolutes. He lived in a different world from the people around him; the fantasy world of genteel Victorian Ladies and Gentlemen which his parents had embodied as he longingly gazed out at them from the confines of the nursery. It was as the British politician Leopold Amery said: he was always caught up in "his own original thought-world."²²

The foremost consequence of Churchill's unconventional personality traits was that throughout his political career— and to his constant astonishment and dismay—he was one of the most fiercely disliked men in all of Great Britain. Of course, he was also greatly admired, but the sharpness of his mind and tongue, coupled with his obdurate refusal to subordinate his convictions to the exigencies of party consensus, was violently resented by his contemporaries. In debate, moreover, he neither gave nor asked for any quarter, and, given his wit and forensic skill, that frequently meant that his opponents suffered dreadful drubbings at his hands. The Conservatives, who were naturally hostile to him to begin with, reacted like maddened bulls to his pointed Parliamentary barbs. "I like the marital and commanding air with which the right hon. Gentleman treats facts," he would say of one of their leaders. "He stands no nonsense from them."[23] And of the decimated Tory contingent in Parliament he would declare, "Call them not the party Opposite but the party in that corner."[24] No wonder that on one occasion the entire Conservative representation got up and walked out of the chamber when Winston rose to speak, or that on another a backbencher hurled a book at him which struck him in the face.[25] Even outside of Parliament his personality excited violent emotions. Twice within the space of one week in 1909, for example, perfect strangers attempted to attack him with whips because of his well-publicized ambivalence about woman suffrage.[26]

Churchill found all this animosity both distressing and incomprehensible. His belief, as he had once written to Cockran, was that "in this country . . . we make it a rule & keep it to some extent never to bring politics into private life or private life into politics. . . ."[27] Such was the totality of his involvement in public affairs, however, that his private life and his politics were frequently indistinguishable.

Such vicissitudes aside, Churchill made a fine showing at the Board of Trade, inaugurating three major programs designed to mitigate the consequences of unemployment: labor exchanges, job insurance, and public works projects. As Professor Henry Pelling of Cambridge University has said in summing up Winston's two years as the Board's President, he proved to be "a man equalled only by Lloyd George among his contemporaries in his capacity to diagnose and effectively to treat the worst social evils of his day."[28]

In January 1910 came another general election. The Liberals, having failed to make an appreciable dent in many of the nation's problems over the course of the previous four years, more or less resigned themselves to losing some of their majority. They remained in power, however, and Churchill was offered the plum position of Home Secretary in the new administration. This was the senior secretaryship of state, an office with broad responsibilities across the spectrum of British life, including immigration, public order, and the prison system. Having once been imprisoned and having found the experience almost intolerable ("I certainly hated every minute of my captivity more than I have ever hated any other period in my whole life"[29]), Winston was eager to improve conditions for the convicts in British penal institutions, and he introduced many humane reforms. He ran afoul of controversy, though, when it came to dealing with labor unrest, and he was blamed for using excessive force in contending with a series of railroad and mining disputes. Studies of his actions have demonstrated that he behaved much more in a spirit of moderation than of belligerency; indeed, he was criticized by the Conservatives and the *Times* for his leniency in dealing with some violently restive coal miners in Wales. Despite his restraint, however, what must, in the light of scholarship, be termed a myth has grown up and persisted about the truculence of his conduct; even today many British working men revile his memory because he supposedly "called out the troops at Tonypandy."

A much less serious episode has come down to us through history as The Siege of Sidney Street. This fracas involved three or four anarchists who in January 1911 killed three policemen and then holed up in an old building, 100 Sidney Street, in London's East End. When Churchill learned that the gang had been cornered, his spirit of adventure got the better of him and he leaped out of his bath, hastily got dressed, and hurried to the scene. There his presence proved something of an embarrassment: ". . . my position of authority . . . attracted inevitably to itself direct responsibility. I saw now that I should have done much better to have remained quietly in my office. On the other hand, it was impossible to get into one's car and drive away while matters stood in such great uncertainty, and moreover were extremely interesting."[30] Eventually two of the anarchists were killed when 100 Sidney Street caught fire and, on Churchill's orders, was permitted to burn. But the reputed leader of the gang, one Peter the Painter, was never found. Still, in the final analysis, Churchill's presence probably saved lives, for it was he who prevented an overzealous fire chief from trying to extinguish the burning building while the desperados were actively firing from the windows. He was nevertheless roundly criticized in Commons for having so undignifiedly mixed in beneath his echelon; hap-

pily, there was as much amusement as there was vitriol in the
censure that was meted out.

In July 1911 while Churchill was still at the Home Office,
the German gunboat *Panther* appeared off the Moroccan port
of Agadir, which was widely recognized to be within the
French "sphere of influence." This action not only provoked
an international crisis, it also inspired the Home Secretary to
write an amazingly prophetic strategy paper on how the next
European war would have to be fought in its initial stages.
He foresaw the Schlieffen Plan, the German sweep through
Belgium, and the timetable on which the outcome of the battles would depend. When the crisis passed but Germany continued to be menacing, Prime Minister Asquith came to the
conclusion that his most talented and energetic cabinet colleague could most profitably be employed in a military department. In late September, accordingly, he offered to make
Winston First Lord of the Admiralty.

The next three years of Churchill's political life were unquestionably his most productive until 1940. He and "Clemmie"
had had a daughter, Diana, and a son, Randolph, in 1909 and
1911 respectively, so he was happy in his family life as well.
He was supremely challenged by his work; his task, as he saw
it, was speedily to reorganize Britain's sea power so that it
could cope with any eventuality of modern warfare, and he
dealt ruthlessly with those who espoused the status quo. When
a group of hoary old admirals asserted that his innovations
were undercutting the traditions of the Royal Navy, he dismissed them from his office with a brusque: "And these traditions, what are they? Rum, sodomy, and the lash. Good morning, Gentlemen."[31] But when war did come, even the hoary
old admirals had to join the rest of the nation in acknowledging that the fleet was ready. So did a hoary old colonel: "I
have never liked Winston Churchill," Teddy Roosevelt wrote
an English friend, "but in view of what you tell me as to his
admirable conduct and nerve in mobilizing the fleet, I do wish
that if it comes your way you would extend to him my congratulations on his action."[32]

"Everything tends toward catastrophe and collapse," Churchill wrote Clementine as the war clouds broke. "I am interested, geared up & happy. Is it not horrible to be built like
that? . . . I pray God to forgive me for such fearful moods of
levity. Yet I wd do my best for peace, & nothing wd induce
me wrongfully to strike the blow. . . ."[33]

He did do his best for peace, but on Tuesday evening,
August 4, 1914, the British ultimatum to Germany on the subject of Belgian neutrality expired, and Foreign Secretary
Edward Grey uttered his famous requiem for nineteenth-
century civilization: "The lamps are going out all over Europe;
we shall not see them lit again in our lifetime."

Like almost everyone else in Europe except Grey, Churchill
carried a hopelessly romantic concept of war into the *abattoir*
of 1914–18. His memories were of cavalry charges and flashing
sabers, and the prospect of renewed conflict excited him tremendously. Lloyd George, then Chancellor of the Exchequer,
remembered seeing him just after midnight on August 5:
"Winston dashed into the room, radiant, his face bright, his
manner keen, one word pouring out on another. . . . You could
see that he was a really happy man."[34]

But if the First Lord went into World War I with a much
greater degree of enthusiasm than many of his contemporaries,
he was also much quicker to recognize and recoil from the
grim, depersonalized process of mass slaughter that war had
become. In addition, he attempted to do something about it.
Less than six months after the first Battle of the Marne, he sent
Asquith a memorandum: ". . . my impression is that the position of both armies is not likely to undergo any decisive change
—although no doubt several hundred thousand men will be
spent to satisfy the military mind on this point. . . . Are there
not other alternatives than sending our armies to chew barbed
wire in Flanders . . . ?"[35] He certainly thought there were. He
undertook, for example, to promote the development of a
more efficient barbed wire chewer called a "land ship," the
forerunner of the tank; he brought the brilliant old retired
Fleet Admiral "Jacky" Fisher back to the Admiralty as First
Sea Lord; most important, he conceived a naval operation
against the weakly defended Turkish fortifications at the

Dardanelles that would link Britain and France with their Russian allies, isolate the Central Powers in the eastern theater, and, he hoped, contribute to a speedy termination of the war. The concept was brilliant, but despite Churchill's efforts it was bungled in the execution. Fisher grew more and more alarmed over the losses the Navy was sustaining, and after many stormy confrontations with his beleaguered First Lord he melodramatically resigned. His demission precipitated a political crisis and Asquith had to turn to the Conservatives in order to form a new government. One of their conditions for co-operation was that Churchill be replaced, and on May 27, 1915, he was effectively removed from power.

"When I was young," Churchill told his doctor in 1944, "for two or three years the light faded out of the picture. I did my work. I sat in the House of Commons, but black depression settled on me."[36] This was the dreaded "black dog" of depression that was to afflict Churchill throughout his life. Even in 1969, the memory of the Dardanelles disgrace was still painful to his widow: "When he left the Admiralty he thought he was finished... I thought he would die of grief."[37] "I knew everything and could do nothing," Churchill himself wrote:

... The change from the intense executive activities of each day's work at the Admiralty to the narrowly-measured duties of a counselor left me gasping. Like a sea-beast fished up from the depths, or a diver too suddenly hoisted, my veins threatened to burst from the fall in pressure. I had great anxiety and no means of relieving it; I had vehement convictions and small power to give effect to them. I had to watch the unhappy casting-away of great opportunities, and the feeble execution of plans which I had launched and in which I heartily believed. I had long hours of utterly unwonted leisure in which to contemplate the frightful unfolding of the War. At a moment when every fibre of my being was inflamed to action, I was forced to remain a spectator of the tragedy, placed cruelly in a front seat. . . . Marvellous organizations of railroads, steamships, and motor vehicles placed and maintained tens of millions of men continuously in action. Healing and surgery in their exquisite developments returned them again and again to the shambles. Nothing was wasted that could contribute to the process of waste. The last dying kick was brought into military utility.[38]

✕ Although Winston discovered painting as a means of occupying his mind and had his new daughter, Sarah, to brighten his mornings, he finally could not bear the burden of despair and inactivity any longer. On November 18, 1915, he crossed over to France as a Lieutenant Colonel in the Oxfordshire Hussars to serve as a battalion commander in the line. From the trenches in March 1916 he wrote his wife, "Sometimes . . . I think I wd not mind stopping living very much—I am so devoured by egoism that I wd like to have another soul in another world. . . ."[39]

Churchill's exile from power lasted over two years, and even when he was named Minister of Munitions in the Lloyd George coalition in the summer of 1917, his responsibilities were still much more limited than they had been when the war began. In his new office, however, Winston did have the opportunity to correspond on a regular basis with high officials of the newly cobelligerent United States, and in his opposite number at the War Industries Board, Bernard Baruch, he found a friend he would cherish until he died. Together he and Baruch established many joint committees to allocate important war materials among the Allies. Foremost among these was the International Nitrate Executive, of which Churchill was named the head. "I now became the Nitrate King," he exulted, "the greatest there will ever be."[40]

By the summer of 1918 the preponderance of Allied resources in men and matériel had tipped the scales against the Central Powers and the end of the war, if not exactly imminent, was imminently foreseeable. On the Fourth of July, London's Central Hall opposite Westminster Abbey was the scene of an exuberant commemoration of Anglo-American friendship. Speaking for Great Britain, Churchill said, "We desire to express to our American kith and kin our joy and gratitude for the mighty aid they are bringing to the Allied cause. . . . The presence at this moment in Europe of a million American soldiers . . . is an event that seems to transcend the limits of purely mundane things and fills us with the deepest awe."[41]

Three and a half weeks later Winston was one of the guests

of honor at a Gray's Inn dinner being given for the War
Ministers. The principal speaker was Lord Curzon, and Sir
Robert Borden and General Jan Smuts were on hand to represent Canada and South Africa. Toward the end of the evening
the youthful American Assistant Secretary of the Navy, who
was on an inspection tour of the western-front nations, was,
to his "horror," called upon to speak for the United States. He
managed to come up with a few innocuous sentences which
accomplished their purpose without in any way being particularly memorable. Churchill certainly retained no recollec-
tion of the little speech, nor even of the young fellow who
made it. Had he been even more farsighted than he already
was, he would have paid closer attention, however. For
twenty-three years later he and Franklin D. Roosevelt were
destined to meet once again.[42]

World War I came to an end on the eleventh hour of the
eleventh day of the eleventh month of 1918. On the tenth day
of the first month of 1919 Churchill was named Secretary of
State for War and Air in the new Lloyd George postwar coalition. His first concern in his new office was for the success of
the White Russians in their battle against what he termed "the
foul baboonery of Bolshevism." British, American, French, and
Japanese troops had entered Russia after the treaty of Brest-
Litovsk in order to make sure that port facilities and ammunition dumps did not fall into German hands. Churchill wanted
these troops actively to assist the Whites, and he traveled to
Paris in February to discuss the issue of their intervention or
withdrawal with President Woodrow Wilson.

Winston's hatred of communism was perfectly natural to
him. The Marxist creed represented a view of the world precisely antithetical to his own nineteenth-century aristocratic
beau ideal. But relatively few people felt as strongly as he did
about the matter, especially among the Liberal and Labour
rank and file. Churchill's mission to Paris, therefore, was sym-
bolic of an increasing divergence between his views and those
of most of his political colleagues.

The meeting with Wilson took place on Valentine's Day,
but it was hardly a love feast. Wilson said that all Allied troops
should be withdrawn, countering Churchill's protests with the

solid argument that there were simply not enough Allied troops in Russia to stop the Bolsheviks, even if all of them stayed there, and adding that none of the Allies was prepared to consider an increase in its manpower commitment. The issue of fighting the Communists accordingly remained unresolved, but the trip to Paris was still not a total loss from Winston's point of view; it gave him his first opportunity to meet Bernard Baruch face to face.

On his return to England from France, Churchill took up again his long-standing interest in military aviation. As Minister for Air he now had a perfect excuse to go flying, and he needed one because Mrs. Churchill objected violently to his participation in this still-dangerous activity. Her objections were particularly vehement now that Winston was the father of four; a daughter, Marigold Frances, had been born four days after the Armistice. But Clementine protested in vain. Churchill had spent nearly two hundred hours in the air by 1919, always in the company of highly skilled military pilots, and he argued that "my nerve, my spirits & my virtue" had all benefited from the experiences.[43] Now, furthermore, he was specifically responsible for the readiness and development of His Majesty's Air Forces—it was a matter of Duty. Only a harrowingly narrow escape from what looked to be certain death cured him of his compulsion.

It was mid-July of 1919, a beautiful summer afternoon. Churchill and his copilot, Colonel Jack Scott, took off from Croydon Aerodrome and climbed without incident to just about one hundred feet. Suddenly, as Churchill was about to come out of the second of a series of standard clearing turns, the aileron controls failed, and the plane plummeted earthward in the grip of a notoriously fatal sideslip. "I saw the sunlit aerodrome close beneath me, and the impression flashed through my mind that it was bathed in a baleful yellowish glare. Then in another flash a definitive thought formed in my brain, 'This is very likely Death.' "[44] In truth it was only very nearly Death; Colonel Scott's quick action in switching off the ignition just before the plane struck the ground prevented it. The plane was utterly demolished and Scott broke both legs, but there was no fire or explosion and Churchill walked away from the wreckage with nothing more than a collection of bruises. Only a few hours later, in fact, he was presiding at a House of Commons dinner in honor of General Pershing, who presented him with the American Distinguished Service Cross for his work as Minister of Munitions. In accepting the award, Churchill observed, "From the moment the Germans in their vanity and folly drove the United States to draw the sword there was no doubt that Germany was ruined, that the cause of freedom was safe, and that the British and American democracies would begin once again to write their history in common."[45]

". . . next day I found myself black and blue all over," Winston remembered,[46] but he attended Pershing's military review in Hyde Park just the same. His American escort was a quietly observant young temporary colonel named George Marshall, who had served on the AEF Commander's staff in France and was shortly to become his aide.[47] "What a magnificent body of men never to take another drink," Churchill said to him as the doughboys marched past, thus serving notice that he would not soon be reconciled to the U.S. innovation of Prohibition.[48]

Winston continued at the War Office until 1921, when Lloyd George asked him to take over as Secretary of State for the Colonies. His primary concern in his new post was with the Middle East, where a mass of British, French, Turkish, and Arab interests needed untangling. To this end Churchill organized a conference in Cairo at which T. E. Lawrence (of Arabia) served as his technical adviser. Remarkably satisfactory results rewarded his labors, and toward the end of his sojourn in the Levant he went to Palestine to reaffirm his support for Zionism and the Balfour Declaration.

Back in England the Lloyd George coalition was crumbling; the Conservatives held disproportionate power within its ranks and the newly emergent, equally powerful Labour party assailed it from without. Great Britain, furthermore, was in the grip of a severe postwar economic depression, so a political shake-up seemed more or less inevitable. A general election was called for the autumn of 1922, but just before the campaigning began Churchill was felled by an attack of ap-

pendicitis. He recovered sufficiently to give only a few en-
feebled speeches at Dundee, and when the results were in he
found the Liberal party virtually destroyed and himself, as he
put it, "without an office, without a seat, without a party, and
without an appendix."⁴⁹

For the next two years he was out of Parliament, and the
"black dog" reappeared. His distress over his inactivity was
aggravated by a number of personal losses of extreme gravity:
Marigold died at age three of a throat infection; Jennie died
at age sixty-seven of a hemorrhage; and Bourke Cockran
passed away in 1923 at age sixty-nine. These afflictions were
offset somewhat by the birth of the Churchills' last child,
Mary, in 1922, and Winston put his idle hours to use by com-
piling *The World Crisis*, a six-volume history of World War I
and its consequences. Still, being out of the mainstream of
public life was odious to him, and he made repeated efforts
to get back into the House of Commons. In May 1923 he
fought a by-election in Leicester West as a Liberal and lost by
over four thousand votes to a Labourite. In February of the
following year he broke with the Liberals over the question
of socialism and stood as a "Constitutionalist" in the Abbey
Division of Westminster, which included the Houses of Parliament, Buckingham Palace, and much of London's theater district. This contest, taking place as it did right in the center of
Britain's social and political capital, aroused tremendous interest, and Winston was able to count among his partisans
many actresses and chorus girls. The ladies from Daly's Thea-
tre sat up all night addressing envelopes on his behalf, for
example, and he recollected several years later that "it was
most cheering and refreshing to see so many young and beautiful women of every rank in life ardently working in a purely
disinterested cause not unconnected with myself."⁵⁰ The outcome was less cheering and refreshing though: Churchill
polled 8,144 votes and his opponent polled 8,187.

Finally, in October 1924, there was another general election,
and Churchill was returned for the Epping Division of Essex
as a Constitutionalist with decidedly Conservative leanings.
The Tories had even supported his candidacy. The new (Conservative) Prime Minister, Stanley Baldwin, welcomed the

prodigal son back into the fold by offering Winston the post of Chancellor of the Exchequer. This was the office that Lord Randolph had risen to at his political zenith, and his son gratefully and happily accepted it. He served competently if without his customary élan for five years, mired in what he looked back on as "a bog of sums." Only during the General Strike of 1926 did he become embroiled in violent controversy, having taken on the job of "publisher" of the temporary government newspaper (all others being shut down), the *British Gazette*. The *Gazette* had a life span of barely more than two weeks, but what it lacked in longevity—and objectivity—it more than made up for in spirit. The left and the workers regarded it as being downright inflammatory, but Churchill defended his lack of impartiality with the ringing declaration: "I decline utterly to be impartial as between the Fire Brigade and the fire."[51] Even after the strike ended, strong feelings of resentment continued to be projected in his direction, and on one occasion when the Labour benches became particularly rowdy as he rose to speak he wagged his finger at them and shouted, "I warn you!" This only provoked louder hisses and catcalls. "I warn you!" he persisted, as the bedlam level was reached and exceeded. "If you let loose on us another General Strike, we will let loose on you—another *British Gazette!*"[52] The jeers and catcalls dissolved into laughter; it was much easier to disagree with Churchill than to dislike him, although, as always, there were many people who managed to do both.

The struggle between Conservatives and Labourites continued throughout the late 1920s, and in the spring of 1929 Stanley Baldwin's party was voted out of office. Churchill retained his seat at Epping, but now he was only a private member in opposition. He was also nearly fifty-five years old, and it was a time for taking stock, for reflection. Almost thirty years had passed since he had last seen his mother's homeland. Bourke Cockran was dead, but Bernard Baruch stood ready to take up where he had left off. With the dust from the general election settling around him, Churchill's thoughts turned again to the other side of the Atlantic. It was a good moment to cut loose and explore.

CHAPTER FIVE

Hearst and Hollywood

IF IT WAS "profit not pleasure" Churchill pursued when he went to the United States in 1900, his object on his next journey twenty-nine years later was precisely the reverse. "I want to see the country," he wrote Baruch in June. "... I have no political mission and no axe to grind...."[1] In July he added, "I do not want to have too close an itinerary. One must have time to feel a country and nibble some of the grass...."[2]

Of course, grass-nibbling in the Churchillian style was a considerably more ambitious operation than that usually associated with pastures and milk cows. Winston was to sail to Quebec in August, travel by private Canadian Pacific Railroad car across the continent to Vancouver, enter the United States at Seattle in September, motor in easy stages down to Los Angeles, and then work his way east to the Grand Canyon, where another private railroad car, this one provided by the head of the Bethlehem Steel Corporation, would carry him and his party onward to Chicago and New York.

And quite a party it was: Winston himself, his brother, Jack, his son, Randolph, age eighteen, and his nephew John, age twenty—the four men of the Churchill family. (Jack's younger son, Peregrine, at age sixteen was still classified as a boy and therefore did not qualify for inclusion.) They were a motley yet oddly congenial crew: John, moonfaced, musical, artistic, cherubic, and with just a trace of the satyr in his eyes; Randolph, dazzlingly handsome, dazzlingly opinionated, a fierce partisan of his father and ardently studying to follow in his footsteps; Jack, vague, quiet, inoffensive, the classic

"little man" somewhat bemusedly adrift among eruptive con-
sanguineal peaks; and Churchill, weathered, tempered, but
still pursuing and pursued by his ferocious ambition, still short
of his ultimate goal, the hunched-over doggedness and firm-set
jaw revealing hints of the indomitability that would immor-
talize him in a decade's time.

With the smoke puffs from Winston's cigar leading the way,
the Churchill Expedition to North America set off from London for Southampton like an Anglicized version of the Tooner-
ville Trolley. They boarded the *Empress of India* on August 3,
and arrived in Quebec after a week's voyage. On August 17
they were at Niagara, where Winston described the Falls as
being "bigger, better, and grander" than on his first visit
(which apparently took place on his way back to New York
from the Midwest in January 1901).[3] On August 24 they were
at Winnipeg (which was also bigger, better, and grander than
it had been twenty-nine years before); on August 31 it was
Calgary; and on September 7 they arrived in the United States.

The Expedition's arrival on American soil was fraught with
peril, for it signaled the first encounter of Churchillian thirst
with U.S. Prohibition. Randolph's luggage bulged with flasks
of whisky and brandy,[4] but, since the party was armed with a
diplomatic visa and a letter of introduction from no less a
personage than the former Vice President, then United States
Ambassador to Great Britain, Charles G. Dawes, no trouble
was expected. These documents, on being duly presented to
agents of the U.S. Customs Service as the Expedition's boat
from Vancouver glided into Puget Sound, naturally resulted
in the Churchills' suitcases being subjected to one of the most
ruthlessly thorough searches ever inflicted on an impatient
band of travelers. "My uncle got so angry I thought he would
explode," John remembered. "'What are you looking for?' he
shouted. 'I have already told you that we have nothing to declare. The point of this letter from the ambassador is to assure
you of my integrity.'" The astounding reply was that the
Customs men were looking for guns and ammunition, and
after an interval of stunned disbelief Churchill commented,
"Monstrous! Absolutely monstrous!"[5]

Poor Jack, meanwhile, having revealed that he was carrying a camera and some photographic plates, was being grilled mercilessly on his intentions vis-à-vis secret American military installations (if the plates were not exposed)[6] and on his proclivities toward the purveyance of pornography (if they were).[7] Finally there came the ultimate affront from the chief of the inspecting crew: "How many cigars?" Had Churchill been prone to apoplexy, the course of history might have been drastically altered on that otherwise tranquil Saturday in the Pacific Northwest.

Randolph, with his flasks concealed in his attaché case, finally passed through the gantlet of inspections to the quayside, only to be there accosted by "an attractive young lady from some paper" who rather peremptorily demanded, "Do we see you now or on the train?" An Etonian Old Boy fully eighteen years of age and a student at Christ Church College, Oxford, Randolph had the facility for elevating his nose to heights considerably more lofty than are deemed physiologically feasible and then looking down it at what he regarded as upstartism and impertinence. It was from just such an eminence that his reply, "I'm not sure you see us at all," wafted down. But the young lady persisted: "Are you going to marry an American wife?" and from still more stratospheric regions Randolph responded that he had no intention of discussing his "matrimonial plans."[8] He then walked majestically away, leaving the energetic cub reporter to try her luck with his father.

Winston, although a good deal more formidable, was also a great deal less stuffy than his son and had no objection to spending ten minutes in conversation with an attractive female; thus her persistence was rewarded. "He was rather captivated, I am afraid," Randolph recorded with despairing ennui.[9] In the interview Winston diplomatically declined to comment on Prohibition, but he did permit himself the rather sly observation: "We realize one hundred million pounds a year from our liquor taxes, which amount, I understand, you give to your bootleggers."[10]

The Churchill party now proceeded to their hotel, accompanied, oddly enough, by the Chief of Customs, who, along with the hotel manager, proceeded to offer the astonished Britons a choice selection of beer and champagne. It was not with "the ultimate consumer" that the government concerned itself, the Americans explained, but with the suppliers of the noxious distillates and brews.[11]

The Expedition was scheduled to depart Seattle by train for southern Oregon late Saturday night, but before they left Winston had the pleasure of an unexpected reunion with one John McGill, who had served under him as a sergeant and section commander in the Malakand Field Force in 1897. He also had the even greater pleasure of meeting a Mrs. Ted Lee, whose father, Joseph McKenna, had worked in a South African mine where Churchill had taken refuge as he attempted to make good his escape from Boer territory.[12] Mrs. Lee's father was the "Mac" Winston had written about in *My Early Life*, the Scotsman who, in addition to concealing the escaped prisoner, had also taken him on a tour of the mine's many shafts and passageways.[13] Touched, Churchill told Mrs. Lee, who had been a small girl in England at the time, that he had often hoped to meet a member of McKenna's family.[14]

After an overnight train journey, the Churchills arrived in Grants Pass, Oregon, and switched to automobiles for the next stage of their trip. It will be best to let Winston describe that morning's drive himself:

Entering California from the north, we travel along the celebrated Redwood Highway. The road undulates and serpentines ceaselessly. On either side from time to time are groves and forests of what one would call large fir-trees. As we go on they get taller. The sense that each hour finds one amid larger trees only grows gradually. . . . Now we are in the heart of the redwoods. . . .
The road is an aisle in a cathedral of trees. Enormous pillars of timber tower up 200 ft. without leaf or twig to a tapering vault of sombre green and purple. So close are they together that the eye is arrested at a hundred yards distance by solid walls of timber.[15]

At the foot of one of the largest redwoods of all (some 370 feet tall) the Expedition halted for a picnic lunch and a swim —"au naturel," according to Randolph—in a "deliciously warm"

stream.[16] Then onward for another forty or fifty miles before
sunset.

Night in the Redwoods is impressive. Every dozen miles or so
rest camps—"motels" as they are called—have been built for the
motorist population. Here simple and cheap accommodation is provided in clusters of detached cabins, and the carefree wanderers on
wheels gather round great fires, singing or listening to the ubiqui-
tous wireless music.[17]

On Monday, September 9, the caravan got rolling at 10:00
A.M., and about three hours later entered the vineyards of
George de Latour in the Napa Valley. De Latour, a transplanted
Frenchman, operated a large—and legal—winery, its legality
arising from the polite fiction that its stock of well over a
million gallons was destined for purely sacramental consump-
tion. "The Constitution of the United States, the God of Israel,
and the Pope—an august combination—protect, with the triple
sanctions of Washington, Jerusalem and Rome this inspiring
scene," Winston reported. "Nevertheless, there is a fragrance
in the air of which even the Eighteenth Amendment cannot
deprive us."[18] Like most transplanted Frenchmen, the Churchills' luncheon host was homesick for his motherland; he was
also distinctly unenamored of California—"*Fleurs sans odeur,
femmes sans pudeur, et hommes sans honneur*," was his suc-
cinct summation.[19]

Not far from M. de Latour's establishment, the Expedition
stopped again, arrested this time on the outskirts of Oakland
by a large sign promising "Good Eats and Soft Drinks."

Yielding to these allurements, I am supplied with a glass of "near
beer." This excellent and innocent beverage is prepared in the following way.

Old-world beer is brewed, and thereafter all the alcohol in excess of one-half of 1 per cent is eliminated and cast to the dogs.
The residue when iced affords a pleasant drink indistinguishable in
appearance from the naughty article, and very similar in flavour.
But, as the less regenerate inform us, "it lacks Authority." I was told
that sometimes distressing accidents occur in the process of manufacture. Sometimes mistakes are made about the exact percentage,
and on one melancholy occasion an entire brew was inadvertently
released at the penultimate stage of manufacture, to spread its

maddening poison through countless happy homes. But, needless to say, every precaution is taken.[20]

Cheerfully sedated by their day's intake of temperance beverages, the Churchill men headed on toward the San Francisco Peninsula. "I had been dozing," Winston unself-consciously admitted, "and awoke with a start to find myself in the midst of the ocean." He was not suffering an alcoholic hallucination. "As far as the eye could reach on all sides in the gathering dusk nothing but water could be seen. The marvellous road was traversing an inlet of the sea . . . by a newly constructed bridge *seven miles long*, and only a few feet above the waves."[21] The bridge was in fact the causeway which served as the forerunner of the Oakland Bay Bridge, completed seven years later.

Thanks to Baruch's good offices, the Expedition had comfortable quarters awaiting them in the Peninsula suburb San Franciscans somewhat sardonically refer to as "Heavenly Hillsborough." It's not that Hillsborough is less than heavenly, it's just that it takes its celestial similitude very seriously. Even Churchill referred to it as "the garden suburb of San Francisco notables,"[22] the specific notables in his case being Mr. and Mrs. William H. Crocker of banking eminence. Whether you took it very seriously or not, however, the Crockers' garden— along with the rest of their estate—was nothing to be sardonic about—not, at least, as far as Randolph was concerned. "It is quite lovely and absolutely gigantic," he marveled.[23] It was in the garden that the Churchills ate lunch on Tuesday, with Mrs. Crocker's daughter, Mrs. Henry Russell, as their hostess. Randolph found Mrs. Russell "most delightful . . . and very well informed." When she betrayed an extensive knowledge of the mechanics of stock transactions, though, he modified his opinion considerably: "I don't find this very attractive in a woman."[24]

Winston, meanwhile, had other things on his mind; and sightseeing was foremost among them. To Crocker he confided, "I have read and heard so much about Seal Rocks that I surely do not want to miss seeing them."[25] The sense of urgency in his words was attributable to the fact that his Bay Area schedule was already very full and that, furthermore, several files of important correspondence had now caught up with him and were demanding his attention. Tuesday afternoon, accordingly, he spent working. On Tuesday evening he was guest of honor at a dinner given under Crocker's auspices at the Pacific Union Club. There Randolph found that his time too was at something of a premium, for he met "a very attractive married lady (about 23)" and arranged to go riding with her the next morning at nine. ". . . It is already 3 A.M.," he scribbled in his diary later that night. "I must try to get my beauty sleep."[26]

On Wednesday the British Consul General gave a luncheon for Winston at the Bohemian Club, after which the press was granted an interview. Jews and Arabs had recently been engaged in serious fighting in the British protectorate of Palestine, and the reporters wanted Churchill's analysis of what the situation portended. "The Arab and the Jew must and will learn to live together," he told them. "The Arabs have nothing against the Jews. The Jews have developed the country, grown orchards and grain fields out of the desert, built schools and great buildings, constructed irrigation projects and water power houses, and have made Palestine a much better place in which to live than it was before they came a few years ago. . . . The Arabs are much better off now than before the Jews came," he continued, "and it will be a short time only before they realize it."[27]

It was a rare failure of prophetic insight.

With the fourth estate taken care of, Winston at last was free to go observe the famous San Francisco seals, but to his great dismay there were none to be seen when he arrived at the famous San Francisco Rocks. "The rocks were occupied only by large and dreary birds," he recollected, "and when I asked a bystander when the Sea Lions would appear, he replied gaily in Italian 'Damfino,' meaning no doubt 'in due course.'"[28] (*Damfino*, of course, is no more an Italian word than blandness is an Italian trait; it is an Americanism with which Churchill was not familiar, a four-word phrase signifying that the speaker is without any information pertinent to the question he has just been asked.)

Winston's disappointment over the seals was mitigated somewhat when Crocker got the Chairman of Pacific Telephone and Telegraph to connect him with Clementine at Chartwell: "I take up the instrument. My wife speaks to me across one ocean and one continent—one of each. We hear each other as easily as if we were in the same room, or, not to exaggerate, say about half as well again as on an ordinary London telephone. I picture a well-known scene far off in Kent, 7,000 miles away. The children come to the telephone. I talk to them through New York and Rugby. They reply through Scotland and Canada. Why say the age of miracles is past? It is just beginning."[29]

Further miracles were in the offing. That evening Churchill was the guest of Dr. W. W. Campbell of the University of California's Lick Observatory, who offered him the opportunity of viewing Saturn and its famous rings. Winston was skeptical, however: "We all know how astronomers have mapped the heavens out in the shape of animals. We can most of us—by a stretch of the imagination—recognise the 'Great Bear,' but still one can quite sympathise with those who call it 'The Plough'*—one is as like it as the other. . . ." Employing one of his most engaging locutions, Churchill continued, "In this mood [of skepticism] I applied myself to the eyepiece." To his amazement, though, Saturn, rings and all, appeared like a brilliant beacon in the field of view, and he "gazed with awe and delight upon this sublime spectacle of a world 800 million miles away."[30] This was his first real exposure to astronomy, and his mind responded with intense excitement to the vistas it presented. He engaged Dr. Campbell in a lengthy animated discussion about the nature of the cosmos, and he came away from it stimulated and impressed: "It appears that outside our own universe, with its thousands of million suns, there are at least two million other universes, all gyrating and coursing through the heavens like dancers upon a stage. I had not heard of this before, and was inspired to many thoughts sufficiently commonplace to be omitted here. I was disturbed to think of all these universes which had not

* Or "The Big Dipper," as in the United States.

previously been brought to my attention. I hoped that nothing had gone wrong with them."[31]

On Thursday morning Winston & Co. departed the Bay Area for the Crocker home at Pebble Beach, where they spent the night. The next day was Friday, the thirteenth, a fittingly ominous date given the fact that it was to witness the first encounter between Winston Spencer Churchill and William Randolph Hearst in the bowels of the latter's fabulous castle-cum-game-preserve-cum-ranch-cum-fantasy-creation above the Pacific, San Simeon. This encounter had been arranged by Baruch, who had suggested in a letter to Winston that he might find Hearst an interesting personality. "I should be very glad to visit Mr. Hearst . . . if you think he would like to have me,"[32] Churchill had replied in a letter dated July 10, and Baruch had gone to work. On the twentieth Churchill wrote him, "I have now received a very pleasant invitation from Mr. Hearst."[33] The matter was settled.

Despite the ease with which the meeting had been planned, both parties still approached it rather gingerly because of the newspaper baron's well-known and widely disseminated opposition to the British viewpoint on, among many other things, naval parity, which was a particularly live issue at the time. To state the dispute simply, Hearst—and perhaps most other Americans—felt that Great Britain was balking at limitations on naval armaments because it wanted to retain maritime superiority over the United States. The British argued, however, that the size of the U.S. Navy was absolutely no concern of theirs and that they simply wanted to build enough warships to protect the sea lanes that brought them their food. The question was most decidedly still unresolved when the Churchill Expedition arrived at San Simeon, but, fortunately for international relations, their host had more immediate problems to contend with.

Given the eminence of his British guests, Hearst had not felt it possible to permit his mistress, the movie star Marion Davies, to be his hostess at San Simeon. This both infuriated Marion and at the same time subjected the Churchills to the rather less stimulating attentions of the press czar's wife, Millicent. Randolph, for one, found her "quite too charming,"[34] and practically gave up his breakfast one morning when she declared, "The relationship between Voltaire and Frederick the Great is not unlike that between Brisbane and Mr. Hearst."[35] Meanwhile, down at her beach house in Santa Monica, Marion made it a point to throw one of her wildest parties, and she was heard to remark very loudly on one occasion that the Churchills "should have come down here. They'd have had a lot more fun."[36]

As it turned out, the Churchills were to have the best of both worlds. Winston Spencer and William Randolph, with Baruch to oversee their entente by telephone from New York, found that they quite hit it off with one another.[37] Randolph and John, meanwhile, were hotly pursuing some of the prettier Hearst house guests with great competitive zeal, and, when John got the better of Randolph with respect to one particularly attractive young lady, Winston could not keep silent. "You know," he said with great mock solemnity to his son and nephew, "I think it is just as well we are leaving soon because Johnny seems to be making unexpected progress."[38] But later that evening, son and nephew got a full dose of a much less genial father and uncle respectively when they mistook Winston's guest bungalow for one sheltering two distinctly more approachable persons of considerably less extended acquaintance. Churchill was always a very light sleeper, and when Randolph clambered across the transom of his bedroom window, the former Chancellor of the Exchequer treated him and his cousin to a loud blast of the sort of rhetoric that, slightly modulated, was to inspirit an embattled England eleven years later. ". . . We both retired feeling very sheepish and fed up," John remembered.[39]

On Tuesday, September 17, an Anglo-American motorcade wound its way two hundred miles south from San Simeon to Hollywood, Churchill and Hearst in the lead car, Jack in his customary limbo in the second, and John and Randolph, suitably abashed, in the third. Hearst, of course, was an extremely powerful man in the motion-picture industry, and since 1925 he and Louis B. Mayer had served as the effective rulers of the MGM empire. The Churchills thus had the perfect entree into Hollywood society. "Draw up a list of all the film stars you would like to meet," Hearst had told John and Randolph, "and I'll get them to come along for a banquet."[40]

Winston was very favorably impressed by the Los Angeles of 1929, describing it as "a gay and happy city." He was particularly struck by the life-on-wheels that even then was the *sine qua non* of an Angelino's life. "The distances are enormous," he wrote. "You motor ten miles to luncheon in one direction and ten miles to dinner in another. The streets by night are ablaze with electric lights and moving signs of every colour. A carnival in fairyland."[41]

The day after Churchill's arrival, Hearst and Mayer gave a lunch for him at MGM. A twenty-piece orchestra played while twenty-five chorus girls, a singer, and several of Metro's stars entertained. The chorines had Randolph nearly slavering; he found "all of them infinitely more attractive than the best in London,"[42] and it must have been with considerable dismay that he watched them being herded off so that his host could introduce the movie colony to his father. In his words of introduction Hearst for the first time gave public expression to the good feelings that had arisen between him and his guest, and Winston responded in a similar vein. Then an MGM executive rose to propose a vote of thanks: "I can only say that I would like to hear [Mr. Churchill's speech] again, and I dare say Mr. Churchill could bear a little of it." From a hole in the ceiling, then, came a recording of Winston's voice, "absolutely perfect in tone and volume," according to Randolph, "and as clear as when he spoke himself."[43] Thus unobtrusively was the practice of bugging foreign dignitaries inaugurated.

The Churchills spent Thursday, the nineteenth, relaxing in Santa Barbara and on Friday the Expedition motored into Hollywood for lunch and a tour of a number of studios. Late in the afternoon they drove out to Marion Davies' beach house for a swim, after which they dressed for a dinner party beneath and alongside the stars. Hearst had been as good as his word; there were stars aplenty: Charlie Chaplin (who was to be a frequent visitor at Chartwell in the ensuing years*), Pola Negri, Harold Lloyd, Billie Dove, Bebe Daniels, Wallace Beery, and—as the saying goes—many many more.[44]

---

* One visit he made is nicely remembered in Sarah Churchill's memoir, *A Thread in the Tapestry*, pp. 35–36.

Most of Saturday, the twenty-first, was devoted to recuperation. The Churchills had lunch with Mayer and then took a
tour of MGM. John and Randolph quickly came to the conclusion that when you'd seen one studio, you'd seen them all,
but their boredom was supplanted by indignation when they
learned that they were to go to a movie that evening while
their sires went out to a nightclub. Winston and Jack, wishing
perhaps to devote a bit more time to recuperation than had
thus far been available, solved the problem by the simple
expedient of switching schedules with their offspring.[45]

⅄ On Sunday, the somewhat rejuvenated senior Churchills
went deep-sea fishing off Santa Catalina Island on the Hearst
yacht. Winston made headlines (albeit small ones) by hook-
ing a 188-pound marlin within half an hour of setting out his
line and then reeling it in in slightly under twenty minutes.
His elapsed time was said to be a record for the local waters,[46]
but John entertained some thoroughly unworthy suspicions to
the effect that his uncle's "good luck" was in large part attributable to some "smart work on the part of [his] hosts."[47]

On Monday, Jack and Winston dined with former Secretary
of the Treasury William Gibbs McAdoo, and on Tuesday all
four Churchills had lunch with Chaplin at the studio where he
was in the process of making *City Lights*.[48] That evening they
attended the premiere of *Cock-eyed World*, starring Victor
McLaglen and Edmund Lowe, a Damon-and-Pythias type of
epic which Randolph described as "the worst film I have ever
seen."[49]

Their Hollywood sojourn concluded, the Expedition bade
farewell to Mr. Hearst, Miss Davies, Mr. Mayer, Mr. Chaplin,
et al., and rode off into the sunrise in the general direction of
Yosemite National Park. The autumn foliage was at the peak
of its splendor when they arrived, and the memory of it was
one of the most vivid of the journey. On their way to Yosemite
they stopped to have a look at the Mariposa County Court-
house, the oldest still in use in California.[50]

From the High Sierras they motored on to the Grand Canyon's South Rim, where the private railroad car of Churchill's
World War I associate Charles Schwab (President of Bethlehem Steel) awaited them. Taking advantage of a trick of

perspective, Randolph and John stood on their heads about six feet from the edge of the Canyon, thereby giving their parents the impression that they were literally teetering on the brink.[51] Once again Churchillian expletives were heard in the land.

✓ The Churchills arrived in Chicago on October 2 after a two-day journey, and Baruch and Winston had a warm reunion on the station platform. Shepherded by the six-foot-five-inch "Bernie" and a couple of prominent Chicago businessmen, the Expedition saw all the Chicago sights, not excepting the world-renowned Armour meat-packing plant. John found this combination slaughterhouse–assembly-line–cannery a "gruesome spectacle" and was further discomforted when, at the end of the tour, his uncle was presented with a box of luxurious soaps, creams, lipsticks, and cosmetics made out of the inedible remains of what had once been pigs, cows, and sheep.[52] Winston, having seen worse butchery on a much larger scale in India and the Sudan, had no trouble retaining his sangfroid, and several hours after the tour ended he was busily addressing a dinner of the Commercial Club on the still-prickly question of naval armaments.

The Churchills left Chicago for New York on the evening of October 5 under Baruch's supervision—and in another private railroad car of his procuring. On arriving in Manhattan the next day, they took up residence at the Savoy-Plaza at Fifth Avenue and Fifty-ninth Street. John and Randolph lost no time in heading for a fashionable speakeasy called Tony's. They found it disappointingly tame, though, and wrote off New York's fabled underworld as a profound disappointment.[53]

New York's fabled society, however, in the persons of Mr. and Mrs. Condé Nast, more than lived up to its billing. Several days before John and Randolph were scheduled to return to England for the beginning of term at Oxford, the Condé Nasts gave a lavish dinner party for them. John found the evening memorable. "I can only dance well with a good partner," he wrote in his memoirs, "and that night I danced superbly. My partner was Adele Astaire. She attracted me so much that next morning I followed up our meeting with a visit to her home."[54] Alas, nothing came of this initiative.

Winston, meanwhile, was settling back into the world of politics and public affairs. On October 8 he shared the dais at the Bond Club with his dearest friend, F. E. Smith, Lord Birkenhead, a brilliant attorney, former Lord Chancellor, and Secretary of State for India in the same government in which Churchill had served at the Exchequer. Both Winston and Birkenhead spoke on the Palestine question. F. E., as he was called by his close associates, defended the adequacy of Britain's efforts to protect Jewish immigrants from Arab violence. Winston echoed his sentiments and then summed up the British position—and his own: "Nothing will give us the strength and encouragement to go on with our task so much as the sense that those who speak our language and are united to us by the crimson thread of friendship on the other side of the ocean sympathize with our task and comprehend our difficulties. . . ."[55]

Four days later Winston and Jack bade John, Randolph, and F. E. farewell as they sailed off back to England on the Cunard liner *Berengaria*. Then Winston proceeded to the Hotel Weylin at 40 East Thirty-fourth Street, where Great Britain's Prime Minister, Ramsay MacDonald, was in residence and celebrating his sixty-third birthday.

MacDonald, the Labour party leader, was in America on a good-will visit to discuss disarmament; he was the first British Prime Minister ever to visit the United States while in office, and his presence in New York bore witness to the incipient shift of world power toward the North American continent. His diffident manner and evident sincerity made a very favorable impression on the American public, which turned a determinedly blind eye to his leftist affiliation. Churchill found this carefully nurtured naïveté very amusing: "Socialism in the United States is a very wicked thing . . . it is considered altogether un-American. But Mr. Ramsay MacDonald! So dignified, so statesmanlike, so respectable! Such noble sentiments, such earnestness, such high ideals! 'Tell me in confidence,' I am anxiously asked, 'is there any truth in the rumor that he has socialistic leanings?' "[56]

Churchill's arrival at MacDonald's suite coincided with the

appearance of a large cake bearing sixty-three candles, and
the two Britons posed for photographers as the Prime Minister
cut the first slice. "Don't point the knife at him," one of the
reporters jokingly cautioned MacDonald,[57] but since there was
still more than a year to go before Winston was to refer to
the Prime Minister as "the Boneless Wonder," the admonition
was premature.

On Sunday, October 1, Winston and Jack headed south
toward Washington and the Civil War battlefields of Virginia.
On their way they stopped at Gettysburg and then continued
on to Bethlehem, Pennsylvania, to have a look at what Charles
Schwab had wrought in slightly less than twenty years as a
steel manufacturer. In addition to providing former ministers
of the Crown with private railroad cars, Schwab ran a company that in 1929 was producing as much steel as all of Great
Britain. Of course, his corporation's output was in turn only a
third that of U.S. Steel, but for a newcomer to the industry
he was making a reasonably respectable showing. In 1914, as
First Lord of the Admiralty, Churchill had negotiated a secret
deal with Schwab for twenty submarines (secret because the
United States was then a neutral),[58] and later, as Minister of
Munitions, he had personally inspected most of Britain's great
steel concerns. Thus he was familiar with both the man and
the type of operations the man was involved in. Despite this
background, however, Winston was enthralled by the sight of
American technology in action, and his enthusiasm was a
strong echo of that which he expressed in 1895 with respect
to the "means of communication" in New York City. "The first
question that occurred to me on my visit to Bethlehem was:
Where are the men? . . . Nothing must be done by man-power
that can possibly be done by horse-power. . . ."[59]

In Washington, Churchill made a brief courtesy call on
President Hoover, whose feelings of hospitality toward his
visitor may have been somewhat restrained. In 1915, while
Winston was at the Admiralty, British naval authorities had
filed charges of corruption and espionage against Hoover in
his capacity as head of the American Relief Committee in London. They considered that his energetic efforts to send food to
Belgium amounted to an interference with the fleet's blockade

of German-held territory.[60] The charges had been quickly dismissed by a King's Bench judge, however, and since Churchill's visit to the White House was a short one, everything passed off amicably enough, though without any special bonhomie.

Now it was off to the back roads of Virginia. Winston was all his life an avid student of the American Civil War, and one of the projects he had particularly set his heart on was to view at first hand the land where the critical battles had been fought: "No one can understand what happened merely through reading books and studying maps. You must see the ground; you must cover the distances in person; you must measure the rivers and see what the swamps were really like."[61] On leaving Washington, accordingly, he traveled to Richmond. From there it was but sixty miles to the peaceful rural quadrangle where, almost seventy years before, men armed with single-shot rifles had slaughtered one another with a ferocity and a zeal that were not to be seen again until 1914–18: Chancellorsville, Spottsylvania, The Wilderness, Fredericksburg—an area no more than ninety miles square, yet the focus of inconceivable suffering and death. In searching for the location of the famous "Bloody Angle" of the Spottsylvania lines, Winston and Jack asked an old man for directions, and in doing so they acquired a guide. After a pleasant stroll through the tranquil autumn forest, they arrived at their goal. "... 'Here is the Angle,' says our guide. 'Here is where the dead lay thickest. Yes! in this trench they were piled in heaps, both sides together, blue and grey.' "[62]

Not many people suspected it, but as the Churchill brothers were heading northward from Virginia, carnage of a different kind from that they had just investigated, but on no less a scale, was about to be seen in New York.

On Thursday, October 29, 1929, Winston was walking down Wall Street after a luncheon with Baruch uptown. It was typical of his life that he should have been strolling past the Stock Exchange on that particular day. "... A perfect stranger who recognized me invited me to enter the gallery.... I expected to see pandemonium; but the spectacle that met my eyes was one of surprising calm and orderliness ... there they were, walking to and fro like a slow-motion picture of a disturbed ant heap, offering each other enormous blocks of securities at a third of their old prices and half their present value, and for many minutes together finding no one strong enough to pick up the sure fortunes they were compelled to offer."[63]

On Friday the leaders of the financial community met to assess the damage and try to stem the flood. Many of them then went to the Commodore Hotel to hear Winston speak on Anglo-American friendship at the annual dinner of the Iron and Steel Institute. Over the weekend the behind-the-scenes meetings continued, but the market had been mortally stricken. The new week began as badly as the old week had ended, and on Black Tuesday, October 29, the entire bottom fell out with one big reverberating crash. Churchill viewed the catastrophe with amazement and dismay: "... Under my very window a gentleman cast himself down fifteen storeys and was dashed to pieces, causing a wild commotion and the arrival of the fire brigade. Quite a number of persons seem to have overbalanced themselves by accident in the same sort of way. A workman smoking his pipe on the girder of an unfinished building 400 ft. above the ground blocked the traffic of the street below, through the crowd, who thought he was a ruined capitalist, waiting in a respectful and prudently withdrawn crescent for the final act."[64]

The next day Winston stepped aboard the *Berengaria* for a pensive journey home. His return to America after almost thirty years had been tremendously stimulating to him. The boisterous young country he had left behind in 1901 had grown into a robust and rapidly maturing great power. The wealth and vigor of the nation had impressed him from coast to coast, and sometimes it had taken his breath away. He began to understand to just how great an extent Britain's future was bound up with America's, and although he was leaving his mother's country with its commercial and industrial structure in ruins, he did not for a moment question the desirability of that impending association. "The autumn afternoon was bright and clear, and the noble scene stretched to far horizons.... Beyond lay all the cities and workshops off the New Jersey shore, pouring out their clouds of smoke and steam. Around towered the mighty buildings of New York....

"No one who gazed on such a scene could doubt that this financial disaster, huge as it is, cruel as it is to thousands, is only a passing episode in the march of a valiant and serviceable people who by fierce experiment are hewing new paths for man, and showing to all nations much that they should attempt and much that they should avoid."[65]

CHAPTER SIX

The Perils
of Fifth Avenue

ALAS, THE FINANCIAL DISASTER proved to be a "passing episode" of considerable longevity, and for Winston, back in England, the Depression signaled the imminent demise of a principle he had cherished since the first day he walked into Parliament. Free Trade was dead in all but theory, and before long even he had to acknowledge the fact. This saddened him, as did, in far greater measure, the death of F. E. Smith in September 1930. "As usual when out of office," moreover, "he was becoming out of sorts." A colleague noted that he looked gloomy and "incredibly aged."[1] The "black dog" reappeared. Most significant of all, Winston was headed for a serious confrontation with the leadership of the Conservative party over the question of India. Stanley Baldwin and his colleagues had decided to support the MacDonald government's policy of eventual Dominion status for Britain's most important colony. Churchill found such a prospect repellent, both on the merits and as a matter of personal conviction. The loss of India would be a fatal knife-thrust for his concept of British civilization, and he was prepared to go to any lengths—compatible with that concept—to prevent it. Early in 1931, accordingly, he resigned from the Conservative Business Committee, or Shadow Cabinet, and officially commenced a period of more than eight years in the political wilderness. Some six months later, running as a Tory, he retained his seat in Parliament in the general election that saw the MacDonald-Baldwin National government win 554 seats in the House of Commons. Party lines were so blurred in the

96

new coalition that there was no occasion for Winston to cross the floor yet a third time, but it came as no surprise to him or to anyone else when he was excluded from the reshuffled cabinet. Once again, as in 1915, he found himself on the sidelines, and there was nothing to prevent him from looking toward America for both a forum and some income. Times were hard all over, after all, and he too had need of extra money.

"My lecture tour in the States has been fully booked up," he wrote Baruch in the summer of 1931, "and the Agency have had no difficulty in letting the largest halls at the highest prices."[2] Large halls and high prices were a necessity if Winston was going to cover his expenses and still have something left over, for his entourage this time included both Clementine and Diana. In addition, there was the more than moderately intimidating figure of Detective Sergeant Walter H. Thompson of Scotland Yard, the man who had been assigned to protect Churchill during the violent period of the Irish Free State Act negotiations of 1921–22 and had stayed with him, off and on, ever since. Thompson's inclusion in the tour was necessitated by solid evidence that an organization called the Indian Terrorist Society, headquartered in San Francisco, had formulated definite plans to assassinate Winston while he was in the United States. The cause of their enmity, of course, was Churchill's position on self-government for the Asian subcontinent, and the threat they posed would have been credible even without Scotland Yard's concrete information about a plot.

The only problem about Thompson's presence in Winston's retinue was that he was an employee of the state while his charge was just an ordinary Member of Parliament making an unofficial journey for personal gain. Churchill accordingly agreed to pay all Thompson's expenses, and the British government agreed to continue paying his salary. It was not a strictly orthodox arrangement, but then orthodoxy had never been Winston's strongest suit.

The assassination threats should have served as an omen that this visit to America was not going to go smoothly. The

problems began even before Churchill left England. His first
lecture was scheduled for Friday evening, December 11, in
Worcester, Massachusetts, and he had booked with Cunard
for December 2. The India question was being debated in
Commons that day, however, and so alternate arrangements
had to be made. Given the fact that Winston had three traveling companions and a tight schedule, this was no easy matter,
and it ultimately developed that the only ship that could get
his wife, his daughter, his bodyguard, and himself to New
York by December 11 was the German liner *Europa*. Now not
only was this a German boat, it was also one of the North
German Lloyd Fleet that had wrested the Blue Riband of the
Atlantic from Cunard, and for Churchill to travel on it, especially at what the New York *Times* called "the height of the
'Buy British' campaign,"[3] was like Carrie Nation traveling in
a club car. Winston was furious: "He cursed and swore and
banged his cane about. . . ."[4] But there was nothing to be
done, and he had to bear in silence the inevitable Parliamentary brickbats his political opponents sent flying in his
direction.

The *Europa* sailed on December 5, with perhaps just a
touch more smoke than usual coming from its stacks.

Despite the ignominy, the crossing was a pleasant one, and
even Thompson was impressed with the service. "I shall not
pay the Germans another compliment," he wrote more than
twenty years later, "and I am relieved here to report that I
do not need to. But they can run a ship and I'll never say
they can't."[5]

The Detective Sergeant was distinctly less impressed with
American journalists. He had risen before dawn on December
11 in order to clean and reload his revolvers prior to debarka-
tion. Suddenly a loud knocking on his stateroom door startled
him out of his ballistic reverie. He flung the door open to find
himself face to face with several dozen male and female reporters who had come out to the *Europa*, still at sea, with the
pilot and quarantine officials. "Hey, where's Winnie?" they
demanded. It was quite a confrontation: some forty hungry—
in more ways than one, probably—American newspaper people who had been up all night on a small boat in filthy

December weather versus the stolid Thompson, half-dressed, heavily armed, and aggressively British.

It was no contest. One reporter drew a chilling thumbnail sketch of this formidable police officer:

> ... He has the fresh high color of the Englishman, cold blue eyes, slicked down hair, the thick neck of a wrestler, and huge fists dangling on large arms like [Bill] Tilden's, a hand's length too long. He stands with legs apart and set like a boxer. He blocks a doorway. His conversation is curt, civil, and in talking he has a habit of rubbing his knuckles into the palm of the other hand.[6]

Thompson told the press that they would have a chance to see Churchill before the ship docked, but that on no account could he be disturbed now. He stepped back into his stateroom to find a steward "making up the place with suspicious enthusiasm." It was a reporter in disguise. "I just picked him up under the arms, planted him hard outside ... and slammed the door."[7]

From that moment on, where newspaper people were concerned, Sergeant Thompson was perpetually—almost psychotically—on his guard.

As a former newspaperman himself, however, Churchill responded with tolerant amusement to his bodyguard's report of the morning's antics. He "had a certain sympathy with it all that I didn't feel."[8] As for the reporters, they finally tracked down their quarry in the *Europa's* sun-deck reception salon. According to the New York *Times*, Churchill "looked very well. His cheeks were tinged with a pinkish glow and his eyes twinkled as he sat ... puffing a cigar...."[9] After an extensive question-and-answer session, Winston stepped outside to pose for photographers. Then it was through Customs and Immigration at the Fifty-eighth Street Pier, a quick motorcycle escort to the Waldorf to drop off the bulk of the luggage, and down to Grand Central Station for the train to Massachusetts. That evening at the Worcester Economic Club Churchill launched his tour with a speech on "The Destiny of the English-Speaking Peoples." With Clementine and Diana he then returned to New York, where, on Saturday, he and Baruch had a happy reunion.

As Winston's next speech was to be at the Brooklyn Academy of Music on Monday night, he and Clementine permitted themselves a day of rest on Sunday. By late evening, with dinner eaten, he was drowsily contemplating the possibility of bed. Then Baruch telephoned to say that a couple of colleagues from the old War Industries Board were at his apartment, and to ask if Churchill wanted to come over and see them. Churchill did, and since it was purely an unscheduled social call, he did not want Thompson along. The Sergeant had other ideas and expressed them in no uncertain terms. At this, he recalled, Winston "became very agitated with me and in his determination to make this one call all alone, he was supported by his wife. . . . Never once in my entire life had I allowed one of my charges to tell me what I was to do or not to do. But this time, because of their insistence, and perhaps influenced psychologically by my own newness to America, I allowed the Churchills to set their wish and judgment over mine. . . ."[10]

It was just after 9:30 P.M.

Churchill descended thirty-nine floors to the lobby of the Waldorf and then remembered that he did not know Baruch's exact address. The telephone book, he discovered, revealed only an office listing. He hesitated a moment, then decided to plunge ahead regardless. He reasoned that he could recognize Baruch's building if he saw it, and he knew that it was on the east side of Fifth Avenue somewhere in the vicinity of number 1100. The Waldorf doorman hailed a taxi for him and off he went.

Winston was unfamiliar with traffic lights—they were not introduced in England until the late 1930s. Thus, to his preoccupation with finding Baruch's apartment, there was added a marked degree of irritation as the cab fitted and started uptown in obedience to flashes of red and green. North of One-hundredth Street he saw that the building numbers were in the 1200s and he instructed the driver to make a U-turn and proceed slowly southward while he once again scrutinized the passing façades. One small building looked familiar, and the cab made another U-turn and pulled up in front. The doorman recognized Churchill immediately and told him that he too had served against the Boers in South Africa. But no, he was sorry, Mr. Baruch did not live there. Had Mr. Churchill checked in the telephone book?

Along with orthodoxy, Churchill had never been abundantly blessed with patience. The cab made yet a third U-turn and resumed its southward course—whenever the stoplights permitted. It was now nearing 10:30. Every time the taxi had to stop, Winston got a little more irritated. Baruch would be worried about him; he must get there soon.

The cab was now back in the 900s, between Seventy-sixth and Seventy-seventh streets. Winston saw another house that looked familiar and told the driver to stop. Given the maddening interference of the reds and greens, another U-turn would just take too much time; he would cross the avenue and inquire while the taxi waited.

Churchill opened the left rear door and stepped out onto the street. He looked north at a car approaching from about two hundred yards away and hurried toward the center of the road to get out of its path. Had he been in London, where people drive on the left, any cars approaching from the south would now have passed behind him on the west side of the avenue. But he was not in London, and "at this moment habit played me a deadly trick." He suffered a split second of disorientation and continued looking uptown for approaching traffic after crossing the middle of the road. Mario Contasino, driving north on the right side of Fifth Avenue at slightly better than thirty-five miles per hour, was horrified to see a man's figure suddenly materialize less than ten feet in front of him, and in the three-tenths of a second it took him to react, those ten feet had been reduced to none.

"There was," Churchill later wrote, "one moment—I cannot measure it in time—of a world aglare, of a man aghast. I certainly thought quickly enough to achieve the idea *'I am going to be run down and probably killed.'* Then came the blow."[11]

Very quickly a police officer appeared at the scene and took charge:

"What is your name?"
"Winston Churchill. . . ."

"What is your age?" asked the officer, adhering to his routine.
"Fifty-seven," I replied. . . .
The constable proceeded to demand particulars of the accident.
. . . I said "I am entirely to blame; it is all my own fault."[12]

Churchill was lifted onto the floor of a taxicab and driven three blocks east to Lenox Hill Hospital. En route he noticed with alarm that he seemed to be suffering from total paralysis, but by the time the cab arrived at Lenox Hill feeling was beginning to return to his arms and legs.

After the customary financial interrogation American hospitals are given to, Winston was admitted and Dr. Otto Pickhardt, a famous consulting surgeon, was summoned to perform a thorough examination to determine if their were any internal injuries. Clementine was notified, and she and Thompson hurried uptown—"This is what happens when police officers permit themselves to do things contrary to their own judgment," the Sergeant fumed.[13] Meanwhile, the senior resident, Dr. Bloom, was treating Churchill's visible injuries.

"We shall have to dress that scalp wound at once. It is cut to the bone."
"Will it hurt?"
"Yes."
"I do not wish to be hurt anymore. Give me chloroform or something."
"The anaesthetist is already on the way."[14]

When the patient awoke he found his wife and Baruch smiling down at him. He had suffered a sprained right shoulder, lacerations of the forehead and nose, and multiple contusions. Given the circumstances, he had gotten off very lightly indeed, and he knew it: "I do not understand why I was not broken like an eggshell or squashed like a gooseberry. . . . I certainly must be very tough or very lucky, or both."[15]

But he was also, as noted, fifty-seven, and a long, painful convalescence lay ahead of him. During the first few days at Lenox Hill his recovery was impeded by a slight attack of pleurisy, but by Wednesday it was clearing and by the weekend he was sitting up and able to read. Flowers and telegrams poured in from all over the English-speaking world, and King George himself telephoned to find out how Winston was doing.

It was a gracious gesture on the part of His Majesty, but it only aggravated Sergeant Thompson's difficulties with the press. In their efforts to gain entry to the injured man's room, newspapermen disguised themselves as doctors and orderlies while newspaperwomen affected to be dieticians or nurses. One enterprising reporter even went so far as to conceal himself in a bin of fresh linen. Only Thompson's carefully honed xenophobia and constabulary suspiciousness kept the wolves outside the door.

Mario Contasino, meanwhile, was anxiously keeping tabs on the condition of the man he had inadvertently run over. A young unemployed truck driver from Yonkers, Contasino went to the hospital every day to inquire about Churchill's health. Taking a cue from Sergeant Thompson, the hospital staff became suspicious of him after the first couple of visits, but when, after questioning, he revealed his connection with the patient, they became friendlier. Clementine was informed of his concern, and she and Winston asked that he be shown up to the room the next time he appeared. On Sunday afternoon, December 20, accordingly, a nervous Contasino was ushered past a glowering Thompson into the Churchills' presence. He talked with them for half an hour or so and disclosed that he had been out of work for two months. Churchill expressed concern lest the publicity surrounding the accident hinder him in his efforts to find a job, and he offered to provide some financial assistance. Contasino, a strong-principled second-generation Italo-American whose family had come over from Potenza in the 1880s, declined with thanks, whereupon Winston presented him with an autographed copy of his latest book in the World Crisis series, *The Unknown War*. "I never want to drive again," said Contasino with operatic remorse as he accepted the volume, but the Churchills urged him to put the incident in the past and carry on, and he agreed eventually that that would be best.[16]

The day after Contasino's visit, Winston left the hospital to return to the Waldorf. He was still not ambulatory, the *Times* noted, but he "appeared to be in good spirits and shook hands

heartily with the several physicians and nurses who cared for
him while he was in the hospital."[17]

Appearances may have been deceiving in this case. Churchill's lecture tour lay in ruins all around him: "the largest
halls at the highest prices" had to be reserved all over again,
dates had to be shifted around or eliminated, expectations of
income had to be drastically scaled down, and all the while
expenses precipitously mounted. Being run over had happily
proved not to be a calamity for Winston, but it was quite
enough from his point of view that it now amounted to an
enormous inconvenience.

He spent his first Christmas in America a semi-invalid, and
a few days before New Year's he interviewed a young British-
born woman named Phyllis Moir, who had applied for the position of his traveling private secretary. Miss Moir was met at the
door of Apartment 39A of the Waldorf Towers by "a tall lanky
man with an angular cockney face" who "eyed me suspiciously
and gave me a professional once-over."[18] She introduced herself, and Thompson, "a little reluctantly," allowed her inside.
After a few minutes he showed her into a large elegantly fur-
nished drawing room. "At first I thought the room was un-
occupied. Then, buried in an enormous Queen Anne armchair
by a blazing fire, I caught sight of a humpty-dumpty sort of
figure reading a letter. . . . A deep livid gash in his forehead
gave him the air of a sorely wounded warrior and the droop
of his powerful shoulders betrayed a weariness which the
jauntiness of his attire could not disguise."[19]

"I understand you are willing to accompany me on my pere-
grinations," Churchill said to her after a hiatus of several minutes. Then, abruptly, "You shouldn't have sent me the origi-
nals of these letters—your letters of recommendation. Why,
they might have got lost."

"I am not by nature a timid person," Miss Moir noted a
decade later, "but Churchill literally floored me. Never in my
life have I felt so unimportant beside another human being."[20]
Winston told her that he was leaving for Nassau shortly and
would be gone about three weeks. Would she be ready to start
work on his return? She said yes, and just that quickly the
interview was over.

Departure for the Bahamas was set for New Year's Eve, and on the thirtieth, Churchill held his first post-accident press conference in his suite. The *Times* correspondent found him "pale, nervous and shaky"[21]—and not particularly sanguine. "I am pessimistic about how humans conduct the matters of the world," he said. And he added mournfully, "From now on you may take it for granted that England will be a definite full-blooded protectionist country." As to himself, he admitted that he had not been feeling well enough to keep up with current affairs. "It has been like in Mark Twain's diary," he told the reporters. "Got up, washed, went to bed."[22]

✳In Nassau the warm sun of the subtropics aided Winston's recovery, but he was still very slow to mend. On January 14, for example, almost two weeks after his arrival and more than a month after his accident, he was still unable to lift his hands above the level of his elbows, and his doctor strongly recommended that he prolong his stay in Nassau for at least ten days. On the eighteenth he wrote Baruch, "I have found the business of recovery a great deal slower than I had hoped during those first buoyant days at the hospital. A very considerable nervous reaction overtook me here, with neuritis in the arms and much feebleness of body and spirit. . . . I am still very weak and have to spend at least eighteen hours out of the twenty-four horizontal . . . there is no doubt that I have received a shock which will take long to master. . . ."[23]

Feeling fitter but still a long way from full recovery, Churchill sailed back into New York Harbor on January 25. Phyllis Moir was standing ready at her post in the Waldorf, braced for the onslaught of typing and dictation that she knew was in store for her.

"A terrific commotion in the hall outside heralded the Churchills' arrival. Their comings and goings are always accompanied by volcanic disturbances. The door of the apartment was ceremoniously opened by the manager and the Churchill family trooped in, Diana chattering shrilly, Mrs. Churchill telling Mr. Churchill he ought to lie down, and Mr. Churchill calling loudly for his mail, his secretary and a Scotch and soda."[24]

All three were immediately forthcoming, and having read

the first, drunk the third, and supplied the second with enough
work to last a fortnight, Winston was free to turn his attention to the press, members of which had gathered at the hotel
to speak to him. "The world today is ruled by harassed politicians absorbed in getting into office or turning out the other
man," he told the reporters, "so that not much room is left for
determining great issues on their merits. . . . It is a great de-
lusion to think that the people have the kind of government
they want in any country of the world now."[25]
His disposition seemed no sunnier than when he left.

On Thursday evening, January 28, Churchill's lecture tour
was finally resumed. Along with two thousand other people,
Mario Contasino was in the audience at the Brooklyn Academy of Music as Winston relaunched his personal campaign
for closer ties between the British Commonwealth and the
United States: "England and America are going in the same
direction. They have the same outlook and no common dis-
cords. Why then do we not act together more effectively? Why
do we stand gaping at each other in this helpless way,
ashamed that it be said that America and England are working together, as if that were a crime? We must be the strong
central nucleus at the council board of the nations."[26]
Churchill allowed himself two days' rest after this speech
in order to gather strength before going on the road. Six weeks
of virtually uninterrupted travel lay ahead of him.
The grind began Sunday, the thirty-first, with a train journey
to Hartford. Arriving shortly after noon, Winston, Clementine,
and Diana were greeted by a representative of the Mark
Twain Memorial and Library Commission and given lunch.
Then, at 3:00 P.M., Winston mounted the dais at Bushnell Auditorium and was introduced to another two-thousand-plus
audience by Connecticut's Governor Wilbur Cross. He reiterated his appeal for Anglo-American unity, making particular reference to the bond of language exemplified by his most
revered former friend and Hartford's most distinguished former resident: ". . . identity of language comes home with
special force to those in this city. Here is the center of the
great Mark Twain literature that has flowed out and is still

flowing over all the English-speaking peoples around the entire globe."[27]

Lecture completed, the Churchills piled into an automobile and headed off for Springfield, Massachusetts, where they boarded the overnight train for St. Louis. After a Monday-evening lecture there, the next stop was Chicago on Tuesday for an address on "The World Economic Crisis" at the Union League Club. According to the *Tribune*, there was an extraordinarily distinguished gathering of solid men of Chicago,"[28] and their equally solid wives, of course—fifteen hundred people in all. In speaking of the global depression, Winston gave his listeners a foretaste of the sentiments Franklin D. Roosevelt would express in his inaugural address one year, one month, and one day in the future: ". . . whatever we do, do not let us fail in the supreme duty—the duty of good courage. . . . My confidence in the British Empire is as great as my confidence in the United States. We still have the everlasting fundamentals to deal in and to consider. In the words of one of your own statesmen [Cockran, of course] 'The earth is a generous mother. She will produce food for all her children if they will but cultivate her soil in justice and in peace.' "[29]

In Cleveland on Wednesday, Churchill repeated his Chicago speech and then got together with a group of businessmen at the Mid-day Club for an informal round-table discussion. Like Miss Moir, the assembled company executives found Winston a little intimidating in face-to-face conversation, and he finally had to chide them gently to get them to shake off their diffidence. "Now, come now," he said after a series of particularly timid questions, "this isn't the American free speech I've heard so much about—or that my mother always boasted about."[30] This jab broke the ice, and for the next hour he traded good-natured verbal punches with his hosts over such sore subjects as tariffs, war debts, and naval armaments. Toward the end of the session he was asked about the prospects for long-term peace. "We are not through with wars," he answered sepulchrally. "We will have another one. . . ."[31]

The next stop after Cleveland was Toledo on Thursday, February 4, and after Toledo came Detroit—and trouble. Detroit was one of the three eastern cities—Chicago and New

York were the other two—where an assassination attempt was considered most likely to occur. Thompson was backed up by a large squad of local detectives, uniformed policemen, and agents of the Secret Service. No attempt was made, as it turned out, but the Indian population of the city subjected the Churchills to a·constant stream of vituperation: twice their car was stoned and once a bag of human excrement was thrown into the lobby of their hotel.[32] It was with considerable relief, therefore, that they entrained for Chicago on the morning of the sixth.

Winston's host in the windy city was the windy publisher of the Chicago *Tribune*, Colonel McCormick, and much to Thompson's satisfaction all local excursions were accomplished in the Colonel's specially constructed armored car. On the evening of the sixth the recently deposed utilities czar Samuel Insull introduced Churchill to an overflow crowd at Orchestra Hall and then sat back to listen as Winston delivered his "English-speaking Peoples" (as distinguished from his "Economic Crisis") address. "Round upon round of applause, spontaneous and vehement, followed the closing words," according to the *Tribune* correspondent. "The handclapping was so prolonged and the attitude of the audience so manifestly intimate and affectionate that the English statesman felt impelled to rise again and utter a few words expressive of his gratitude for the cordial and understanding reception which Chicago has given him in recent days."[33]

In such an atmosphere, danger seemed remote.

Orchestra Hall gradually emptied, and about twenty minutes after the end of the speech Winston and Clementine entered the lobby on the way to McCormick's car. They stopped to talk to a small group of admirers who had lingered behind to meet them after the rest of the crowd had left. Some twenty feet away was the glass-doored entrance to the hall. Thompson and several Chicago detectives were nearby. Suddenly, what Thompson remembered as a "very correctly dressed Indian" hurried through the doors with his right hand in his coat pocket.[34] "His intention was to kill my man and you could see this in his eye," Thompson recalled. In an instant the British detective had his gun out and started advancing toward the potential killer. When the Indian saw him coming he swerved around and bolted for the exit, crashing through the glass doors and into the arms of two alert plainclothesmen. "All of us got cut up a bit," Thompson noted laconically, and in the confusion a would-be accomplice ran off down the street and escaped.[35] Winston, meanwhile, viewed the proceedings with a disapproving scowl, as though he found the Indians' lack of martial spirit reprehensible.

Nothing daunted, the Churchills departed Chicago a couple of hours later for New York, and back in Manhattan Winston gave two speeches—the "Crisis" on Monday, February 9, at the Hotel Astor and the "Peoples" on Tuesday at Carnegie Hall. The Astor address was given before the New York Economic Club and an audience of fifteen hundred people including old friends Baruch and Schwab and newer acquaintances John D. Rockefeller, Jr., and Henry Morgenthau. After speaking, Churchill threw the floor open to questions and engaged in a lively back-and-forth for over an hour. The final question of the evening was: "Would you become an American citizen if we could make you President of the United States? I know our Constitution disqualifies you, but we can amend that." Winston twinkled and replied, "There are various little difficulties in the way. However, I have been treated so splendidly in the United States that I shall be disposed, if you can amend the Constitution, seriously to consider the matter."[36]

Before his Carnegie Hall engagement on Tuesday, Churchill and Al Smith, a newly announced Presidential aspirant (or, perhaps, fellow Presidential aspirant, in light of the above), went on an excursion to the top of the brand-new Empire State Building. There the two politicians exchanged profound observations appropriate to men of their station. Mr. Churchill: "I have never been so high before." Mr. Smith: "And I don't suppose I shall ever get any higher myself."[37]

After New York came Rochester and then Washington, where the Churchills took up residence at the British Embassy. The ambassador in these years was the ultrapunctilious Sir Ronald Lindsay, and it seems safe to say that Winston's stay in his official domicile aged him as few things—including possibly his accumulated years—had up to that time. As was his custom, Churchill insisted on working in bed in the mornings, and it was thus Sir Ronald's painful duty to discuss each day's inevitably chaotic agenda with him in his boudoir. Miss Moir remembered the bizarre aspect of such planning sessions: "These two made the oddest contrast, the immensely dignified diplomat standing extremely ill at ease at the foot of the old-fashioned four-poster and the Peter Pan of British politics sitting up in bed, a cigar in his mouth, his tufts of red hair as yet uncombed, scanning the morning newspapers."[38]

Winston gave his "Crisis" talk to the "most critical" of his U.S. audiences[39] at Constitution Hall on Friday, the twelfth, but received "prolonged and deafening" applause nevertheless.[40] While in Washington he also paid his second call on President Hoover and attended a dinner party given by Daisy Harriman. At the table he was seated next to Alice Roosevelt Longworth, the late Theodore's sharp-tongued daughter. Despite her lineage, Mrs. Longworth seems not only to have taken to him but even to have engaged in a little flirtation as well. When he asked her to state her opinions about Prohibition, for example, she leaned over and murmured, "I would rather whisper them to you."[41] (Of course, this may simply have been because bad language from a lady was still unacceptable in polite society.)

"After dinner was over," Churchill remembered, "the whole company formed a half-circle around me, and then began one of the frankest and most direct political interrogations to which I have ever been subjected. The unspoken, but perfectly well-comprehended condition was that any question, however awkward, might be asked, and that any answer, however pointed, would be taken in good part. For two hours we wrestled strenuously, unsparingly, but in the best of tempers with one another. . . . Nowhere else in the world, only between our two people, could such a discussion have proceeded. . . ."[42]

On Valentine's Day the Washington *Post* reviewed Winston's Friday speech in an editorial. It was rather a jaundiced critique, all things considered, but it also accurately reflected Churchill's by now firm conviction that England's future welfare was inextricably bound up with, and perhaps even dependent upon, her special relationship with America.

Winston Churchill, former chancellor of the British exchequer, is in the United States for the general purpose of trying to hitch the British wagon to the American star. The way to solve the problems of the world, he told a Washington audience Friday night, is to strike a working agreement between Great Britain and the United States. Unity of the English-speaking people has become a great British ideal.

Not many years ago political and economic unity with the Yankees would have been repulsive to British statesmen. . . . Now the tables are turned and Mr. Churchill is trying to flatter the United States into taking over some of Great Britain's liabilities.

It is rather strange for a debtor to offer a partnership to his creditor. What contribution has Britain to make to the cooperative bond that Mr. Churchill suggests for the two countries?[43]

After a Washington Press Club luncheon in his honor on February 16, Winston embarked upon the most grueling period of his tour. He was still not completely recovered from his automobile accident, and the distances between what were usually only one-night stands were immense. Nashville, New Orleans, Cincinnati, Grand Rapids, Indianapolis, Ann Arbor— east, west, north, and south the Churchills traveled. Fifteen years later Winston looked back on this episode, "living all day on my back in a railway compartment and addressing in the evening large audiences," and he concluded, rather startlingly for someone with his background, "On the whole I consider this was the hardest time I have had in my life."[44]

Still, the cities of America impressed him: ". . . What lovely country surrounds the city of Atlanta . . . and who would miss Chattanooga, lying in its cup between the Blue Ridge and Lookout Mountain? . . . In Minneapolis amid its rolling plains my small party had its most appreciative welcome. Cincinnati, I thought, was the most beautiful of the inland cities of the Union. . . . There was a splendor in Chicago and a life thrust that is all its own."[45]

The schedule was backbreaking, but the enthusiasm of American audiences made it bearable. Everywhere the Churchills went they were received with openness and warmth. Atlanta was typical. The *Constitution* reported that the offices of the lecture bureau sponsoring Winston's appearance had been "flooded with requests for seats" from the moment the date of his visit had been announced.[46] On the day of his arrival, February 23, the same newspaper accorded him the following eulogy: "Few speakers of today equal the former chancellor of the British exchequer in eloquence and wit. He commands an unrivalled fund of information about the inner workings of European governments and his views on the future of the civilized world, about the present crisis in economic and social structures and about probable developments in world alignments command respectful attention in the capitals of the world."[47]

There were the customary press conferences, and in the evening the lecture hall was packed with thousands of people. After being introduced by Georgia's Governor, Hugh Dorsey, Winston held the large crowd rapt for over an hour with a recitation of his "Peoples" address. Toward the end of his talk he warned against precipitate cuts in Anglo-American armed strength, noting that "it would be a sad day for our two countries if advocates of full disarmament had their way and something happened to peace. I hope never to see the time come when the force of right is deprived of the right of force." And he concluded with feeling: "Whatever the pathway of the future may bring, we can face it more safely, more comfortably, and more happily if we travel it together, like good companions. We have quarreled in the past, but even in our quarrels great leaders on both sides were agreed on principle. Let our common tongue, our common basic law, our joint heritage of literature and ideals, the red tie of kinship, become the sponge of obliteration for all the unpleasantness of the past."[48]

Before leaving Atlanta Winston reviewed the ROTC cadets at Georgia Tech and spoke to the students. Then it was back on the train and back on his back and off to the next speech in the next city on the list.

The tour wound down in an accelerating spiral of fatigue, and when the Churchills finally staggered back to the Northeast for Winston's last three appearances, all of them were very nearly spent. On their way to New York the news broke that Anne and Charles Lindbergh's infant son had been kidnapped. Perhaps because of their own tragedy with Marigold, Winston and Clementine were deeply shocked, but they were even more dismayed by the sensational way the press played up the crime. Neither of them could understand what seemed to be such wanton public insensitivity, and both refused to make any comment on the case whatsoever. "What about the Lindbergh case?" reporters asked shortly after Churchill's 8:30 A.M. arrival at Boston's South Station on March 10. "I do not wish to comment on it," Winston replied in clipped tones. "Could such a thing have happened in England?" they persisted. "I do not wish to comment on it," Churchill repeated more emphatically, "at all!" The newspapermen turned to more congenial topics, but the responses from their subject, who was "patently tired out" on this the day of his final lecture, came grudgingly if at all. His foremost impression of America at that moment, he said, was that he had "spent only two of the past ten nights in a real bed." As for Prohibition, "There seems to be an enormous feeling of revulsion against it." What about the election of de Valera in Ireland? "I thought it was going to happen some time ago because it was the most unreasonable thing that could happen."[49]

Winston delivered "Peoples" at Symphony Hall that evening and then took the night train back to New York City. He was now at the end of his strength, literally aching to lie down on his berth on the White Star liner *Majestic* and sleep all the way back to England. On Friday, March 11, at dockside he spoke to the American press one last time. The *Times* man found him "obviously tired from the strain of his recent trip."[50] When the reporters were done with him, he trudged aboard the ship and headed for his cabin. Baruch accompanied him and was the last to leave the boat before it weighed anchor. It was nearly midnight now; the hawsers were set loose and two tugboats pushed the *Majestic* into the channel.

Thus, Winston Churchill left America for a fourth, and in a sense final, time. Churchill the man would never return to this side of the Atlantic. Next time he came he would be Churchill the legend.

Part Two

———

FRIEND AND ALLY

CHAPTER SEVEN

Wilderness Years and Finest Hours

THE 1930S ARE KNOWN as Churchill's years in the political wilderness, the time when he stood alone, a prophet without honor in his own country, trying to shake England out of her torpor and alert her to the danger posed by a resurgent Germany. There is a great deal of truth in this picture, but there is another far less edifying portrait that emerges from this period as well, particularly with respect to 1932–36. In this we see a man systematically undermining his credibility and his capacity to be of service with a ruthless efficiency that would be impressive if only the result were not exactly contrary to the intention. On a more subjective level we see a political caricature: a blimpish figure, no longer young, no longer promising, what Lord Beaverbrook referred to as "a busted flush."[1] We see increasing irritability and vituperation and watch in embarrassment as an overweight Pantaloon strives frenziedly and with ever-growing desperation to keep in sight the constantly receding goal of Parliamentary pre-eminence that he has been pursuing vainly all his life.

To suggest that Churchill's failings between 1932 and 1936 seriously limited his influence on British foreign policy between 1937 and 1939 would be to tread carelessly on the treacherous ground of historical conjecture. But while it cannot readily be established that a more respected Winston would have been more successful in attacking the politics of appeasement, it is incontrovertible that Winston as he was, was of virtually no political consequence whatsoever—of no consequence, that is, until events overtook his efforts to forewarn his country and showed that he was right too late for his rightness to have any value apart from personal vindication. The problem was India or, more precisely, Churchill's attitude toward it. On that subject he was guilty of a politician's most deadly sin: failure—or refusal, in his case—to recognize a fundamental rearrangement of the building blocks of power. India for him was still Bangalore, the Malakand Field Force, and the Inter-Regimental Polo Tournament at Meerut; still an inchoate hodgepodge of Maharajahs and Princes, Hindus, Moslems, and Sikhs benevolently superintended and kept from one another's throats by the paternally indulgent hand of the British Raj. It was the brightest jewel in the glorious crown of Empire, and the rise of a coherent nationalist movement with a broad popular base there was something he was temperamentally incapable of acknowledging. He therefore derided the movement—"India . . . is no more a united nation than the Equator"—and discounted it almost completely in his own thinking. The result was that, whenever he argued for the maintenance of the imperial status quo, he was always in effect urging the paradoxical proposition that India should not merely stay the way it was, Gandhi, Congress party, and all, but that it should stay the way it used to be before Gandhi-ism and Congress had appeared on the scene. Rather than confront the fact that the only real Indian issue was *how* the colony could best be granted a degree of self-determination, he persisted in addressing himself to the question of *whether* it ought to be. As a consequence, his contributions to public debate were little more than irrelevant at best, little less than obstructionist at worst. Furthermore, since his contributions were numerous and—Churchill being Churchill—memorable, their cumulative effect on his political reputation during more than five years of heated Parliamentary controversy was disastrous. People, particularly Indians, were and will yet be a long time forgetting his bombastic denunciation of Gandhi as "a seditious Middle Temple lawyer, now posing as a fakir of a type well known in the East, striding half-naked up the steps of the Viceregal Palace . . . to parley on equal terms with the representative of the King-Emperor."[2] Eloquence, especially eloquence in a mistaken cause, can often do an orator more harm than prolixity, and Churchill on India is a case in point. As Liberal party leader Herbert Samuel observed in 1933, "The brilliance of his speeches only makes the errors in his judgment more conspicuous. . . ."[3]

The Government of India Act was finally passed in the summer of 1935 over Churchill's politically dead, or at least prostrate, body. At this time, however, Adolf Hitler was still in the process of consolidating his hold over the people of Germany and did not yet constitute an immediate menace. Thus, during the last half of 1935 and virtually all of 1936, there was time for the wounds of the India debate to heal somewhat and for Churchill to regain some of the stature he had lost. This he proceeded to do in a series of measured speeches on the dangers posed by the all-out intensity of German rearmament, on the March 1936 remilitarization of the Rhineland, and, most particularly, on the singularly ineffectual nature of the British government's response to these developments. Now his eloquence became once again his ally, and in November 1936 his standing in Parliament rose higher than ever on the strength of a devastating and incisive indictment of the Baldwin administration's altogether mushy foreign policy: "The Government simply cannot make up their minds, or they cannot get the Prime Minister to make up his mind. So they go on in strange paradox, decided only to be undecided, resolved to be irresolute, adamant for drift, solid for fluidity, all-powerful to be impotent. So we go on preparing more months and years —precious, perhaps vital, to the greatness of Britain—for the locusts to eat." It was one of his best speeches, and, with the threat from the continent becoming daily more palpable, it seemed that his political star might yet sparkle brightly at the zenith. Less than three weeks after the speech was delivered, however, the abdication crisis came along, and his star was very nearly blotted out.

When it became known that Edward VIII intended to marry not only morganatically but a foreigner and a divorcée as well, the resultant storm of disapproval broke with tropical suddenness and force. All Churchill's instincts of romance and chivalry impelled him to gallop to the King's defense, but like the legendary captains of cavalry he did not look to see if his battalions were behind him as he charged. Even if he had, of course, he would not have slackened his speed, but the fact was that he charged virtually alone. The government and the public at large were adamantly against the proposed marriage, and the people, moreover, were outraged at what seemed to them to be the almost cavalier manner with which Edward had flung away his immense personal popularity and prestige. On December 7, 1936, Churchill was shouted down on the floor of the House of Commons as he tried to plead the King's cause. His political stock fell again to the Government-of-India-Act level, or even lower. Four days later when Edward VIII yielded his throne to George VI, Winston too found himself occupying a lower station in Great Britain's national affairs.

"Of all the political qualities," wrote Robert Rhodes James in his brilliant study of Churchill's pre–World War II career, "persistence is perhaps the most admirable, and among the most difficult. To persist in a political career that appears to others, and even on occasion to the politician himself, as finished, demands exceptional strength of character."⁴ And as the most deadly of the locust years, 1937 and 1938, broke upon the United Kingdom, the strength of Churchill's character was put to its most severe test. To be sure, he had consolations: there was his painting and there were his books. The 1930s saw him publish, among other works, a four-volume biography of his ancestor the Duke of Marlborough, an anthology of his newspaper and magazine articles, and *Great Contemporaries*, a collection of essays on prominent public figures. He also wrote most of his *History of the English-Speaking Peoples* in this period, though its completion and publication were to be delayed for almost a generation by the war. Then, of course, there was his family and the idyllic home life he shared with them at Chartwell in the green Kentish Weald, a strong refuge from political strife where "I built with my own hands a large part of two cottages and extensive kitchen-garden walls, and made all kinds of rockeries and waterworks and a large swimming pool which was filtered to limpidity and could be heated to supplement our fickle sunshine."⁵ All the blessings and consolations in the world, however, could not efface the fact that his country was sliding inexorably toward a terrible abyss and that he, out of office for more than eight years now, could do nothing more than look on helplessly and cry out futile warnings to the uncomprehending land. After the Abyssinian crisis of 1935–36 had served both to alienate Italy from the Western democracies and discredit the League of Nations, the European balance of power in 1937 shifted perceptibly to the east. In May of that year Stanley Baldwin retired as Prime Minister and Neville Chamberlain, the scion of a famous Birmingham political family, succeeded him. In 1938 the real hammer blows began to fall.

The first shock was, for Churchill personally, perhaps the greatest. It was the resignation of Anthony Eden as Foreign Secretary over the question of German infringements of Austrian sovereignty. He received the news toward midnight on February 20. "I must confess that my heart sank, and for a while the dark waters of despair overwhelmed me. . . . From midnight till dawn I lay in my bed consumed by emotions of sorrow and fear. There seemed one strong young figure standing up against long, dismal, drawling tides of drift and surrender, of wrong measures and feeble impulses. . . . Now he was gone. I watched the daylight slowly creep in through the windows, and saw before me in mental gaze the vision of Death."[6]

Hard upon the first blow came the second: the invasion and annexation of Austria by the Third Reich on March 12. "For five years I have talked to this House on these matters—not with very great success," Churchill said in Commons. "I have watched this famous island descending incontinently, fecklessly, the stairway which leads to a dark gulf. . . ."[7] The swallowing up of Austria, he warned, placed Czechoslovakia in a position of great strategic peril; and to undermine Czechoslovakia was to offer Hitler the mastery of Central Europe.

Now it was Neville Chamberlain's turn to disregard a fundamental change in the arrangements of power. For Churchill, who understood so clearly the motions of the weights and springs in the scales of Europe, it must have been maddening to watch the Prime Minister toss away the solid counterpoise of Czechoslovak territorial integrity and accept an insubstantial piece of paper in exchange.

The painful debacle of Munich does not need to be recounted here. Suffice it to say that in September 1938, on the flimsiest of pretexts and without firing a shot, Hitler effectively won control of every hectare of territory between the Rhine and the Vistula. "We have sustained a total and unmitigated defeat," Churchill admonished the House of Commons, and an angry roar of disapproval erupted from the Government benches.

One pound was demanded at the pistol's point [he continued]. When it was given, two pounds were demanded at the pistol's point. Finally, the Dictator consented to take £1 17s. 6d. and the rest in promises of good will for the future. . . . All is over. Silent, mournful, abandoned, broken, Czechoslovakia recedes into the darkness. . . . I do not grudge our loyal, brave people . . . the natural, spontaneous outburst of joy and relief when they learned that the hard ordeal would no longer be required of them at the moment; but they should know the truth . . . they should know that we have sustained a defeat without a war . . . they should know that we have passed an awful milestone in our history, when the whole equilibrium of Europe has been deranged, and that the terrible words have for the time being been pronounced against the Western Democracies: "Thou art weighed in the balance and found wanting." And do not suppose that this is the end. This is only the beginning of the reckoning. This is only the first sip, the first foretaste of a bitter cup which will be proffered to us year by year unless, by a supreme recovery of moral health and martial vigour, we arise again and take our stand for freedom as in the olden time.[8]

Nineteen thirty-nine was a vortex spiraling ever more rapidly downward toward Armageddon. On the Ides of March, German troops advanced upon the emasculated remnants of the Czechoslovak nation and completed the bloodless conquest the Prime Minister of Great Britain had initiated six months before. Now, however, the scales fell from Neville Chamberlain's eyes, and before the month was out both England and France extended unconditional—and, in the event, unavailing—guarantees to Poland, which was plainly the next country on Hitler's list. One week into April Mussolini invaded Albania, and one week into May he entered into a Pact of Steel with his German compeer. Almost simultaneously, Maxim Litvinov, a

Jew, "resigned" as Stalin's Foreign Commissar and was replaced by V. M. Molotov. His departure signified—and was clearly meant to signify—that England and France were not the only suitors who might reasonably hope to win the favor of husky Mother Russia, so long a wallflower at the European Ball but now so ardently pursued. Throughout most of the summer the elephantine Slav coquette kept her beaus dangling as she tried to make up her mind, but on August 21 the Gaul and the Anglo-Saxon learned that it was the Teuton whose suit had been granted. The victors of World War I suddenly found themselves forlorn and isolated in the northwestern corner of Europe, sworn to protect an encircled Poland which they could not even reach. On September 1 Hitler attacked and immediately received British and French ultimata to withdraw. On September 3 the ultimata expired, and in London Neville Chamberlain called on Winston Churchill to serve for a second time and in a second world conflict as First Lord of the Admiralty. "So it was that I came again to the room I had quitted in pain and sorrow almost exactly a quarter of a century before.... Once again defence of the rights of a weak state, outraged and invaded by unprovoked aggression, forced us to draw the sword. Once again we must fight for life and honor against all the might and fury of the valiant, disciplined, and ruthless German race. Once again! So be it."[9]

THE WHITE HOUSE   September 11, 1939
WASHINGTON

My dear Churchill:

It is because you and I occupied similar positions in the World War that I want you to know how glad I am that you are back again at the Admiralty. Your problems are, I realize, complicated by new factors but the essential is not very different. What I want you and the Prime Minister to know is that I shall at all times welcome it if you will keep me in touch personally with anything you want me to know about. You can always send sealed letters through your pouch or my pouch.

I am glad you did the Marlboro [*sic*] volumes before this thing started—and I much enjoyed reading them.

[signed] Franklin D. Roosevelt[10]

Thus, scarcely a week into the war, did the President of the United States inaugurate a correspondence that was to last until his death in 1945 and comprise, all told, over seventeen hundred messages. It is intriguing to speculate about what motivated FDR to take this unconventional initiative. He had met Churchill only once, in 1918, and then but briefly (see page 73). Robert Sherwood, in his classic *Roosevelt and Hopkins*, suggests that the President recognized in Churchill the surest guarantee against a negotiated Anglo-German peace —"another Munich"—after what seemed certain to be the speedy subjugation of Poland.[11] This makes sense, but one suspects that the subtly intuitive side of FDR's personality played a part too. However brief his encounter with Winston had been, he remembered it (see page 134), and it is likely that he was very much aware that Churchill was not only half-American by blood but also a vigorous exponent of Anglo-American entente. It is even possible, and certainly tempting, to suppose that Roosevelt perceived early on that Neville Chamberlain would be no better at waging war than he had been at forging peace and that, when his inadequacies became intolerable, Churchill would be the inevitable choice to succeed him. Whatever may have been the intricacies of his calculations, FDR found in Churchill an eager correspondent. "I responded with alacrity," Winston wrote of this first message, "using the signature 'Naval Person.'"[12]

In the event, Poland was extinguished ruthlessly and with dispatch, the *coup de grâce* being administered when Soviet troops crossed her eastern frontier on September 17 pursuant to the Secret Additional Protocol to the Nazi-Soviet Pact of August 23. At the Admiralty Churchill bore into his task with all the vigor of his personality and all the wisdom and experience born of forty years of politics, twenty years of high office, and ten years of involuntary exile from the councils of power. A torrential stream of "minutes" and directives began to flow from his office, and the Admiralty Board, sensing the electricity that now would pulse through His Majesty's naval establishment, signaled the fleet, "Winston is back."

Churchill's minutes make a fascinating study in and of themselves. They reveal not only the breadth and depth of his involvement in his work, but also the tremendous impulsive energy with which he inspirited even the most plodding and cumbersome bureaucracies. "I am certainly not one of those who need to be prodded," he observed. "In fact, if anything, I am a prod."[13] He was a tenacious campaigner for *Action!* and a steam-roller advocate for his concepts thereof. "All I ask," he once admitted in all innocence, "is compliance with my wishes after reasonable discussion."[14]

First Lord to Second Sea Lord, Parliamentary Secretary
and Secretary.   7.X.1939
Will you kindly explain to me the reasons which debar individuals in certain branches from rising by merit to commissioned rank? . . . If a telegraphist may rise, why not a painter? Apparently there is no difficulty about painters rising in Germany!

First Lord to Fourth Sea Lord   12.XII.1939
I am told that the minesweeper men have no badge. If this is so, it must be remedied at once. I have asked . . . for designs from Sir Kenneth Clark within one week, after which production must begin with the greatest speed. . . .

Special Entry Cadetship   8.II.1940
It seems very difficult to understand why this candidate should have been so decisively rejected. . . . One has to be particularly careful that class prejudice does not enter into these decisions. . . .

First Lord to Secretary   (see previous minute)   25.II.1940
I do not at all mind "going behind the opinion of the board duly constituted," or even changing the board or its chairman if I think injustice has been done. How long has it been since this board was re-modelled? . . . Let me have a list of the whole board—with the full records of each member and the date of his appointment.

First Lord to Second Sea Lord and Fourth Sea Lord   24.III.1940
Backgammon would be a good game for Wardroom, Gunroom, and Warrant Officers' Mess, and I have no doubt it would amuse the sailors. . . . Backgammon is a better game than cards for the circumstances of wartime afloat, because it whiles away twenty minutes or a quarter of an hour whereas cards are a much longer business.[15]

Of course by far the great preponderance of Churchill's directives dealt with more vital matters, such as U-boats, the transfer of the British Expeditionary Force to France, the dis-

position of the fleet, and the pursuit of the pocket battleship
Graf Spee. Given the suspicious lack of action on the western
front, the war at sea was just about all the war there was, for
as Roosevelt had feared the only offensive Hitler launched
against France and England during the winter of 1939–40 was
a peace offensive. The destruction of Poland was a *fait accompli*, the Führer argued, and the Reich was demanding no special concessions from Paris or London other than acquies-
cence in that fact. Why not let matters rest where they were?

But Hitler had exhausted his adversaries' gullibility, even if it
had taken him several years of conquest to do it. The same
could not be said with respect to the anxious and obsequious
neutrals who paid him court, however. "Each one hopes that if
he feeds the crocodile enough, the crocodile will eat him last,"
Churchill warned in a radio broadcast on January 20. "All of
them hope that the storm will pass before their turn comes to
be devoured. But I fear—I fear greatly—the storm will not
pass.... There is no chance of a speedy end except through
united action...."16

The storm broke at the beginning of April. On the ninth,
less than a week after Chamberlain had added to his 1938
prophecy of "peace in our time" the equally infelicitous assess-
ment that Hitler had "missed the bus," Germany overran
Denmark and Norway. One month and one day later it was
the turn of Holland, Belgium, and Luxembourg. May 10, 1940:
the "phony war" was over. Provoked beyond endurance by
three years of mismanagement and vacillation, the House of
Commons turned on the utterly discredited Prime Minister.
The prominent Conservative Leopold Amery invoked Crom-
well's injunction to the Long Parliament: "You have sat too
long here for any good you have been doing. Depart, I say,
and let us have done with you. In the name of God, go!"
Lloyd George, a snow-white seventy-seven, joined the attack:
"The Prime Minister ... has appealed for sacrifice.... I say
solemnly that the Prime Minister should give an example of
sacrifice, because there is nothing which can contribute more
to victory in this war than that he should sacrifice the seals of
office."

While Chamberlain did not go like a lamb to the slaughter,

it was clear that a National government including the Labour and Liberal oppositions had to be formed, and neither party would consent to serve under him. At 11:00 A.M. on the morning of May 10, accordingly, he asked Winston and the Foreign Secretary, Lord Halifax, to come to his office. "I have had many important interviews in my public life," Churchill recollected, "and this was certainly the most important. Usually I talk a great deal, but on this occasion I was silent." Chamberlain preferred Halifax as his successor, but knew that Winston would be a far more popular choice; the Foreign Secretary, among other things, was stained with the odium of Munich. Without expressing the idea in so many words, the Prime Minister intimated in a roundabout way that Churchill's differences with Labour over the years might now prove awkward should he be chosen to form a new government. It was a thinly veiled invitation to withdraw, but Winston had not traversed all his years of anguish, despair, and frustration only to toss over his ambitions with a courtly gesture at the moment of their realization. The overture dissipated in the air, but still the principals in the drama sat mute, and "a very long pause ensued. It certainly seemed longer than the two minutes which one observes in the commemorations of Armistice Day." Finally Halifax acknowledged that the gambit to get his rival's support for his own elevation had failed; he broke the silence by stating that his position as a member of the House of Lords excluded him from further consideration. The prize, so long sought, so often gone aglimmering, fell at last to Winston Leonard Spencer Churchill, the public-school failure who had only been good enough for a commission in a cavalry regiment.[17]

The rest of May 10 was spent in a hectic round of meetings and negotiations. Neville Chamberlain, "silent, mournful, abandoned, broken," faded into the background. It was not until three o'clock on the morning of the eleventh that Churchill got to bed. "I cannot conceal that . . . I was conscious of a profound sense of relief. At last I had authority to give directions over the whole scene. I felt as if I were walking with Destiny, and that all my past life had been but a preparation for this hour and this trial. . . . I thought I knew a good deal about it all, and I was sure I should not fail. Therefore, although impatient for the morning, I slept soundly and had no need of cheering dreams. Facts are better than dreams."[18]

During Winston's first weeks in power, however, facts were considerably worse than nightmares. The German army feinted with its right hand and then crashed through the weakly defended region of the Ardennes, piercing the French lines with massive thrusts of armor and mechanized infantry. Churchill told the House of Commons on May 13 that he had "nothing to offer but blood, toil, tears, and sweat," and rarely has a political promise been so punctiliously kept. Despite the courageous leadership of Paul Reynaud, France cracked like a twig. After less than two weeks of fighting, the Germans had reached the Channel. After less than three weeks the evacuation of Dunkirk had begun and the Belgian army had surrendered. One month after Churchill took office Norway ceased to offer resistance and Italy declared war. On June 14 the Germans entered Paris, and on June 22 France lay down her sword. From the Arctic Circle to the shores of Africa, from Gibraltar to the Dardanelles, Britain stood alone.

In *Great Contemporaries* Churchill had described the one man who, more than any other, had infused a vital spirit into the Allied cause in World War I: "Clemenceau embodied and expressed France. As much as any single human being, miraculously magnified, can ever be a nation, he was France. . . . Happy the nation which when its fate quivers in the balance can find . . . such a champion."[19] Now the same words applied with even greater force to himself and Great Britain. Not once, not twice, not just half a dozen times, but time after time, again and again throughout 1940 and '41 he sounded the precise chord that would set the entire nation to sympathetic vibration. He said what the British people felt, what they would have said themselves had they possessed his powers of articulation, and he said it with a lyric majesty and an electric air of conviction that still have the capacity to thrill and inspire. At the culminating moment of his and his country's lives, he expressed not only resolution to England and defiance to England's foes, but a profound peace of mind, a feeling of rightness, a sense that Britain was at last in harmony with fundamental universal forces, that the sickness and putrefaction of the recent past had been washed away, that the nation as a whole had been spiritually regenerated, and that its people had indeed arisen once more to take their stand for freedom as in the olden time.

Here are some of his words:

You ask what is our policy? I will say: It is to wage war, by sea, land and air, with all our might and all the strength that God can give us; to wage war against a monstrous tyranny, never surpassed in the dark lamentable catalogues of human crime. That is our policy. You ask, What is our aim? I can answer in one word: Victory—victory at all costs, victory in spite of all terror, victory however long and hard the road may be; for without victory there is no survival. . . .

Even though large tracts of Europe and many old and famous States have fallen or may fall into the grip of the Gestapo and all the odious apparatus of Nazi rule, we shall not flag or fail. We shall go on to the end, we shall fight in France, we shall fight on the seas and oceans, we shall fight with growing confidence and growing strength in the air, we shall defend our island, whatever the cost may be, we shall fight on the beaches, we shall fight on the landing grounds, we shall fight in the fields and in the streets, we shall fight in the hills; we shall never surrender, and even if, which I do not for a moment believe, this island or a large part of it were subjugated and starving, then our Empire beyond the seas, armed and guarded by the British Fleet, would carry on the struggle, until, in God's good time, the new world, with all its power and might, steps forth to the rescue and the liberation of the old.

. . . These cruel, wanton, indiscriminate bombings of London are, of course, a part of Hitler's invasion plans. . . . This wicked man, the repository and embodiment of many forms of soul-destroying hatred, this monstrous product of former wrongs and shame, has now resolved to try to break our famous island race by a process of indiscriminate slaughter and destruction. What he has done is to kindle a fire in British hearts, here and all over the world, which will glow long after all traces of the conflagration he has caused in London have been removed. He has lighted a fire which will burn with a steady and consuming flame until the last vestiges of Nazi tyranny have been burnt out of Europe, and until the Old World—

and the New—can join hands to rebuild the temples of man's freedom and man's honour, upon foundations which will not soon or easily be overthrown.

The gratitude of every home in our island, in our Empire, and indeed throughout the world, except in the abodes of the guilty, goes out to the British airmen who, undaunted by odds, unwearied in their constant challenge and mortal danger, are turning the tide of the world war by their prowess and their devotion. Never in the field of human conflict was so much owed by so many to so few. . . .

And finally:

What General Weygand has called the Battle of France is over. I expect that the Battle of Britain is about to begin. Upon this battle depends the survival of Christian civilisation. Upon it depends our own British life, and the long continuity of our institutions and our Empire. The whole fury and might of the enemy must very soon be turned on us. Hitler knows that he will have to break us in this island or lose the war. If we can stand up to him, all Europe may be free and the life of the world may move forward into broad sunlit uplands. But if we fail, then the whole world, including the United States, including all that we have known and cared for, will sink into the abyss of a new dark age made more sinister, and perhaps more protracted, by the lights of perverted science. Let us therefore brace ourselves to our duties, and so bear ourselves that, if the British Empire and its Commonwealth last for a thousand years, men will still say, "This was their finest hour."[20]

It is hard from this vantage point in time to grasp how very close to extinction Western civilization was in 1940–41; indeed, rich as we are now in material things and secure as we are in a world where general war has been discredited as a sensible concomitant of foreign policy, we are free to indulge ourselves in airy speculations about whether our cultural survival was really such a very good thing. Whether one wishes to praise or condemn the principal saviors of the West, however, one can hardly escape acknowledging who they were. At a time when all of Europe was either hostile, subject, or rigidly neutral, when all Asia was hostage to either Russian or Japanese tyranny, when all the oceans were sharply contested by both surface and subsurface enemy armadas, and above all when the only Horatius standing at the bridge was a nation outnumbered, outgunned, outmanufactured, and outorganized by its adversaries by factors of three or four to one—two men, by virtue of their political acuity and their skill in mobilizing the human resources of their countries, were responsible for bringing about the eventual worldwide resurrection of the democratic ideal. The two were Churchill and Roosevelt, and the story of World War II is in good part the product of their constant collaboration.

It was clear to Roosevelt from the outset that the United States had a great deal more than a mere emotional stake in Britain's future, and with the fall of France his constant concern became to bring American influence to bear on the outcome of the war in Europe in the only way—and to the greatest extent—possible: through matériel and shipping. Churchill for his part was careful to do nothing that might allay Roosevelt's fears of the possible consequences of a British collapse. In a message dated June 15, 1940, he wrote: "Although the present government and I personally would never fail to send the fleet across the Atlantic if resistance was beaten down here, a point may be reached in the struggle where the present ministers no longer have control of affairs. . . . The fate of the British fleet . . . would be decisive on the future of the United States because if it were joined to the fleets of Japan, France, and Italy, and the great resources of German industry, overwhelming sea power would be in Hitler's hands. He might, of course, use it with merciful moderation. On the other hand he might not. . . ."[21]

Hitler's inclinations toward merciful moderation were soon demonstrated to be minimal as words like "Blitz" and "Coventry" took on new significations. But the Battle of Britain was fought and won, and, as England moved into her first winter under siege, her Prime Minister had one cause, at least, for rejoicing. "I did not think it right for me as a foreigner to express any opinion upon American politics while the election was on," he wrote Roosevelt on November 6, "but now I feel that you will not mind my saying that I prayed for your success and that I am truly thankful for it."[22]

One of the first fruits of FDR's success was Lend-Lease. On December 17 he said to reporters, "Now, what I am trying to do is eliminate the dollar sign. . . . Well, let me give you an illustration. Suppose my neighbor's home catches fire, and I have a length of garden hose. . . ."[23] On December 29, in a Fireside Chat, he said, "We must be the great arsenal of democracy." In January 1941 he sent two emissaries to London, the first, his right-hand man, Harry Hopkins, whom Churchill practically smothered with attention, and the second, his recently defeated Republican opponent, Wendell Willkie. With Willkie went a handwritten note: "Dear Churchill . . . I think this applies to you people as it does to us: Sail on, Oh Ship of State!/Sail on, Oh Union strong and great./Humanity with all its fears/With all the hope of future years/Is hanging breathless on thy fate. . . ."[24] Churchill replied to this note in a worldwide radio broadcast on February 9, the day the House of Representatives passed Lend-Lease: ". . . Put your confidence in us. Give us your faith and your blessing, and, under Providence, all will be well. We shall not fail or falter; we shall not weaken or tire. Neither the sudden shock of battle nor the long-drawn trials of vigilance and exertion will wear us down. Give us the tools, and we will finish the job."[25] On March 8 the tools were provided; the Senate passed Lend-Lease 60 to 31, and from Churchill to Roosevelt came this glad and eloquent epitome: "Our blessings from the whole British Empire go out to you and the American nation for this very present help in time of trouble."[26]

Further help—from an unexpected quarter—was now forthcoming. On the Wilhelmstrasse in Berlin one dictator prepared meticulously to attack another. Operation Barbarossa, the invasion of Russia, was to be the capstone of Hitler's *Drang nach Osten*, and it was scheduled to commence on May 15. Late in March, however, Yugoslavia, in response to clever prodding by the British Secret Service, defied a German takeover attempt, and Hitler, infuriated, reacted with a violence and a brutality that were unusual even for him. Yugoslavia must be treated with "unmerciful harshness," he commanded,[27] and from April 6 to April 13 it was. The conquest of Greece was undertaken simultaneously, and by the end of the month all the Balkan states were in Axis hands. But there had been a price to pay, not so much in blood and treasure, as in time.

In order to avenge himself on the Yugoslavs, Hitler had com-
promised the achievement of his paramount goal. Even as the
plans for the castigation of southeastern Europe were being
hastily put into effect, he told his subservient generals, "The
beginning of the Barbarossa operation will have to be postponed up to four weeks."[28] In the event, the delay was until
June 22, so when Germany struck eastward she not only took
on a second formidable adversary while the first was still unquelled, but did so with barely three months of warm weather
in which to make good her cause.

It was one year to the day from the surrender of France.
Britain was no longer alone.

Of course, under normal circumstances, with Stalin as one's
friend one had no need of enemies. But as even the old
Communist-baiter Churchill recognized, with Hitler as one's
enemy one's friends were where one found them. "... Can
you doubt what our policy will be?" he asked in a radio
broadcast on the day of the invasion. "We have but one aim
and one single, irrevocable purpose. We are resolved to destroy Hitler and every vestige of the Nazi regime.... Any
man or State who fights on against Nazidom will have our
aid. Any man or State who marches with Hitler is our foe.
... That is our policy and that is our declaration...."[29]

The policy was more than mere posturing, the declaration
more than mere words; right from the beginning they meant
that Britain would have to share Lend-Lease matériel with
the Soviet Union, and even contribute supplies of her own.
This fact, along with the enormous strategic repercussions of
Russian belligerency on Anglo-American planning, made a
face-to-face meeting between Churchill and Roosevelt virtually essential. In July, Hopkins made a second trip to London to lay the groundwork and then went on to Moscow for
a week. His return journey across the Atlantic was accomplished in the company of the Prime Minister aboard His
Majesty's Ship *Prince of Wales*, whose ultimate destination
was Placentia Bay near the small town of Argentia in Newfoundland. "You'd have thought Winston was being carried
up into the heavens to meet God!" FDR's envoy recollected,[30]

and he took advantage of Churchill's excitement to the extent of winning thirty-three dollars in Canadian money off him at backgammon. At this juncture the Prime Minister may have regretted his advocacy of the game as First Lord, but the chances are that he was too keyed up over the prospect of what he believed to be his first meeting with the President to experience much in the way of self-reproach. Of course, as the reader knows, he had met Roosevelt before, and even a President Roosevelt as well, but his memory for presidents was better than his memory for assistant secretaries of the Navy. He wrote the Dominions' prime ministers that although he and FDR had been in constant and intimate contact since 1940, they had not yet set eyes on each other. Roosevelt got wind of this and was a bit miffed,[31] and Churchill himself amended his memory retroactively in *The Gathering Storm* (written in 1947) by referring to the Gray's Inn encounter and remarking on how he had been struck by FDR's "magnificent youth and strength."[32] Fortunately for their relationship, and for the world, both men had more important things to worry about in the summer of 1941 than unintentional personal slights, and on August 9 their *second* meeting took place amidst great pomp and cordiality aboard the American cruiser *Augusta*. As the tenth was a Sunday, interdenominational services were held on the quarterdeck of the *Prince of Wales* with Roosevelt and Churchill seated side by side. "We ended with 'O God Our Help in Ages Past,'" Winston wrote in *The Grand Alliance*. "Every word seemed to stir the heart. It was a great hour to live...."[33]

From the Placentia Bay Conference came the Atlantic Charter and, perhaps more important, the beginnings of serious though still covert Anglo-American military collaboration, at least on the planning level. While England struggled on against the Germans in the air and in North Africa, a new menace to both English-speaking powers was becoming ever more tangible in the Far East. "The Jap situation is definitely worse," FDR wrote Churchill on October 15, "however in spite of this you and I have two months of respite."[34]

His prediction was a week shy of being accurate.

————

When it was 10:00 A.M. in Honolulu on December 7, 1941, it was 9:00 P.M. in England. Churchill was at Chequers having dinner with U.S. Ambassador John Winant and Lend-Lease plenipotentiary Averell Harriman. The radio was tuned to the evening news and toward the end of the transmission something was said about an attack by the Japanese upon American shipping in Hawaii. The item did not make any particular impression on Churchill, but Harriman was concerned. Then, in the best British tradition, the butler, who had been listening to his radio rather more attentively in the kitchen, came in and confirmed that the United States had indeed and at last been drawn into World War II. Within five minutes Churchill was on the phone to Washington. "It's quite true," Roosevelt told him. "We are all in the same boat now."[35]

"So we had won after all," Churchill reflected gratefully. "England would live; Britain would live; the Commonwealth of Nations and the Empire would live.... Once again in our long island history we should emerge, however mauled or mutilated, safe and victorious.... Being saturated and satiated with emotion and sensation, I went to bed and slept the sleep of the saved and thankful."[36]

His first thought on awakening the next morning was to come, for the fifth time, to the United States.

CHAPTER EIGHT

Grand Allies

IN ASSESSING THE EVENTS of December 7 Robert E. Sherwood concluded, "It may well be said that those in high authority in both the United States and Britain made two original errors of calculation; they greatly underrated Japanese military strength and daring, and they greatly overrated Japanese political astuteness."[1] Of the two errors the second is much the more comprehensible, for if war is the continuation of diplomacy by other means, then the attack on Pearl Harbor ranks immeasurably higher as a diplomatic blunder than it does as a military master stroke. Even if the American fleet's three aircraft carriers had not been at sea that Sunday, thus escaping Admiral Yamamoto's grasp, for Japan to launch herself alone against the United States and the British Commonwealth in the Pacific and Indian oceans was, as Churchill put it, an "irrational act." He had said as much as far back as April in an admonitory telegram to the Japanese Foreign Secretary: "... If the United States entered the war at the side of Great Britain, and Japan ranged herself with the Axis Powers, would not the naval superiority of the two English-speaking nations enable them to dispose of the Axis Powers in Europe before turning their united strength upon Japan? ..."[2] But the Japanese were no better at taking Churchill's warnings than the British had been, and now the punishment they would suffer for their recklessness was merely a matter of, in Churchill's words, the "proper application of overwhelming force."

Of course, from Japan's point of view Pearl Harbor and

the attacks launched simultaneously throughout Oceania and Asia could be regarded as a desperately risky, yet still justifiable, attempt to redress at one stroke the unfavorable balance of power obtaining in a region of the world which the Japanese considered properly their own. No such rationale can explain the action of Germany and Italy in the wake of Japan's gamble, however; if the Rising Sun's surprise offensives were irrational, then the German and Italian responses to them were downright lunatic.

Pearl Harbor had not by any means solved Franklin Roosevelt's problems with isolationism in the United States. The isolationist philosophy was primarily Europe-oriented, its fundamental tenet being that America should stay out of what was just another in the endless series of Old World quarrels that the founders of the New World had crossed the Atlantic to escape. The Pacific, however, was entirely a different matter—that was "our" ocean; it contained the Philippines and the Aleutians as well as the Hawaiian Islands, and on its far shore lay China, in which the United States had long had a proprietary interest. Many isolationists felt that Roosevelt's failure to pursue a more aggressively interventionist policy in the Far East was just as reprehensible as his readiness to involve America in the *totentanz* of Europe, and for such people Pearl Harbor was in no way a political setback. Thus FDR on December 8 did *not* ask the Congress to declare war on the Axis but on Japan alone; he left the task of making the United States a full-fledged belligerent in World War II to Hitler and Mussolini. Of course, being a politician who was not without a degree of guile, Roosevelt did this in the knowledge that, insane as it seemed, the two dictators had every intention of doing what he wanted them to do. The Japanese codes had been broken and messages between Tokyo and Berlin had been subject to regular interception by American radio technicians for almost a year. One of these messages, sent a week before Pearl Harbor, contained Ribbentrop's assurance that if the Japanese "became engaged in a war against the United States, Germany would of course join in the war immediately,"[3] and if four days counts as "immediately," that is precisely what Germany did.

How can we account for this unaccountable and ultimately suicidal action? It was certainly not a question of Germany feeling compelled to honor her word; such a compulsion had long been considered outré on the Wilhelmstrasse. No, the dispositive factors appear to have been suitably squalid and banal: ignorance, petulance, and miscalculation. The ignorance and the petulance were Hitler's—about the United States's military-industrial capacity, and in reaction to America's open support of the Axis's enemies. The miscalculation was general throughout the German High Command; almost every prominent Berlin official believed that the United States would be obliged by Japan's audacious coup to concentrate most of its power in the Pacific theater and to reduce or even discontinue its "interference" in the conflicts of Europe.[4]

It was precisely to make sure that this did *not* happen that Churchill proposed to Roosevelt on December 9 that he come immediately to the American capital. As he said in *The Grand Alliance*, "We [in Britain] were conscious of a serious danger that the United States might pursue the war against Japan in the Pacific and leave us to fight Germany and Italy in Europe, Africa, and the Middle East."[5] That these British anxieties—and German hopes—were not entirely without foundation is evidenced by the fact that on the day after Pearl Harbor all Lend-Lease shipments to England were suspended indefinitely.[*]

Roosevelt's reply to Churchill's message was understandably somewhat muted; with the United States in the throes of an emergency crash program of mobilization, he as President could not contemplate the prospect of a precipitate descent by the Prime Minister on Washington with unrestrained enthusiasm. He made a few propitiatory noises in his answering telegram, but the gist of it was that, since Winston's presence in America could not possibly be kept secret, his suggested visit would expose him to unacceptable dangers on the return journey. Churchill was having none of this; he was the King's First Minister and a veteran of the cavalry charge at Omdur-

---

[*] They were resumed almost immediately, however.

man. He wasn't going to be put off by a couple of submarines. Besides, he had already been across the Atlantic and back once without incident, and even if the Germans found out about his presence in the Western Hemisphere this time, they still would not know how, when, or by what route he would return eastward. As for the advisability of acquiescing in FDR's tactfully indirect attempt to put him off for a month or two, Churchill was quite specific: the time for diplomatic niceties vis-à-vis America was past; "now that she is in the harem, we talk to her quite differently."[6] "We do not think there is any serious danger about return journey," he wired Roosevelt on December 10. "There is, however, great danger in not having a full discussion on the highest level." Just in case this wasn't sufficiently direct he added, "I feel it would be disastrous to wait for another month before we settled common action. . . . I had hoped to start tomorrow night. . . ."[7] On receipt of this telegram FDR was wise enough to bow gracefully to the inevitable. "Delighted to have you here at the White House," he wired back.[8]

On December 12 Churchill boarded his special train and headed for the west coast of Scotland, where the newly commissioned battleship *Duke of York* was awaiting him in the Firth of Clyde. In his party of over eighty military and civilian officials were the Minister of Supply, Lord Beaverbrook; the First Sea Lord, Admiral Pound; the Chief of the Air Staff, Air Marshal Portal; former Chief of the Imperial General Staff, Field Marshal Dill (soon to head the British delegation to the Combined Chiefs of Staff Committee); Churchill's personal physician, Sir Charles Wilson; his personal assistant, Commander C. R. ("Tommy") Thompson, R.N.; and his "other" Thompson, our redoubtable friend from Scotland Yard.

In stormy weather the *Duke of York* headed down the Irish Channel toward the Bay of Biscay. The seas were so rough, however, that the destroyer escort could make no more than six knots. For two days, as the impatient Prime Minister put it, the flotilla "paddled along," until Admiral Pound, who was in over-all command, came to the conclusion that they "were more likely to ram a U-boat than to be torpedoed by one" under prevailing conditions. He ordered, therefore, that the battleship cast off its destroyers and run through alone at the best speed possible, which was barely twenty knots in the teeth of the gale-force winds.

In Washington, meanwhile, Mrs. Roosevelt was surprised to hear from her secretary, Malvina Thompson (also called "Tommy"), that for the first time since they had moved to the White House her husband had asked for a list of the people who had been invited to dinner over Christmas.[9] On December 19 FDR himself told her that certain very important visitors were expected and that arrangements must be made to lodge them for several weeks. The visitors' identities were not revealed though, and it was only at the last minute that the First Lady and her staff learned what was in store for them.

Had Mrs. Roosevelt been a reporter or a diplomat instead of the President's wife, she probably would have been less in the dark, since the fact that Churchill was en route to America was common knowledge in both Washington's and London's inner—and even not-so-inner—circles.[10] The details of his itinerary, however, and his mode of travel in particular were strictly classified. Thus, although many people were expecting him, only a very few knew when or under what circumstances he would materialize.

Shortly after noon on December 22, in response to rumors that an announcement of some importance was imminent, reporters began to gather in the lobby of the Executive Office Building, just across from 1600 Pennsylvania Avenue. By three there were nearly two hundred of them there, but as afternoon dragged on into evening with nothing whatsoever to report, their numbers dwindled. Those few who resisted the lure of the cocktail hour were amply rewarded for their constancy at 6:45: they were ushered into the office of FDR's Press Secretary, Stephen Early, and told matter-of-factly, "Gentlemen, the Prime Minister of Great Britain, Mr. Churchill, is now with Mr. Roosevelt in the White House. He arrived by air, and the President met him at an airport near Washington."[11]

By air? No, nothing had happened to the *Duke of York*; it

was just that Winston had gotten a little itchy. According to his own account in *The Grand Alliance*, he and his party "were all impatient after nearly ten days at sea" to end their journey.[12] Wilson's diary gives a slightly different version however: "...Before we anchored in Chesapeake Bay the P.M. was talking about steaming up the Potomac to Washington. Now he was like a child in his impatience to meet the President. He spoke as if every minute counted. It was absurd to waste time; he must fly...."[13] And fly he did, from Hampton Roads to Washington National Airport. FDR met him there and they drove directly to the White House, arriving about an hour before Early made the official announcement.

The Prime Minister was established in the Northeast Suite on the second floor of the Executive Mansion, across the hall from the suite occupied by Hopkins; next door the Monroe Room had been converted to house his extensive array of maps. The President's quarters were at the far end of the corridor. Inspector (he had been promoted) Walter Thompson and Commander Tommy Thompson were also housed on the second floor, where, it may be assumed, they frequently encountered the secretarial Tommy Thompson, and perhaps even the noted Scots canine Fala, as they went about their duties. Given these almost connubial living arrangements, there was a great deal of informal visiting about up and down the second-floor hallway, and "informal" may perhaps be a serious understatement. Shortly after his arrival Churchill had gone upstairs to unpack and immerse himself in a tub of water, two or three baths being an inviolable part of his daily routine (remember the 1900 panegyrics on Anglo-American cleanliness). Inspector Thompson meanwhile poked around the sitting room, "determining heights, distances, telephone locations, exposed risks," and so on. He heard his charge emerge from the bathroom and fix himself a drink. Then came a knock on the door. "See to that, please, Thompson," said the Prime Minister, and Thompson did. "That" turned out to be Franklin D. Roosevelt in his wheelchair, coming to make sure that his guest was comfortably accommodated. He looked over Thompson's shoulder into the room, the Inspector tells us, at first curiously and then with an expression of mingled disbelief and shock. There was Churchill; pink, naked, cigared, and smiling, with a large towel in one hand and his drink in the other. "You see, Mr. President," he beamed, "I have nothing to hide."[14]

Can this story be believed? As nothing very momentous hinges on the issue and as the imprudence of imputing an untruth to Inspector Thompson is self-evident, I am disposed to conclude that it can. Hopkins certainly repeated his version of it (in which Churchill's words are: "The Prime Minister of Great Britain has nothing to conceal from the President of the United States") often enough to raise at least a presumption in favor of its veracity. As against such considerations, however, there is the testimony of Churchill himself. Robert Sherwood once screwed up the courage to ask him pointblank whether the story was true or false. He was told that it was "nonsense," that Churchill "never received the President without at least a bath towel wrapped around him." As to the declaration of total candor: "I could not possibly have made such a statement as that. The President himself would have been well aware that it was not strictly true."[15] Truth, however, is an elusive quality, and perhaps what is most important in this very unportentous context is that whatever the actual facts may have been, the possibly apocryphal facts are perfectly consistent with Winston Churchill's personality. More significant, they are perfectly consistent with the extraordinary, almost bucolic, lack of ceremony that characterized the relationship of these two heads of government. For this, much of the credit goes to Hopkins, who once described himself as "a catalytic agent between two prima donnas."[16]

Winston and FDR *were* prima donnas of course, but in the best possible sense of the term—like Galli-Curci and Tebaldi. Both men were patrician, both were "acquainted with grief," and both had overcome almost insurmountable obstacles in rising to their high stations. They had many interests in common—history, biography, the out-of-doors, the Navy—and each had a lively respect for the accomplishments of the other. But the most crucial factor in their association was not their similarities but their profound differences. Both were *rarae aves* and each regarded the other with a sort of child-like fascination. Roosevelt's easiness, warmth, and protean subtlety were qualities Churchill could only envy and admire, while Churchill's vigor, eloquence, and Promethean fecundity of mind totally captured FDR's imagination. To say that they enjoyed each other's company would be to understate egregiously; they reveled in it. Had they been private citizens their friendship would have been perfect, so neatly did the facets of their personalities interlock. As statesmen, however, the degree of intimacy they could permit themselves was limited. Both had responsibilities to which personal feelings were manifestly subordinate. Winston did indeed have something to hide; nothing dark or terrible, to be sure—simply the inescapable concomitants of the fact that Britain's interests and America's were not identical. In Churchill's eyes the United States was not only the determinative factor in the struggle against the Axis but also the guarantor of Britain's status as a great world power. Being farsighted almost to the point of clairvoyance, he was well aware that a period of American hegemony was at hand, and his prime objective was to secure for the British Empire a partnership therein. Roosevelt by contrast came out of the long tradition of American political idealism that stretched back through Wilson and Lincoln to the Founding Fathers. However "political" he might be in practice, he was actuated by the simple and unsordid motives spelled out in the Declaration of Independence, the Gettysburg Address, Wilson's Fourteen Points, and his own Four Freedoms. The very concept of Empire was incompatible with his principles, and while he would not use American power to undermine the British colonial establishment, he certainly had no intention of helping to perpetuate it.

Thus the lines were drawn. Churchill, being far more impulsive and unguarded than FDR, allowed his affection for the President free reign within the limits of his responsibilities. He saw Roosevelt as a savior—and something of a father figure as well. His natural instincts were reinforced, moreover, by the knowledge that the closer he and FDR became, the better it would be for Britain. Roosevelt, on the other hand, was compelled both by nature and by circumstance to maintain his distance. He too knew that the United States was about to take its place in the world, and as President he intended that it should do so unencumbered, even by the most adoring of allies.

Here then, very briefly, were the dynamic tensions of the Roosevelt-Churchill relationship: a great mutual attraction and a sincerely reciprocated affection, in uneasy harness with differing political ideologies and conflicting national objectives. That the relationship endured as well as it did, given its intensity and the severity of the strains placed upon it over four years of war, is strong testimony to the depths of the feelings that served as its foundations.

We may leave open the question whether Churchill was stark naked or modestly betoweled when Roosevelt came into his suite; the important point is that both men were eager to begin work. They talked while Churchill dressed and then proceeded to the President's study, where the evening's dinner guests were gathered. It was a small group of people that first night: the British Ambassador and Lady Halifax, Mr. and Mrs. Cordell Hull, Mr. and Mrs. Sumner Welles, Lord Beaverbrook, Mrs. Roosevelt, and Hopkins. As he was to do every evening of Churchill's stay, the President prepared the predinner cocktails himself and then was accompanied by the Prime Minister to the elevator. "I wheeled him in his chair ... as a mark of respect," Churchill related, "and thinking also of Sir Walter Raleigh spreading his cloak before Queen Elizabeth."[17] The analogy is apt, for FDR, as a head of state was on the same level as the British Monarch, a fact that Churchill never disregarded: almost always it was "Winston" and "Mr. President" when the two men addressed each other (FDR, of course, would have been tempted to use the familiar even with the Pope), very infrequently was it "Winston" and "Franklin."

After dinner the Arcadia Conference—for so this meeting was officially called—began in earnest. Here for the first time the concept of a joint Anglo-American operation against French North Africa was presented to United States officials. Roosevelt liked the idea, a fact that gave Churchill tremendous satisfaction, and the discussion ended at midnight without a note of discord having been heard. The President, it appeared, did not have his eyes fixed firmly on the Pacific; Japan had not even been discussed.

"Since Churchill knew of Roosevelt's habits of going to bed early," Sherwood tells us, "he made a pretense [while at the White House] of retiring himself at a fairly reasonable hour; but Roosevelt knew that his tireless guest and Hopkins would go on talking and he did not want to miss any of it so he stayed up much later than usual."[18] This is precisely what happened on the night of December 22; the two leaders, Beaverbrook, and Hopkins continued their consultations until 2:00 A.M. When Churchill returned to his room he was so keyed up with excitement that he asked Wilson if he could take a sleeping pill: "I must have a good night." The doctor assented and then went downstairs with Beaverbrook, who was pretty excited himself. "I have never seen that fellow in better form," he said of the Prime Minister. "He conducted the conversation for two hours with great skill."[19]

Arcadia had gotten off to a splendid start.

The smooth sailing continued on the twenty-third. In addition to the fact that Churchill found himself virtually barricaded in his room by the avalanche of fan mail and Christmas presents pouring in from all over the United States, he also had the satisfaction as he lay in bed that morning of reading the unanimously enthusiastic American newspaper commentaries on his arrival. The reaction of the New York *Times* was among the more restrained: "From the depths of its heart this country will bid Sir Winston* welcome. . . . We clasp his hand and say: Here is not only a great man and a good man. Here is a son returning to his mother's land."[20] At the first meeting of the British and American Chiefs of Staff, meanwhile, the vital question of United States intentions vis-à-vis the European Theater of Operations was quickly and happily resolved. General Marshall and Admiral Stark presented their opposite numbers with a position paper which read in part: "notwithstanding the entry of Japan into the war, our view remains

* One mark against the *Times*: Churchill did not become "Sir Winston" until 1953.

that Germany is still the prime enemy and her defeat is the key to victory...."[21] At midday Churchill, Roosevelt, and Hopkins inaugurated their custom of lunching privately together, a custom that was observed every day of Churchill's stay in Washington except December 26, when, as will be seen, Winston had more pressing business to attend to. "It was at the lunches that most of the major problems were thrashed out," Sherwood relates, "so that when the President and the Prime Minister went into the full dress meetings they were often already in agreement."[22]

At 4:00 P.M. Churchill and Roosevelt held their first joint press conference, although on this occasion FDR might just as well have been on the moon for all the attention that was paid to him. The reader will remember that it was almost ten years since the American press had had a crack at Churchill, and it is fair to say that a lot had happened in the interval. The President made a brief opening statement and then introduced his star attraction:

I am sorry to have taken so long for all of you to get in, but apparently—I was telling the Prime Minister—the object was to prevent a wolf from coming in here in sheep's clothing. (Laughter) But I was thereby mixing my metaphors, because I had suggested to him this morning that if he came to this conference he would have to be prepared to meet the American press, who, compared with the British press—as was my experience in the old days—are "wolves" compared with the British press "lambs." However he is quite willing to take on a conference, because we have one characteristic in common. We like new experiences in life.... Steve [Early] and I first thought that I would introduce the Prime Minister, and let him say a few words to you good people, by banning questions. However the Prime Minister did not go along with that idea, and I don't blame him. He said that he is perfectly willing to answer any reasonable questions for a reasonably short time, if you want to ask him.[23]

They certainly did want to ask him, but first they wanted to see him, and Roosevelt passed their request along. Then, according to the official transcript of the press conference, "Applause greeted the Prime Minister when he stood up, but when he climbed onto his chair so that they could see him better, loud and spontaneous cheers and applause rang through the room."[24]

It is depressing but nonetheless instructive to compare a Churchill—or, indeed, a Roosevelt—press conference with the ones national leaders engage in today. It is not so much the presence of wit and directness that distinguishes the earlier encounters—although it certainly does—but the sense one gets even from a transcript that it is a human being speaking rather than a pre-programmed committee. A few examples:

Q. Do you think the war is turning in our favor in the last month or so?

A. I can't describe the feelings of relief with which I find Russia victorious, the United States and Great Britain standing side by side. It is incredible to anyone who has lived through the lonely months of 1940.
It is incredible. Thank God.

Q. Mr. Minister (sic), can you tell us when you think we may lick these boys?

A. If we manage it well, it will take only half as long as if we manage it badly. (Loud laughter)

Q. How long, sir, would it take if we managed it badly?

A. That has not been revealed to me at this moment. We don't need to manage it badly.

Q. How long if we manage it well, sir?

A. Well, it would be imprudent to indulge in a facile optimism at this time.

Q. Mr. Prime Minister, in one of your speeches you mentioned three or four of the great climacterics. [There were four: the Battle of France, the Battle of Britain, Lend-Lease, and the invasion of Russia.] Would you now add our entry into the war as one of these, sir?

A. I think I may almost say [affecting a Texas drawl] "I sure do." (Loud laughter)[25]

It was a bravura performance and it got rave reviews. Arthur Krock summed up the consensus first impression: "the skill and success with which he met the questions of the American press; and his candor, alertness of intellect and con-

centration on the task in hand ... matched the reputation Mr.
Churchill has acquired for all three."[26]

Until dusk on December 24 there was little to suggest that
the Christmas spirit had descended on the White House.
True, Anne O'Hare McCormick in her column in that morning's New York *Times* had said of the President's house guest,
"His round apple-cheeked face and the shrewd twinkle in his
eye suggest the most familiar visitor at this season,"[27] but all
through the day the talk among the Allied leaders was exclu-
sively of war. With the coming of darkness, however, there
came a welcome respite. Together with Mrs. Roosevelt and
the Crown Prince and Princess of Norway—whose subjects
were observing Christmas under German supervision—Roosevelt and Churchill came out onto the South Portico of the
White House for Washington's annual tree-lighting ceremony.
It was the Prime Minister's first public appearance since his
arrival and about thirty thousand people had gathered outside the gates to get a glimpse of him and the President. First
there were carols, "Silent Night" and "O Come All Ye Faithful." Then, looking out at the crowd massed together in the
dim twilight of their first wartime winter, Roosevelt pressed
a switch and the Community Tree, until then only a black
silhouette against the illuminated spire of the Washington
Monument, blazed into life. The President spoke:

Fellow workers for freedom ...
... when we make ready our hearts for the labor and the suffering and the ultimate victory which lie ahead, then we observe
Christmas day—with all of its memories and all of its meanings—
as we should. ...
We have joined with many other nations and peoples in a very
great cause. ... One of their great leaders stands beside me. ... He
and his people have pointed the way in courage and in sacrifice ...
and I am asking my associate, my old and good friend, to say a
word to the people of America, old and young, tonight. ...

Churchill responded:

... I spend this anniversary and festival far from my country,
far from my family, and yet I cannot truthfully say that I feel far

from home. . . . I cannot feel myself a stranger here in the center and at the summit of the United States. I feel a sense of unity and fraternal association which, added to the kindliness of your welcome, convinces me that I have a right to sit at your fireside and share your Christmas joys.

But the time available for sharing Christmas joys was limited. The tree lit, the greetings spoken, the two men returned indoors and got back to the business of the war.

Christmas Day offered two short breaks in the round-the-clock work schedule. Churchill and Roosevelt took time out from the morning conferences to attend an eleven o'clock service at the Foundry Methodist Church. "It is good for Winston to sing hymns with the Methodists," said Roosevelt,[28] and Churchill heartily agreed. "I'm glad I went," he confided to Wilson after the service. "It's the first time my mind has been at rest for a long time. Besides," he added characteristically, "I like singing hymns."[29] Inspector Thompson was less enthusiastic about the excursion, largely because of the, to his mind, excessive security precautions the Secret Service insisted upon—"as if a huge consignment of gold bullion were being moved to a bank down a street where known groups of gangsters with machine guns were waiting for the right moment to strike."[30]

From church the conferees went directly back to the White House and work, toiling throughout the afternoon and evening until it was time for Christmas dinner. Fully sixty people sat down at the table, Halifax, Beaverbrook, and the Crown Prince and Princess among them. FDR said that there would be no speeches, but he took the opportunity to observe that the King and Queen of England had dined in the same room two and a half years before. That occasion, he said, had marked the beginnings of the Anglo-American partnership now so solidly established. (Earlier in the day he had taken a moment to write to Clementine Churchill: "Our very warm Christmas greetings. It is a joy to have Winston with us. He seems very well and I want you to know how grateful I am to you for letting him come."[31])

Churchill was silent and withdrawn during dinner, and afterward he got up and asked to be excused. The problem was not with his digestion; it was just that he had a particularly important project pressing on his mind. "The two democracies were to be joined together" and "he had been chosen to give the banns."[32] The next day, in other words, he was going to address the Congress. "I had never addressed a foreign Parliament before. Yet to me, who could trace unbroken male descent on my mother's side through five generations from a lieutenant who served in George Washington's army, it was possible to feel a blood-right to speak to the representatives of the great Republic in our common cause...."[33]

Still, he was nervous. As he left the White House, Inspector Thompson reminded him to make sure he had his speech glasses, and on Capitol Hill Wilson sat with him in a small room off the Senate floor as he waited to be introduced. He paced up and down the room, going over and over his address in his mind even though he was planning—as always—to speak from extensive written notes. Suddenly he stopped pacing and wheeled around to face his physician, "his eyes popping." "Do you realize we are making history!?"[34]

Accompanied by the officers of the Senate, he entered the chamber at 12:30, whereupon "everyone rose and cheered," Inspector Thompson remembered. "When Americans cheer they cheer all over.... For myself, usually cool, I felt such an enormous pride I... hated to think how good my aim would have been if I had had to use my revolver."[35]

He didn't have to, however, and, as the expectant audience stilled, Winston got up to speak.

Members of the Senate and the House of Representatives ... the fact that my American forebears have for so many generations played their part in the life of the United States and that here I am, an Englishman, welcomed in your midst makes this experience one of the most moving and thrilling of my life, which is already long and has not been entirely uneventful.

I wish indeed that my mother, whose memory I cherish across the veil of years, could have been here to see me. By the way, I cannot help reflecting that if my father had been American and my mother British, instead of the other way around, I might have got here on my own. In that case, this would not be the first time you have heard my voice. In that case I would not have needed any invitation, but if I had it is hardly likely that it would have been unanimous. So, perhaps, things are better as they are. . . .

The laughter rolled up toward him. It was going well, and he began to warm to his theme. He gave a broad overview of the war situation and described the tasks facing the English-speaking peoples. Then he turned his attention to Japan, and the atmosphere in the Senate Chamber became tense with anticipation.

After the outrages they have committed upon us at Pearl Harbor, in the Pacific islands, in the Philippines, in Malaya and the Dutch East Indies they must know that the stakes for which they have decided to play are mortal. When we look at the resources of the United States and the British Empire, compared to those of Japan, when we remember those of China . . . and when also we observe the Russian menace which hangs over Japan, it becomes . . . difficult to reconcile Japanese action with prudence or even with sanity.

What kind of a people do they think we are?

At this, a roar went up on Capitol Hill such as has probably never been heard before or since. The Congress "rose to its feet as one man," according to Wilson, "and stood cheering as if they would never stop."[36]

"Is it possible," Churchill continued when the commotion had subsided, "that they do not realize that we shall never cease to persevere against them until they have been taught a lesson which they and the world will never forget?"

He was nearing the end, and he chose for his peroration what was to become a constant theme:

Duty and prudence alike command . . . that the germ centers of hatred and revenge should be constantly and vigilantly curbed and treated in good time and that an adequate organization should be set up to make sure that the pestilence can be controlled at its earliest beginning before it spreads and rages throughout the entire earth. . . .

Then, in closing:

It is not given to us to peer into the mysteries of the future. Still I avow my hope and faith, sure and inviolate, that in the days to come the British and American people will for their own safety and for the good of all walk together in majesty, in justice and in peace.

"He stood still for a moment at the end," Inspector Thompson recollected, "then turned and sat down. There was an instant of dead silence. Then, as the Americans say, 'all hell broke loose.' Something great for all the English-speaking peoples all over the world had happened in those minutes. . . ."[37] Senators and representatives, cabinet officers and Supreme Court justices, ambassadors and civil servants, all cheered and waved—and the Prime Minister basked in their approval. They were still cheering as Churchill stepped from the rostrum, exchanged V signs with Chief Justice Stone,[38] and was shepherded from the chamber by Majority Leader Alben Barkley. He was sweating freely, but he had clearly triumphed. "I hit the target all the time," he reported jubilantly to Wilson.[39] He was so elated that even the prospect of a luncheon of fried chicken, mashed potatoes, and peas with congressional leaders—archisolationist Burton K. Wheeler among them— didn't phase him. He told the legislators that the response his remarks had evoked was "the finest compliment I have ever received," and almost a decade later the glow still lingered. "What I said was received with the utmost kindness and attention," he wrote in *The Grand Alliance*. "I got my laughter and applause just where I expected them."[40] And back at the White House, FDR allowed as how his visitor "had done quite well."[41]

But the effort—indeed, the accumulated effort that had gone into the days since December 7—had taken its toll. Early in the morning of the twenty-seventh Churchill, like any good Briton trying to sleep in an overheated American building, rose to open a window. The "air-conditioning," as he explained it, had failed temporarily and the heat had become "oppressive."[42] The window refused to budge, displaying a bulldog tenacity comparable to that of its immediate adversary. But the Prime Minister persevered and, after great exertion, emerged victorious. As he was savoring his triumph he noticed a dull pain over his heart that went down his left arm.[43] He thought of sending for Wilson but decided against it, owing to the lateness of the hour and to the fact that the pain soon stopped. Wilson was called the next morning and made a thorough examination. He found no evidence of a thrombosis, but it was clear to him that the symptoms were those of a coronary insufficiency. Far less clear, though, was what he could realistically do about them. Prescribing six weeks of complete rest—the textbook treatment—was clearly out of the question. Quite apart from its geopolitical repercussions, such a recommendation would probably do little more than add apoplexy to his patient's existing catalogue of maladies. Even a timid "you have been overdoing things" provoked an outburst. "Now, Charles, you're not going to tell me to rest. I can't. I won't. Nobody else can do this job. I must."[44] In the end Wilson had to settle for a feeble "you mustn't do more than you can help in the way of exertion for a little while,"[45] and Churchill went galloping off back to work.

And so there was no letup. If anything the pace intensified; conferences, cables, and decisions devoured the next two days, and on the evening of the twenty-eighth Wilson's cardiac case departed for Ottawa by train to address the Canadian Parliament and similarly not exert himself until New Year's Eve. "It is true that he seems to revel in every minute of the long day," the troubled physician wrote in his diary, "but little things, straws in the wind, warn me that a price must be paid for flouting nature."[46]

Wilson's fears may have been justified, but nature seemed disposed to forgive the debts Churchill was running up. He was in his element; "a jovial kewpie puffing a cigar," as one reporter put it,[47] and the trip to Canada made him jollier still. He was received enthusiastically, given several opportunities to speak French (his version of it at any rate*), shepherded around from one dignitary to another, and provided with a platform in the Canadian legislature from which he could gleefully recall General Weygand's June 1940 prophecy that England would "have her neck wrung like a chicken" within

---

* Churchill stood no nonsense from French grammar. After a meeting with French leaders in 1915, for example, Prime Minister Asquith wrote in his diary: "Winston was very eloquent in the worst French anybody ever heard. 'S'ils savent que nous sommes gens qu'ils peuvent conter sur' was one of his flowers of speech." (The Earl of Oxford and Asquith, *Memories and Reflections,* vol. 2, p. 61.)

three weeks if she fought on alone against Germany. "Some chicken!" he snorted to peals of laughter. "Some neck!"

It may have been "Some consolation!" to Wilson as he and Winston boarded their Washington-bound train on the evening of the thirty-first that, even if Canada had not been exactly restful for his patient, it at least had served as a tonic.

Churchill's visit to America was the occasion for all sorts of firsts, reverently dug up and printed by newspapers from coast to coast: first visit of a British Prime Minister during wartime, first speech by a foreign head of government to a joint session of Congress, first joint press conference of British and American leaders, first meeting of a President and a Prime Minister on Christmas Eve, etc., etc., down to the most trivial precedents imaginable. The first that is least likely to be succeeded by a second, however, belongs to a stretch of railroad tracks situated on the west bank of the Connecticut River in Vermont, about halfway between Brattleboro and Vernon, just north of the Massachusetts line. There, according to the New York *Times*, for the first and only time in history a British Prime Minister celebrated the arrival of a new year "on a train travelling through a foreign country thousands of miles from his homeland."[48] And it was in fine style that he celebrated it too. As the train pulled out of Brattleboro he strode into the dining car, "cigar in place, glass in hand" (contents: whisky and soda),[49] and proposed a toast to the crowd of reporters and staff aides gathered there: "Here's to 1942. A year of toil. A year of struggle. A year of peril. But a long step forward toward victory." Then he clasped hands with Chief Air Marshal Portal on his right and RAF Corporal Wilfred Homer on his left; Portal and Homer clasped the hands of the men next to them and a human chain quickly formed. Statesmen, soldiers, journalists, and railway conductors—Americans, Britons, Canadians, and Australians—all partook of the foolhardy yet transcendent human ritual of smiling in the face of Time, and the words of "Auld Lang Syne" reverberated out into the silence of the New England winter. "God bless us all," said Churchill when the singing had ended. "May we all come through the year in safety and with honor."[50]

As historic firsts go, this one had much to recommend it.

Eight hours and fifty-six minutes into 1942 Churchill's train pulled into Union Station. The Prime Minister strolled briskly down the platform, stopping at the locomotive and reaching up his hand to the engineer. "Thank you very much," he said to the astonished railwayman, "a very enjoyable ride."[51] Then he was off again at a smart clip through the crowded station concourse, Secret Service men trotting to keep up with him. Halifax greeted him and together they entered a limousine and headed for the White House.

Over in Virginia, meanwhile, eight trusted parishoners of Christ Church, Alexandria, were hurriedly delivering engraved white cards to longtime members of the congregation, many of whom were still sleeping off the effects of New Year's Eve. "Be at the Church for a special service at 11 A.M.," the couriers whispered conspiratorially. "Tell no one. There will be two very distinguished guests."[52]

Built in 1773, Christ Church had the distinction of having had George Washington as one of its founders, and promptly at eleven the first President's family pew, number 59, was occupied by the thirty-second President and Winston Leonard Spencer Churchill. The service began with "My Country 'Tis of Thee." Then came Washington's "Prayer for the United States" and the "In Time of War" prayer from the English prayer book. After the rector of Christ Church had delivered his sermon, FDR and Churchill drove to Mount Vernon to lay a wreath on Washington's tomb. Then it was back to business, with a vengeance.

Ever since Churchill's arrival in Washington work had been proceeding on a draft declaration of war aims to be signed by all the countries fighting against the Axis. It had been provisionally called "A Declaration by Associated Powers," but as this was not particularly euphonious and as similar phraseology during World War I had produced rumbles in Congress about "entangling alliances," Roosevelt early in the morning of December 31 had changed "Associated Powers" to "United Nations." He showed his house guest the revision on January 1 and Churchill was delighted with it. It brought to his mind some lines from Byron's *Childe Harold* which he brought to the President's attention:

Here, where the sword United Nations drew,
Our countrymen were warring on that day!
And this is much—and all—which will not pass away.

That same day the two men, along with Chinese Foreign
Minister T. V. Soong and the Soviet Ambassador, now re-
habilitated, Maxim Litvinov, signed the final draft of the document. During the next twenty-four hours the signatures of
the twenty-two other nations then at war with Germany were
collected, and at 3:00 P.M. on January 2 the Declaration
was made public. By itself, as Churchill noted, the document
was not going to win any battles, "but it set forth who we were
and what we were fighting for,"[53] and it was as good a way
as any to begin what was certain to be a long and arduous
year for the most prominent signatories. In addition, the Declaration contained one very significant passage which was to
acquire still greater significance as the war progressed: the
pledge of all who signed not to make a separate peace.

January 2 and 3 were devoted largely to setting up what was
to be a short-lived unified command in the Southwest Pacific
under General Wavell and to the creation of the highly dur-
able Anglo-American Combined Chiefs of Staff Committee.
The exhaustion Wilson had been fearing, however, was now
beginning to show itself. Even Churchill was forced to admit,
although perhaps not in so many words, that he was badly in
need of some time off. "My American friends thought I was
looking tired and ought to have a rest," he wrote,[54] and plans
were made for him to spend a few days at the villa of Lend-
Lease administrator Edward Stettinius in Pompano, some
thirty miles south of Palm Beach, Florida.

This was splendid news from Mrs. Roosevelt's point of view,
for, much as she respected and admired the Prime Minister,
she regarded him as being prodigal with his own health ("It
was astonishing to me that anyone could smoke so much and
drink so much and keep perfectly well"[55]) and an out-and-out
calamity with respect to her husband's. Those late-night talk
sessions in Hopkins' room, she felt, were draining FDR's
strength: ". . . I was always glad when [Mr. Churchill] departed, for I knew that my husband would need a rest, since

he had carried on his usual hours of work in addition to the unusual ones Mr. Churchill preferred."[56] On top of this was the fact that Mrs. Roosevelt, always very shy to begin with, found her British visitor terribly intimidating. "I have to confess that I was frightened of Mr. Churchill," she wrote after his death in 1965.[57] On one particularly protracted evening, for example, she became so concerned over the lateness of the hour that she went to the Monroe Room and asked the Navy officer on duty there to go into Churchill's study and tell him that it was time the President retired. The lieutenant indicated respectfully that it might be more appropriate if she delivered such a message herself and turned away for a moment to open the nearby door. On turning back, however, he found that the First Lady had fled.[58]

On January 3, in what was essentially a diversionary ploy designed to establish his presence in Washington prior to his departure, Churchill emerged from the White House and posed in the Spanish Garden for some twenty-five news photographers. The officially stated purpose of this unusual midwinter outing was "squirrel feeding," and Harry Hopkins' nine-year-old daughter, Diana, along with the always co-operative Fala, was on hand to lend credibility. No squirrels got fed, however, because Churchill was wearing one of his "siren suits," the zippered coveralls which had excited great curiosity among members of the press every time he had appeared in them, as for instance during his New Year's Eve train trip from Ottawa. This was the reporters' first opportunity to get the facts on these sartorial oddities, and the Prime Minister, forgetting his original mission, obligingly demonstrated their various features, zipping and unzipping innumerable fasteners and praising the garment's ready-to-wear convenience. "I can get into it in half a minute," he declared as the correspondents reverently noted down his words.[59] Thus the White House squirrels went hungry; but the diversionary ploy was successful. The next day, as pictures of Winston and his coveralls —datelined Washington—appeared in newspapers across the country, he, along with General Marshall, was safely on his way to Florida. He was in particularly good spirits, moreover;

he had just come from the Oval Office, where he and Beaver-brook had listened to FDR read the State of the Union Message which was to be delivered before the Congress on January 6. The speech represented a massive commitment on the part of the United States to an all-out effort against the Axis powers, and the two Englishmen lapped it up voraciously. As Roosevelt reported to Hopkins later in the day, "It went over big."[60]

Pompano agreed with Churchill. ". . . Winston basks half-submerged in the water like a hippopotamus in a swamp," Wilson noted with satisfaction.[61] A total news blackout on the Prime Minister (which was to remain in effect until he had returned safely to England) had been instituted, and despite the presence of several reporters and photographers in the vicinity of the villa grounds, his sojourn in Florida remained a well-guarded secret. This was a great consolation to Inspector Thompson, whose usual anxieties had been considerably aggravated by the Prime Minister's unshakable intention to do all his swimming in the nude. "It's quite private here," he told his pained bodyguard, who for the moment was playing Britannus to his Caesar. ". . . I have only to step out of the back door into the sea." "But you can be seen through field glasses, sir," Thompson remonstrated. To which Churchill retorted, unanswerably, "If they are that much interested, it is their own fault what they see."[62]

Some people, of course, *were* that much interested, one of them being an attractive—and very ambitious—young woman reporter who offered the Secret Service man guarding the Stettenius beach a week's enjoyment of her nocturnal favors in exchange for an interview with the "someone of great importance" who was staying at the villa. Thompson overheard the proposition and watched fascinated from an upstairs window as the sentry strove with his conscience while at the same time trying to convince the lady in question to surrender her citadel on less Draconian terms. No compromise could be reached, however; the Secret Service man, to his everlasting credit—and anguish—withstood the formidable temptations confronting him. Both Churchill's privacy and the enterprising young journalist remained unviolated.[63]

The Prime Minister's repose was disturbed only once, by "quite a large shark," which presumably had other things than an exclusive interview on its mind. Although it was "only" a ground shark, according to the staff at the villa, Churchill "was not wholly reassured," reasoning that it "is as bad to be eaten by a ground shark as by any other."[64] He kept to the shallows for a while, calling out to his anxiously watching bodyguard, "Keep sending me bulletins, Thompson." Eventually the shark swam off, and Winston exulted, "My bulk has frightened him into deeper water."[65]

On the political front, he got into deeper water himself. The problem was that Wendell Willkie, at the time somewhat at loggerheads with FDR, had asked to see him. Roosevelt was distinctly unenthusiastic about the idea, and so Churchill, remembering Willkie's 1941 visit to London, tried to arrange a clandestine rendezvous. He directed that a call be put through to the Willkie law firm in New York. "I am so glad to speak to you," he said on being connected. "I hope we may meet. I am travelling back by train. . . . Can you not join the train and travel with me for a few hours? Where will you be on Saturday next?"

"Why, just where I am now, at my desk," a distressingly familiar voice responded.

"I do not understand," said Churchill.

"Whom do you think you are speaking to?" asked the voice.

"To Mr. Wendell Willkie, am I not?" he answered.

"No," said the voice, "you are speaking to me, Franklin Roosevelt."[66]

So much for the clandestine rendezvous. When Churchill got back to Washington he checked with Hopkins to see if FDR had taken umbrage. The answer was that "no harm had been done,"[67] and Willkie did finally get to see the Prime Minister.

Shortly after midnight on January 10 Churchill boarded a special train and headed north, arriving in Washington on the morning of the eleventh. Two final days of conferences followed, and much to Winston's satisfaction it was formally agreed that Britain and America would henceforth proceed

on the basis that "only the minimum of forces necessary for
the safeguarding of vital interests in other theatres should be
diverted from operations against Germany."[68]

With grand strategy fixed, the moment of departure drew
near, and a farewell dinner was held in the White House on
the evening of the thirteenth. Among the guests, many of
whom had been invited long before Churchill's visit had even
been contemplated, were some Roosevelt cousins, a woman
from the British Embassy, and the reasonably well-known
author Louis Adamic. Mr. Adamic proved to be quite impres-
sionable; every gesture, every grimace, every chance remark
he witnessed that night was invested for him with the most
momentous significance. He went on to write a fatuous and
ultimately very silly book about his experience, which not
only contributed nothing to history but also gratuitously
libeled the Prime Minister. Churchill for his part probably
never did a more profitable evening's work, for after the
book's publication, in 1947, he was awarded twenty thousand
dollars in damages.[69]

January 14 was the final day. Churchill, FDR, and Hopkins
had one more meal together in the evening and got so caught
up in last-minute business that Winston was an hour late in
leaving. Shortly before ten the two Americans accompanied
the Prime Minister to a secret train waiting on a siding at
Sixth Street and bade him a very fond farewell. As the train
pulled out for Norfolk and the *Duke of York,* Churchill pock-
eted a letter for his wife from Hopkins: "You would have been
quite proud of your husband on this trip. First because he was
ever so good natured. I didn't see him take anybody's head off
and he eats and drinks with his customary vigor, and still dislikes the same people. If he had half as good a time here as
the President did having him about the White House he
surely will carry pleasant memories of the past three weeks."[70]

He had had at least as good a time; as he wrote Roosevelt
on his return to London, "I was terribly sorry to leave you
and . . . there is not a moment of it that I did not enjoy."[71]

The Grand Alliance had been launched in grand style.

CHAPTER NINE

The Darkness Before

EVEN THOUGH THE ACCESSION of the United States to the Allied battle line meant that the war was won, the trend for the United Nations in the early days of 1942 was precipitately downward. America belligerent was not the same as America combatant, nor could it be for several months at least. Meanwhile dreadful forfeits had to be paid in all the theaters of the conflict. In the Pacific and Indian oceans the Japanese tide of conquest rolled inexorably southward, inundating the Philippines, the East Indies, Indochina, and the innumerable islands north and east of Australia. Even the "impregnable fortress" of Singapore, its guns pointing uselessly toward the sea, fell to the forces of the Rising Sun. In Europe the Axis powers were still enjoying their "fleeting hour of brutish triumph," and in North Africa Erwin Rommel marched implacably toward the Nile. In Russia "General Winter" could do little more than hold the Germans in position, and when spring came a new and monumental Wehrmacht offensive would certainly be launched.

The one thing that can be said for such cold blasts of adversity is that they compel men and nations to huddle more closely together and put aside, if only for the moment, their more ephemeral differences. Thus on his sixtieth birthday on January 30 the unfailingly resilient Roosevelt was able to wire the sixty-six-year-old Churchill in the midst of all the bleakness, "It is fun to be in the same decade with you."[1] And three weeks later he added, "I hope you will be of good heart in these trying weeks."[2]

But even between Roosevelt and Churchill there were dis-
agreements brewing which defied the unifying effects of catastrophe. Among these India was perhaps the most nettle-
some, if not the most consequential. FDR had first raised the
subject—which was self-admittedly outside the areas of both
his competence and his responsibility—during Churchill's visit
to Washington. The Prime Minister, however, had "reacted so
strongly and at such length that [Roosevelt] never raised it
verbally again."[3] He returned to the attack in writing, though,
on March 10 when he proposed in a personal letter to Churchill that a temporary sort of federal scheme, modeled on the
American colonies' 1783 Articles of Confederation, be set up
in the subcontinent. He concluded the letter by saying, somewhat inconsistently, "For the love of Heaven, don't bring me
into this, though I do want to be of help. It is, strictly speaking, none of my business. . . ."[4]

We can imagine Churchill in the privacy of his bathtub mut-
tering a heartfelt "Amen!"

FDR apparently soon forgot that India was none of his
business, or else he decided that it was, for on April 12 he
sent Churchill a very strongly worded telegram via Hopkins in
which he reiterated his Articles of Confederation proposal—
which was, frankly, simple-minded—and pressed the Prime
Minister to take a more conciliatory line with the Indian nationalists. Even in 1949, when Churchill finally sat down to
write of this incident, he was still angry about it. In words
of unprecedented bitterness where the President was concerned he characterized Roosevelt's plan as "idealism at other
people's expense and without regard to the consequences of
ruin and slaughter which fall upon millions of humble homes.
. . ."[5] To FDR he wrote in a more moderate tone: "You know
the weight which I attach to everything you say to me, but I
did not feel I could take responsibility for the defence of India
if everything had again to be thrown into the melting-pot at
this critical juncture. . . . Anything like a serious difference
between you and me would break my heart. . . ."[6]

At this point in the development of affairs Hopkins, who was
in England, stepped in. He made it clear to his chief that no
purpose was being served by the attempt to bring American

pressure to bear on the India question, and Roosevelt, for the time being, desisted.[7]

Another sphere in which the thinking of the President and the Prime Minister showed signs of divergence was Russia. In a March 18 telegram to Churchill, FDR said, "I know you will not mind my being brutally frank when I tell you that I think I can personally handle Stalin better than either your Foreign Office or my State Department. Stalin hates the guts of all your top people. He thinks he likes me better, and I hope he will continue to do so."[8] Churchill did not respond to this complacent effusion, but it must have caused him serious misgivings. It is easy to be charming from the top of one's own mountain, and Roosevelt was a master at it; it is even easy to be charming from one peak to another, as long as the second peak is smaller and appertains to one's own massif. But charm does not travel well from range to range, and furthermore it is usually irrelevant. Churchill understood what FDR did not: Stalin did not traffic in likes and dislikes. Hitler was anathema to the Marshal, for example, but that had not prevented him from signing a treaty with Germany, nor indeed from adhering to it scrupulously until the day his nation was invaded. Stalin did not hate and Stalin did not love; Stalin calculated. Coldly, ruthlessly, he assessed the dispositions of power and acted, and although his assessments varied widely in their accuracy, his coldness and ruthlessness were immutable. He was not the sort of man one "handled," yet Roosevelt, long accustomed to handling everybody in one way or another, set out to win him over; and increasingly in this connection he came to regard Churchill as an obstruction. The President's motives were certainly of the purest, but he was moving down darker corridors than he imagined, and he would not be warned.

The final area of controversy is the one that has received the greatest amount of publicity over the years: the so-called Second Front. Here the reader may formulate his own strategic opinions. You are possessed of virtually unlimited resources in terms of manpower and matériel, but the number of ships and landing craft at your disposal severely restricts the uses you may make of them. The shortest route to the heart of the enemy is also the most formidably defended and requires an enormous concentration of force. If you choose to strike directly at the heart, therefore, you must forgo attacks on the limbs or on the "soft underbelly" where significant though not conclusive victories may be won at less risk. Alternatively you may choose to divide your forces and undertake operations on the periphery while slowly accumulating at the proper place the strength required for a thrust at the center. Sooner or later you must strike at the vital organ; the question is, very simply, how soon? If you build up slowly to a massive attack while harassing the enemy on his frontiers, you risk prolonging the war and wasting the lives of your soldiers. If you stake everything on the one big stroke, on the other hand, you risk a defeat of staggering proportions against enemy forces which, like yours, will be concentrated for the critical clash. The issue thus reduces itself as follows: do you content yourself for two years with the achievement of secondary objectives, preparing meanwhile for the assault on the principal fortress, or do you go for the kill right away and risk having to start all over again from the beginning—or even stalemate—if your offensive does not succeed?

Stripped of all hyperbole and all politically inspired special pleading, this is what the Second Front question was basically about, and Churchill himself characterized the American and British approaches to it: "... the American mind runs naturally to broad, sweeping, logical conclusions on the largest scale. ... The British mind does not work quite in this way. ... In war particularly we assign a larger importance to opportunism and improvisation, seeking rather to live and conquer in accordance with the unfolding event than to aspire to dominate it often by fundamental decisions. There is room for argument about both views. The difference is one of emphasis, but it is deep-seated."[9]

The difference, moreover, had to be resolved. Early in April Churchill tested the ground: "Perhaps when the weather gets better I may propose myself for a weekend with you and flip over. We have so much to settle that would go easily in talk."[10] In May Molotov visited London and Washington, discussing Russia's postwar boundaries in the first capital and the absolute necessity for a Second Front in the second. Once again

FDR's eagerness to establish relations of trust and amity with the Soviet Union influenced him to be especially sympathetic. "... Molotov's visit is, I think, a real success," he wrote Churchill, "because we have got on a personal footing of candor and as good friendship as can be acquired through an interpreter. ... I am more than ever anxious that Bolero [the code name for the cross-Channel invasion build-up] proceed to definite action in 1942. ... I am especially anxious that [Molotov] carry back some real results of his mission and that he will give a favorable account to Stalin...."[11]

This telegram must have caused the Prime Minister considerable anxiety. Not only did the President seem to be letting Soviet needs dictate Anglo-American strategy, he also appeared to be operating on the unconscious assumption that Russia, in fighting Hitler for her national survival, was somehow doing Britain and the United States a favor. On June 13, accordingly, Winston wired Roosevelt that "in view of the impossibility of dealing by correspondence with all the many difficult points outstanding, I feel it is my duty to come to see you. ...."[12] FDR replied the same day that such a visit would be welcome, and less than ninety-six hours later Churchill was on his way.

This time he flew, in a Boeing flying boat, the *Bristol*. He was accompanied by the Chief of the Imperial General Staff, Alan Brooke; the War Office's Director of Plans, Brigadier Stewart; his own Chief of Staff in his capacity as Minister of Defence, General Ismay;* and the two Thompsons and Wilson. The journey took twenty-seven hours, during which the Prime Minister inaugurated the Churchill system of dealing with jet-lag, or prop-lag, as it then was. "Ignoring Greenwich Mean Time and Local Time alike, he announced that he intended to go by Stomach Time."[13] As a consequence, he had just finished a hearty dinner when the *Bristol* began its descent toward the Potomac at around 5:30 P.M. Eastern War Time—10:30 P.M. in London and Winston's stomach—on June 18. As was his

* Churchill's official title during the war was: Prime Minister, Minister of Defence, and First Lord of the Treasury.

custom, he plopped himself down in the copilot's seat and
"supervised" as Captain Kelly Rogers guided the big plane
earthward. At one point he thought it prudent to advise the
Chief Pilot that the *Bristol* and the top of the Washington
Monument were identical distances from the ground. He suggested, furthermore, that it would be "peculiarly unfortunate"
if the British delegation to the second Washington Conference
were to proclaim its arrival "by hitting this of all other objects
in the world."[14] Rogers dutifully noted the admonition and
landed without incident a few minutes later. Army Chief of Staff
George Marshall and Ambassador Halifax were on hand to greet
the erstwhile navigator in the absence of the President at Hyde
Park, whither Churchill was to fly the next morning. Two hours
after his arrival, Stomach Time notwithstanding, Winston found
himself the guest of honor at a lavish dinner at the British
Embassy. Undaunted by the meal he had just eaten en route,
he grappled manfully with a new quota of nourishment and
then stayed up until 1:00 A.M. (local) talking animatedly on the
verandah.

On June 19 Churchill's celebrated courage was put to some
of its sternest tests of the war. First, his plane made "one of
the roughest bump landings I have ever experienced" at New
Hackensack Airport near Hyde Park. Then came the real peril:
FDR took him and Commander Thompson off to the Roosevelt
family estate in his specially rigged Ford V-8 convertible for
a hair-raising game of cat-and-mouse with the anxiously pursuing Secret Service. Having finally succeeded in shaking off
his would-be protectors, the President treated his guests to
some of the best views to be seen from the cliffs above the
Hudson, occasioning them more than a few "thoughtful moments" when he "poised and backed on the grass verges." The
Prime Minister managed to retain his sangfroid throughout
these trials and, "though I was careful not to take [the President's] attention off the driving," he was even able to initiate
discussion on a number of the most important pending issues.[15]

Among these was "Tube Alloys" or what the Americans referred to as "S-one"—the development of an atomic bomb—
and after lunch the two leaders and Hopkins retired to Roosevelt's den to explore the matter in depth. "The room was dark

and shaded from the sun," Churchill recollected. "Mr. Roosevelt was ensconced at a desk almost as big as the [room]. Harry sat or stood in the background. My two American friends did not seem to mind the intense heat."[16] Work on "Tube Alloys" had been in progress since 1939, and since October of 1941 British and American scientists had been working on it jointly. Now the facts seemed to point definitely toward feasibility, but the next step, if taken, would entail an enormously large allocation of resources to build and operate Uranium-235 production facilities. It was known that the Germans were working on the manufacture of heavy water (an oxide of the hydrogen isotope deuterium which is used to sustain an atomic reaction by slowing down the motion of neutrons). This being the case, there was really no alternative but to go ahead with an Anglo-American program, and it was decided that, despite the enormous cost, an all-out effort would be made to develop a fission weapon as soon as possible at a location somewhere in the United States. With this portentous decision taken, Roosevelt and Churchill went cheerfully off to have tea at the cottage of Laura Delano.

Dinner found the President in black tie and Winston in his siren-suit coveralls, or "rompers," as he called them. The contrast was so stark that even Churchill had to acknowledge it, but FDR laughed off his apologies and everyone fell to. Next morning the Prime Minister was seen padding barefoot around the Roosevelt lawn in his bathrobe. Rarely have all the niceties of protocol been so studiously observed.

After lunch on the twentieth the President showed Churchill his "Library," which was really a rambling and bottomless collection of Roosevelt memorabilia. Prominently displayed was the newest acquisition: the edition of Churchill's Complete Works that Winston had sent over from London a week before. Afternoon conferences and dinner followed the library tour, and then it was off by train for Washington and what everyone thought would be the official commencement next day of the Second Front debate.[17]

Unlike "Tube Alloys," the Second Front was a matter of widespread public discussion. Presidential Press Secretary

Early, in fact, had stated in announcing Churchill's arrival on the eighteenth that conjecture to the effect that cross-Channel operations would be discussed during the impending talks was "perfectly justified."[18] Conjecture was just about all the public could do in connection with this visit by Churchill, however. In contrast to his previous trip he kept a very low profile, and even his presence at Hyde Park was kept secret. People were sorry not to see—and hear—more of him, but they understood the requirements of security. In any case, as the New York *Times* pointed out, it was "unnecessary to bid welcome to a guest so deeply loved in this country as Mr. Churchill, and so long adopted as our own."[19]

Churchill was now to require all the affection and good will he could muster. Shortly after his arrival in Washington, as he and Roosevelt were talking in the President's study, news came from North Africa which rocked him as few things had in his entire life. ". . . A telegram was put into the President's hands. He passed it to me without a word. It said 'Tobruk has surrendered'. . . ."[20]

Tobruk, which had withstood a seven-month siege in 1941, which had by its resistance thwarted Rommel's plans for the conquest of Egypt, which had been relieved amidst great rejoicing—and after greater sacrifice—the same week that Japan attacked Pearl Harbor, which had become a world-renowned byword for British tenacity and valor: Tobruk, suddenly, shockingly, unaccountably, and in the space of a single day had simply folded, its garrison of some thirty thousand men bowing to barely two-thirds that many troops of the Afrika Korps. Churchill was literally stunned: "This was one of the heaviest blows I can recall during the war. . . . It was a bitter moment. Defeat is one thing; disgrace is another."[21]

Roosevelt proved equal to the occasion; after the long anguished silence that followed on the reading of the telegram he asked, very simply, "What can we do to help?" Churchill replied immediately. With the Suez Canal and the lines of communication to India now directly threatened, there was one supreme and critical need: "Give us as many Sherman tanks as you can spare," he said, "and ship them to the Middle East as quickly as possible." Without wasting a moment the

President called for Marshall, who reported that the Shermans were just coming into production and that the first three hundred had already been issued to divisions of the American army. "Nevertheless," the soldier-statesman continued, "if the British need is so great, they must have them; and we could let them have a hundred 105-mm self-propelled guns in addition."

As Churchill himself observed, reduced for once to the level of platitude, "A friend in need is a friend indeed."[22]

Although Marshall, Hopkins, and Secretary of War Stimson were profoundly reluctant to admit it, the fall of Tobruk ruled out all prospects for an early Second Front. "The discussions in the White House that Sunday continued through lunch and dinner and far into the night," Robert E. Sherwood relates. "Churchill poured out his matchless prose in opposition to the trans-Channel operation in 1942...."[23] With Germany dominating or threatening all of North Africa from the Atlantic to the Nile and but a step or two away from turning the Mediterranean into an Axis-held lake, he carried his point. A new operation, Gymnast, hitherto regarded as a low-priority undertaking in American minds, was abruptly upgraded in status; and though the assault on northern France still supposedly ranked higher in the official scale of values, its true relative weight now that Tobruk had crumbled was obvious to anyone who had access to the conference records. One key sentence said it all: "Forces to be employed in 'Gymnast' would in the main be found from 'Bolero' units which have not yet left the United States."[24] Less than five months after this sentence was written, Gymnast, become Torch, landed Anglo-American troops on the shores of Morocco and Algeria.

Monday, June 22, was a bittersweet day for Churchill. The attempt to storm *Festung Europa* had, to his great relief, been safely relegated to the future—but only as a consequence of a truly calamitous military defeat. Reactions to the surrender of Tobruk were coming in from all over the world, and the news from London was laced with phrases like "no-confidence motion," "vote of censure," and "change of government." Churchill's critics in England were so vocal and angry, in fact, that even the head of the American Office of War Information, Elmer Davis, became concerned. He approached the Prime Minister during the daily luncheon with Roosevelt and Hopkins and suggested that it might be politically advisable for him to cancel the trip to Fort Jackson, South Carolina, that Marshall had arranged for the twenty-fourth, and hurry back to London to confront his detractors. Churchill dismissed such alarmism impatiently; he declared that no more than twenty "malcontents" would go against him on a vote of confidence, and in the event ten days later, the total was only twenty-five.[25]

After lunch Hopkins told Winston that there were a couple of army officers at the White House that day whom the President thought he might like to meet. Marshall and FDR were very high on these two Major Generals, he said, so at 5:00 P.M. Dwight D. Eisenhower and Mark W. Clark were shown into Churchill's room. "I was immediately impressed by these remarkable but hitherto unknown men," Winston wrote,[26] and Eisenhower, who was about to undertake his new assignment in London as Commander of U.S. forces in the European theater of operations, remembered how much he admired the way Churchill, despite Tobruk, was "thinking of attack and victory, not of defense and defeat."[27]

Later on Monday the President and the Prime Minister issued their first public statement since the latter's arrival, declaring that their common objective was "the earliest maximum concentration of Allied war power upon the enemy,"[28] but disclosing precious little else. It was even news that Churchill was in Washington, and only a speech by Hopkins delivered that night in New York revealed that he was staying at the White House. The Presidential Press Office was a bit freer Tuesday, acknowledging that Churchill and Roosevelt had met with shipping experts in the course of their consultations, but apart from that modest revelation all cards were kept very close to the vest. As the young Washington correspondent of the *Times*, James Reston, bluntly expressed it, "The plain and simple truth about these important discussions is that only a few people know what has gone on since Mr. Churchill arrived, and they are not telling what they know."[29]

———

Dinner on Tuesday evening was both a pleasant and an unplanned occasion. It had originally been intended for Churchill to depart for Fort Jackson in the early evening and dine aboard the President's train, but the sleeping car which was to have carried him had somehow gotten damaged in the capital's railroad yards, so the traveling party had supper at the White House instead. During the meal FDR turned to Wilson: "You, Sir Charles, do not know the South Carolina sun in June. Be careful of the Prime Minister tomorrow."[30]

Wilson thought no more about the admonition until the next morning when the reconstituted train had pulled into a siding near Fort Jackson and the troops that Marshall wanted Churchill to see had begun their maneuvers. Then the General handed him a telegram. SECRET, it read. TO BE DELIVERED TO GENERAL MARSHALL IMMEDIATELY UPON HIS ARRIVAL AT CAMP JACKSON STOP YOU AND SIR CHARLES WILSON ARE IN COMMAND STOP ENOUGH SAID STOP ROOSEVELT.[31]

All morning and all afternoon the marching and the war games continued. Six hundred paratroopers leaped out of airplanes, rifles and mortars fired off live ammunition, tanks and mechanized infantry wheeled and clashed and feinted. Churchill loved every minute of it. Wilson withered in the heat.

One of Marshall's objects in exposing Churchill to this display was to convince him that American GIs were ready to pile out of the landing craft onto the beaches of France and slug it out on equal terms with the Germans. In this he was not wholly unsuccessful. At one point, for example, Churchill asked Ismay what he thought of the American performance, and when the British General replied, "To put these troops against continental troops would be murder," Churchill rebutted him. "You're wrong," he said. "They are wonderful material and will learn very quickly."[32] But the operative word was "learn," and Winston reminded Marshall that, in his opinion at least, it took two years to make a soldier.

A pleasantly stimulated Prime Minister, a reasonably satisfied Army Chief of Staff, and a nearly heat-prostrated British physician flew back to Washington on the evening of the twenty-fourth. It was a quarter to four on the morning of the twenty-fifth, however, before the indefatigable Churchill finished a last bit of dictation, bade his near-somnambulent secretary good night, and lay down to get some sleep.

And so, so suddenly, it was the last day of the visit. Churchill joined Roosevelt and Congressional leaders for a meeting of the Pacific War Council and then met with representatives of the Dominions and India. After dinner in the evening the President bade Churchill farewell and set off for Hyde Park. An hour after his departure Hopkins and Harriman accompanied the Prime Minister to Baltimore Harbor, where the *Bristol* was waiting. They encountered a scene of considerable turmoil at the dock as they arrived. Apparently an Irish-American employee of BOAC had been found standing near the *Bristol* fingering a revolver. His presence had been noticed only because he had started mumbling vows to himself to "do Churchill in" along with, in Winston's words, "some other expressions of an unappreciative character."[33] He had been pounced on and disarmed just as the Prime Minister's car was pulling up.

Shortly after midnight on June 26 the flying boat rose out of Chesapeake Bay. It stopped to refuel in Newfoundland in the morning and then resumed its eastward course. At 5:00 A.M. on June 27 it touched down on the water at Stranraer, Scotland. Churchill, with Tobruk lost, the Second Front debate won, and a battle in Commons about to be fought, was back in the front lines.

CHAPTER TEN

Africa Redeemed and Frietchie Recited

A TELEGRAM WAS DELIVERED on July 2, 1942. The sender: Franklin Roosevelt. The recipient: Winston Churchill. The occasion: a vote of confidence in the House of Commons. The result: 475 to 25 in favor of the government. The text: GOOD FOR YOU.[1]

With the din of Parliamentary debate out of his ears, Churchill could turn his attention to the steadily swelling hum of an Allied war machine that was beginning to fire on all cylinders. This engine was already enormously powerful, and potentially it could carry everything before it, but just now, with the eastern piston doing most of the work and the Anglo-American piston having just been obliged to shorten its stroke, it needed a great deal of oil. Someone had to tell Stalin that there would be no Second Front in 1942 and, if not make him like it exactly, at least explain to him why there would be none and what there would be instead.

Pouring oil on troubled Communists was not a task for which one would normally choose a man with Churchill's political background, but as the "one" in this case was Churchill himself, the choice was pretty much preordained. He believed in face-to-face diplomacy—and he relished the challenge. His visit to Moscow was arranged just one month after his return from America. He was going to Cairo in any case in the wake of Tobruk to make drastic changes in the Middle East High Command, and on July 26 he took advantage of a dinner of the War Cabinet with the King to raise the subject of going on to Russia with his colleagues and sovereign. Finding them agreeable, he wired Stalin on the thirtieth, expressing his willingness to come to the Soviet Union, "if you invite me." On the thirty-first Stalin replied, *inter alia*, "I invite you," and the die was cast.[2]

Far off in Washington, Roosevelt must have viewed the impending meeting with no small degree of anxiety. When he had said "Stalin hates the guts of all your top people," there was no implication that the top person to whom he was writing at the time was somehow exempt from this antipathy. To the President's mind the prospect of strong words and bitter recriminations passing between his two colleagues in supreme responsibility was a disquieting and by no means remote one. Before Churchill's departure from London, therefore, he sent him a cautionary telegram: "...We have got always to bear in mind the personality of our ally and the very difficult and dangerous situation that confronts him. No one can be expected to approach the war from a world point of view whose country has been invaded. I think we should try to put ourselves in his place."[3]

FDR need not have worried. Throughout Churchill's stay in Moscow he displayed both firmness and restraint in the face of sharp and continuous provocations to anger. Stalin, having almost single-handedly made it possible for Hitler to concentrate his entire strength on the destruction of Russia, now arrogated to himself the role of injured party in the Grand Alliance: here was the Soviet Union, totally committed along a front of almost two thousand miles, pouring out the last ounce of her wealth and strength in the common cause while Britain and America, unstraitened and uninvaded, shrank from throwing a measly half-dozen divisions across a mere twenty miles of English Channel. "...If the British Army had been fighting the Germans as much as the Russian Army it would not be so frightened of them," Stalin remarked gratuitously at one point,[4] and according to Roosevelt's representative at the meeting, Averell Harriman, the Marshal expressed himself in a similar fashion on every issue raised— that is, "with a degree of bluntness almost amounting to insult."[5] Churchill ignored all the taunts, however, and refuted all the accusations of bad faith. He was playing the better hand, and he knew it. Russia had to fight to stay alive, and her every contribution to the Allied cause was directly and intimately linked to her most vital national interests. If she was fighting more and making greater contributions than England and the United States, it was because her vital interests were more directly and intimately threatened than theirs were, not because she was a more worthy or co-operative ally. If Stalin was displeased with this state of affairs, furthermore, he could derive some small consolation from the knowledge that, apart from geography, there was no factor more glaringly responsible for it than his own leadership; and in Churchill he encountered one ally at least who could not be humbugged or browbeaten into thinking otherwise. It was not Churchill, after all, who had decimated the Red Army officer corps several times over during the Purges; it was not Churchill who had saved Hitler the stresses of a two-front war in 1939; it was not Churchill who had sent millions in food and oil and war matériel to Germany during almost two years of Nazi conquest in the West; and it was not Churchill who, despite ample warning, had refused to fortify Russia's frontiers in the spring of 1941 and prepare for the catastrophic German onslaught.

Thus, after four days of conferences, the Soviet Premier and the British Prime Minister understood each other. Hitler had attacked their countries and that had made them allies. It had not made them friends. They had interests in common but were under no illusions about the extent of them. With Bolero-Sledgehammer* postponed, Stalin had to accept Gymnast-Torch as his only relief in the West. He didn't like it certainly, but there was nothing much that he could do about it. And that was that. "It is my considered opinion," Churchill wrote the War Cabinet, "that in his heart, so far as he has one, Stalin knows we are right, and that six divisions on 'Sledgehammer' would do him no good this year."[6] And to a relieved Roosevelt he reported, "On the whole I am definitely encouraged. . . . Now they know the worst, and having made their protest are entirely friendly. . . ."[7]

* "Sledgehammer" was the plan for an attack on Brest or Cherbourg in 1942.

* Preparations for Torch were now far advanced, and the momentum behind the operation was building rapidly. Late August and early September found the United States and Great Britain in disagreement, however, on the issue of whether the invasion forces should strike at both Algiers and Oran in Algeria or at the latter city alone. The Americans felt that landings near Casablanca and Oran were all that could reasonably be attempted given the resources available and the distances involved. The British, on the other hand, were violently of the opinion that a failure to strike simultaneously near Algiers would undermine the whole strategic value of the operation. By landing in eastern Algeria, they argued, Torch forces might gather in all of French North Africa at a single stroke, and in any case reduce by several hundred miles the distance separating them from Rommel's rearward lines of communication. Telegrams flew back and forth between Washington and London, many of them received and replied to the same day. Finally, by means of various shifts, devices, borrowings, and reshufflings, an accommodation was reached: Oran, Casablanca, *and* Algiers were all encompassed within Torch's geographical configurations. One final series of telegrams sealed the bargain which had been so heatedly yet amicably negotiated:

PRESIDENT ROOSEVELT TO FORMER NAVAL PERSON   4 SEPT. 42
... WE ARE GETTING VERY CLOSE TOGETHER. I AM WILLING TO REDUCE CASABLANCA FORCE BY ... 5000 MEN. SINCE A SIMILAR REDUCTION WAS MADE IN ORIGINAL ORAN ASSAULT FORCE, THIS RELEASES A TOTAL OF ... SOME 10,000 MEN FOR USE AT ALGIERS. ...

FORMER NAVAL PERSON TO PRESIDENT ROOSEVELT   5 SEPT. 42
WE AGREE TO THE MILITARY LAYOUT AS YOU PROPOSE IT. ...

PRESIDENT ROOSEVELT TO PRIME MINISTER   5 SEPT. 42
HURRAH!

FORMER NAVAL PERSON TO PRESIDENT ROOSEVELT   6 SEPT. 42
O.K., FULL BLAST.[8]

Now came "a loaded pause." In Egypt General Montgomery meticulously prepared his troops to meet Rommel's at El Alamein. In England and America, air, sea, and ground forces

for Torch steadily gathered. Last of all, in Russia, German
and Soviet armies battled furiously and without reprieve to
establish once and for all whose will would prevail at the
city of Stalingrad. The tension of waiting mounted day by
day. Then, suddenly, within the space of a single month, in
the Middle East, in northwest Africa, and along the banks
of the River Volga, the hinge turned. On October 23 the
British Eighth Army struck west and routed the Afrika Korps
in less than two weeks of fighting. On November 8 General
Montgomery passed the baton to Eisenhower, and "the Torch
was lit." Again little time was needed; by November 15 Anglo-
American forces stood astride the Tunisian border, and Rommel, reeling backward over twelve hundred miles of desert
before Montgomery's headlong pursuit, was in a vise. On
November 19 Russian forces launched a pincers movement
designed to cut off the German Sixth Army in Stalingrad, and
on the twenty-second the northern and southern prongs met
at Kalach on the River Don, forty miles west of the city.
Whereas his colleague in North Africa was merely bracketed
by hostile legions, the Sixth Army's General von Paulus found
himself hopelessly encircled. Thus in the space of only thirty
days the situation of the Grand Alliance with respect to the
European Axis had been completely revolutionized. Just that
quickly the long series of setbacks and disappointments came
forever to an end. As Churchill himself wrote of this extraordinary turnabout: "It may almost be said, 'Before Alamein we
never had a victory. After Alamein we never had a defeat.' "⁹

Such a drastic alteration of the strategic picture confronted
the Allies with the possibility that they might soon win major
victories without having first concerted plans for exploiting
them. The descent on North Africa, moreover, had prompted
Hitler to overrun the rump territory of Vichy France, and,
with the assassination of Admiral Darlan in Algiers, it became
more than ever imperative to organize the French forces
newly assimilated into the Allied camp. In mid-December,
accordingly, after fruitless efforts to entice Stalin to join them,
Roosevelt and Churchill arranged to meet early in the new
year at Casablanca.

The Casablanca Conference took place in a sort of holiday

atmosphere. Present in addition to the President, Hopkins, the Prime Minister, and the Chiefs of Staff were Lieutenant Colonel Elliott Roosevelt, USA; Lieutenant Franklin D. Roosevelt, Jr., USNR; Captain Randolph Churchill of the British Special Service Brigade; and Sergeant Robert Hopkins, fresh from a Tunisian foxhole. Harold Macmillan, then minister-resident at Eisenhower's headquarters, remembered: ". . . The whole affair . . . was a mixture between a cruise, a summer school, and a conference. The notice boards gave the time of the meetings of the various staffs, rather like lectures, and when they got out of school at five o'clock or so, you would see Field-Marshals and Admirals going down to the beach for an hour to play with the pebbles and make sand castles."[10] Amidst all the sunbathing and family reunions, however, a lot of work got done. Generals de Gaulle and Giraud submitted to a shotgun wedding which took care of the Free French problem, at least for the moment. The British and American military staffs, meanwhile, agreed on Sicily as the first objective after Africa was cleared, and Roosevelt, somewhat to Churchill's surprise, announced publicly that the policy of the "United Nations" vis-à-vis the Axis was one of unconditional surrender. When the conference ended, Winston took the President to Marrakech to see the sunset on the high Atlas, and there painted for him the only picture he assayed during the war. The two men parted company on the morning of January 25, Roosevelt heading back to Washington via Bathurst, Dakar, Monrovia, and Natal, Brazil; Churchill heading back to London via Turkey, Cyprus, Cairo, Tripoli, and Algiers.

As might be expected, both leaders fell seriously ill when they got home. Granted, it was great fun for them being in the same decade together, but the decade in question was their seventh, and they had both been overdoing things. Churchill came down with pneumonia but was so uncooperative about resting that Wilson had to call in Dr. Geoffrey Marshall of Guy's Hospital to help keep his recalcitrant patient in bed. "I call pneumonia 'the old man's friend,'" said the specialist sepulchrally. "Why?" the rebellious Prime Minister asked. "Because it takes them off so quietly," was the answer. Noted Churchill: "I made a suitable reply."[11] As for Roosevelt: "I think I picked up sleeping sickness or Gambia fever or some kindred bug in that hell-hole of yours called Bathurst," he wrote on March 17. "It laid me low...and left me feeling like a wet rag...and after standing it for a week or so I went to Hyde Park for five days; got full of health in glorious zero weather....Tell Mrs. Churchill that when I was laid up I was a thoroughly model patient, and that I hope you will live down the reputation in our press of having been the 'world's worst patient.'..."[12] Two days later FDR sent Churchill a copy of a letter he had received which stated that Winston had come to America with his mother when he was an infant. "I did not know that you came to the United States when you were at the baby carriage age," the President remarked. Churchill replied that Roosevelt's informant was mistaken, and that his first visit—as the reader knows—took place in 1895 when he was twenty. Unruffled, FDR wrote back on March 30, "SOME BABY!"[13]

By now events were moving rapidly. Stalingrad had fallen on January 31, twenty-one Axis divisions having been swallowed up in its forlorn defense. Russian counteroffensives followed all along the eastern front, and by early spring the Germans had been forced all the way back to the line from which their massive attacks of 1942 had been launched. In Tunisia, meanwhile, the vise tightened on the Afrika Korps. Torch forces attacked from the west and the Eighth Army struck from the east. In early May a sick and utterly exhausted Rommel was ordered back to Berlin by Hitler. The fighting continued, but the outcome was a foregone conclusion. On the twelfth, with their backs to the sea, the dispirited remnants of the Axis armies surrendered. The hinge having turned, the ring was now starting to close, and the day before Africa's redemption was completed, Churchill arrived back in the United States to discuss the next steps.

The initiative for this, the Trident Conference, had been entirely the Prime Minister's. "I was resolved to have a conference on the highest possible level," he admitted, and on April 29 he had wired Roosevelt, "It seems to me most necessary that we should all settle together, now ... Sicily and ... exploitation thereof. ... There are also a number of other burning questions which you and I could with advantage bring up to date. ..."[14] The President had responded positively, and on May 5 Churchill and a party of nearly a hundred embarked for America aboard the *Queen Mary*, their fellow passengers some five thousand German prisoners of war on the way to internment.

The "burning question" uppermost in Churchill's mind was whether the victories won thus far in the Mediterranean basin were going to be exploited properly. The American Chiefs of Staff were committed by the Casablanca agreements to Operation Husky, the invasion of Sicily, as soon as operations in North Africa were concluded. After Husky, however, they wanted to pull most Allied forces out of the Mediterranean and concentrate everything for the big operation across the Channel in 1944. Such a plan, to Churchill's mind, was the worst form of strategic coitus interruptus imaginable. Here British and American armies were going to be conquering Italian soil, battering Mussolini's homeland from the air, and bringing the shakiest member of the Axis right up to the point where she would almost inevitably be forced to submit. Just as they prepared to enjoy the fruits of their exertions, though, they were going to be withdrawn and sent far away to sit in idleness for several months before attempting to subdue a much less tractable virago. It was insupportable.

The *Queen Mary* anchored off Staten Island, where Hopkins was waiting with a special train. Churchill, aware that FDR was particularly pressed at the moment because of a John L. Lewis–inspired coal crisis, had offered to put himself up at the British Embassy; but Roosevelt had unequivocally vetoed the idea, and so it was to the White House Winston went.

At 2:30 P.M. on May 12 in the Oval Office the Trident Conference was officially convened. Roosevelt spoke a few words of welcome and then turned the floor over to Churchill, who prefaced his comments by remarking on how greatly things had changed since his last visit to America at the time of the fall of Tobruk. The American military chiefs shifted uncomfortably in their chairs. They did not need to be reminded of Tobruk; it was the collapse of that fortress that had frustrated their plans for an early invasion of France. One could sense a digging in of heels around the table: *this* time there would be no more detours.

Churchill was not unaware of the feeling on the other side of the table, and he said he wanted to make it "absolutely clear" that Britain desired a full-scale cross-Channel invasion "as soon as a plan offering reasonable prospects of success could be made."[15] This reassurance did little to comfort his auditors, since he had said almost exactly the same thing on the day Tobruk fell.*

When Churchill finished speaking, Roosevelt underscored the American position by stating that "the [cross-Channel] operation must be carried out on the largest scale in the spring of 1944."[16] What he meant was: Our Mediterranean forces are not going from Sicily to the Italian mainland. Churchill understood that meaning, but he certainly wasn't about to show that he did—or to acquiesce. As the New York *Times* (another advocate of an early invasion of France) somewhat ruefully acknowledged in announcing his arrival, "Mr. Churchill . . . is a welcome visitor. He is also a potent conferee. . . ."[17]

This time, however, his conference potency would have to make itself felt without the aid of a military disaster. For at 2:15 P.M. on May 13 he received the following telegram from Eisenhower's British deputy, General Alexander: SIR: IT IS MY DUTY TO REPORT THAT THE TUNISIAN CAMPAIGN IS OVER. ALL ENEMY RESISTANCE HAS CEASED. WE ARE MASTERS OF THE NORTH AFRICAN SHORES.[18] Such a message was ample compensation for the loss of a bargaining point.

May 14 provided only one interlude in the ongoing conferences. It was the third anniversary of the Home Guard, and Churchill marked the occasion in a radio speech beamed to Britain. Here indeed was an opportunity to reflect on happy contrasts: the Guard had been organized to protect the British against a German invasion; now an assault against the

* "If a sound and sensible plan [for the invasion of France] can be contrived, we should not hesitate to give effect to it" (June 21, 1942).

Germans was being readied on the very island that had once
been under siege.

May 15 being a Saturday, Roosevelt proposed that Churchill accompany him and Mrs. Roosevelt to Shangri-La, the
Presidential retreat in the Catoctin Mountains of Maryland,
now called Camp David. With Harry Hopkins along as the
fourth passenger, the President's car and its motorcycle escort
set off. Two hours later the procession neared Frederick,
Maryland, and a road sign for Barbara Frietchie Candy moved
Hopkins to quote from Whittier's poem: "'Shoot if you must
this old grey head,/But spare your country's flag,' she said."
I will not attempt to improve on Churchill's account of what
happened next:

When it was clear that no one else in the car could add to this
quotation, I started out:

> "Up from the meadows rich with corn,
> Clear in the cool September morn,
> The clustered spires of Frederick stand" . . .

and sailed steadily on:

> "Up rose old Barbara Frietchie then,
> Bowed with her threescore years and ten;
> Bravest of all in Frederick town,
> She took up the flag that the men hauled down.
>
>   .   .   .   .
>
> "'Halt,' the dust brown ranks stood fast.
> 'Fire!' Out blazed the rifle-blast.
> It shivered the window with frame and sash,
> It rent the banner with many a gash.
> Quick as it fell from the broken staff,
> Dame Barbara seized the silken scarf.
> She leant full out of the window-sill,
> And shook it forth with a right good will.
> 'Shoot if you will this old grey head,[*]
> But spare your country's flag' . . ."

At this point they all joined in the chorus:

* Hopkins' "Shoot if you must" is the correct rendition.

". . . she said."

I went on:

"A shade of sadness, a touch of shame
Over the face of the leader came,
And a nobler nature within him stirred
At the sight of this woman's deed and word.
'Who touches a hair of yon grey head

[he is said to have exclaimed, somewhat inconsistently with his previous instructions]

'Dies like a dog. March on,' he said.

"So all day long through Frederick's street
Sounded the tramp of marching feet,
And all day long that free flag tossed
Over the heads of the rebel host."

I got full marks for this from my highly select American audience, none of whom corrected my many misquotations. . . .[19]

Hopkins was particularly impressed, and on Monday he told Wilson, "While we were still asking ourselves how he could do this when he hadn't read the darned [poem] for thirty years, his eye caught a sign pointing to Gettysburg. That really started him off."[20]

Thoroughly instructed on the intricacies of Civil War strategy, the Presidential party at last arrived at Shangri-La. FDR seized a few free minutes to catch up on his stamp collecting and Churchill, thinking wistfully perhaps of how restorative he would have found a canvas and some oils just then, stayed to observe. "I watched him with much interest and in silence for perhaps half an hour as he stuck [the stamps in his albums] each in its proper place, and so forgot the cares of State." Soon General Bedell Smith arrived, however, fresh from Eisenhower's headquarters, and the President "sadly . . . left his stamp collection and addressed himself to his task."[21]

Taking advantage of another brief respite on Sunday, FDR took out a few hours to do some angling. "No fish were caught," Churchill reported, but the President "seemed to enjoy it very much, and was in great spirits for the rest of the day. Evidently he had the first quality of an angler, which is not to measure the pleasure by the catch."[22]

The only really pressing matter over the weekend involved a nice question of diplomatic protocol. Madame Chiang Kai-shek, at the time in New York, "intimated" to Churchill "that she would be glad to receive [him] there." As an ardent Germany-firster and an unrepentant colonialist, the Prime Minister was not particularly eager to confer with an ardent Japan-firster who was also a militant nationalist, especially since he did not regard Chiang's China as much more than a burdensome irritant. Roosevelt, attempting a compromise, invited Mrs. Chiang to the White House for lunch, but the "invitation was refused with some hauteur. Madame was of the opinion that I should make the pilgrimage to New York." Seeing that FDR was annoyed by this rebuff, Churchill rather impishly offered to meet the lady halfway, say, in Delaware. "This offer was however considered facetious."[23]

If Madame Chiang was not prepared to go two hundred miles to see the Prime Minister, other people in the United States would gladly have gone three times around the world for five minutes with him. Among these were the many American Jews seeking free access to Palestine for their European brethren. On May 16 they took a full-page ad in the New York *Times* and pleaded: MR. CHURCHILL, CHAMPION OF HUMANITY, ONE WORD FROM YOU NOW CAN SAVE THE LIVES OF UNTOLD THOUSANDS.[24] Whether Churchill saw this appeal or not (and, being an omniverous newspaper devourer, he almost certainly did), he continued his staunch support for the Palestinian Jews throughout the war.[25]

On Monday the mountain idyll came to an end, and everyone reluctantly headed back to Washington, arriving at the White House about midday. "In the regretted absence of Madame Chiang Kai-shek," Churchill noted, "the President and I lunched alone in his room, and made the best of things."[26]

Then it was back to work, which for Churchill meant, among other tasks, preparing for his second speech to Congress. In many ways this second address would be more

VISIT OF MR. CHURCHILL TO UNITED STATES OCCASIONS PLEA
TO OPEN GATES OF PALESTINE TO SAVE EUROPEAN JEWS

Mr. Churchill, Champion of Humanity, One Word From You Now Can Save the Lives of Untold Thousands.

Allow the Gates of Palestine to Open—and Multitudes Will be Rescued.

We are fully aware of the burden of responsibilities resting on your shoulders. We know you are in counsel with our great President, devising plans for a speedy and final defeat of the forces of evil and for a glorious victory for all humanity.

We know that your wisdom and the wisdom of our President are today concentrated on the one supreme task of the War—the blueprint of Victory.

Because of your absorption with a gigantic program, there is real danger that you might inadvertently overlook the boast of the cowardly Nazis that they will avenge their crushing military defeats by speeding the process of slaughtering the defenseless Jews of Europe.

We would not deserve to forfeit your respect, if we failed to invite your attention to the imminent danger to which the European Jews are exposed!

Your shining record as an indomitable fighter for the right, though you stood alone, is the outstanding glory of your life—a glory which in turn inspired the gallant British people to miraculous achievements.

"No ships are needed for European Jews to reach Palestine"

Palestine is the nearest and most practical haven. Their voyage does not require ships. It can be reached through Turkey by train or bus. Palestine is not further from Bulgaria than Miami is from New York.

Who is standing in the way of the European Jews' saving themselves?

Shocking facts that must be known.

The Jews CAN Leave Europe

There Is a Place Where Jews Can Go!

Jews Are Not Being Admitted to Palestine for Political Reasons.

The Arab Population Is NOT an Enemy of the Jews!

"We stand before the Bar of History, of Humanity and God"

Archbishop of Canterbury leads public opinion in Great Britain demanding from government immediate action to save remaining millions of European Jews — Bermuda Conference a deep disappointment to many in Great Britain and United States

PLAN OF JEWISH ARMY COMMITTEE ADVOCATED IN THE SENATE

Senator Langer demands the creation of a United Nations Agency to deal with Jewish Problem in Europe.

Join the Crusade for Decency

Churchill—A Friend of Palestine as a New Hebrew Nation.

COMMITTEE FOR A JEWISH ARMY OF STATELESS AND PALESTINIAN JEWS

EXECUTIVE BOARD

GABRIEL A. WECHSLER — National Secretary
DR. MAURICE WILLIAM — Acting Chairman, Executive Board
PETER H. BERGSON — National Director

National Officers

515 Fifth Avenue, New York City — 2117 I St. Street, N.W., Washington, D.C.

This full-page advertisement in the New York *Times* appeared during Churchill's third wartime visit. In addressing Churchill, the Committee for a Jewish Army had in mind his long-standing advocacy of the cause of Zionism (see box, lower left).

important than the first. For one thing, the press and the American public, however well they understood the need for secrecy, were beginning to chafe a little at the near total blackout of news on the Prime Minister's visit. As the *Times* pointedly commented, "There have been no public announcements of any kind concerning the course of the White House talks. . . ."[27] For another (somewhat ironical) thing, despite the tight security, there had been partial leaks from some of the American military conferees to members of Congress, and something had to be done to clear up the many misconceptions that had resulted.

As usual, Churchill was highly apprehensive beforehand. He told Wilson that he viewed his talk as "a great responsibility; a much more difficult speech than the first time I talked to Congress after Pearl Harbour."[28] When the time came, however, everything went off smoothly. He entered the House chamber shortly after 12:30 on May 19 and was accorded a ninety-second standing ovation before he was even introduced. The Speaker, Sam Rayburn, presented him to the assembled senators, representatives, Supreme Court justices, diplomats, VIPs (including Baruch and the Duke and Duchess of Windsor), calling him "one of the outstanding figures of all the earth."

And so he was launched. His words this time were not inspirational, for his object was to enlighten and clarify rather than to enthrall, but it was a Churchillian speech nevertheless, and far from dull. He began:

The fact that you have invited me to come to Congress again, a second time, now that we have settled down to the job, and that you should welcome me in so generous a fashion, is certainly a high mark in my life, and it also shows that our partnership has not done too badly.

After briefly reviewing the events since December 1941, he confessed to the sense of relief he had felt when America finally entered the war:

. . . The experience of a long life and the promptings of my blood awoke in me the conviction that there is nothing more important for the future of the world than the fraternal association of our two peoples in righteous work both in war and peace.

Then, in a tone calculated to make an impression on the people who doubted Britain's commitment to the fight against Japan and on the many Congressional critics of the Germany-first policy, he turned his attention to the Pacific:

> ... let no one suggest that we British have not at least as great an interest as the United States in the unstinting and relentless waging of war against Japan. I am here to tell you that we will wage that war side by side with you . . . while there is breath in our bodies and while blood flows in our veins. . . .

After enlarging on this theme for several minutes, he turned with relish, and humor, from the Pacific to North Africa:

> One continent at least has been cleansed and purged forever from Fascist or Nazi tyranny. The African excursions of the two dictators have cost their countries in killed and captured 950,000 soldiers. . . . There have also been lost to the enemy 6,200 guns and 2,550 tanks and 70,000 trucks—which is the American name for lorry and which I understand has been adopted by the combined staffs in Northwest Africa in exchange for the use of the word petrol in place of gasoline.

He continued his survey of the whole sphere of the war, and when he came to deliver his summation he made use of his weekend travels to deliver a somber and all too accurate warning:

> I was driving the other day not far from the field of Gettysburg which I know well, like most of your battlefields. It was the decisive battle of the Civil War. No one after Gettysburg doubted which way the dread balance of the war would incline. Yet far more blood was shed after the Union victory at Gettysburg than in all the fighting which went before. It behooves us, therefore, to search our hearts and brace our sinews . . . we cannot afford to relax a single fiber of our being or to tolerate the slightest abatement of our efforts. . . . By singleness of purpose, by steadfastness of conduct, by tenacity and endurance such as we have so far displayed, by these, and only by these, can we discharge our duty to the future of the world and to the destiny of man.

Finis. The cheers came rolling up toward the dais. After
several minutes of smiles and V signs, the immensely pleased
Churchill was shepherded away to a luncheon hosted by the
chairmen of the Senate and House Foreign Affairs committees. After eating he met with the committees' membership
for an hour-long question-and-answer session. Then he returned to the White House, where, he was happy to note, "the
President . . . seemed very pleased with me. . . ."[29]

Other reactions to the speech were favorable too, and it definitely accomplished its purpose of informing and clarifying.
It accomplished it so well, in fact, that Hopkins was able to
report to Wilson that the main grievance now on Capitol Hill
was "that the only time they're told anything is when Winston
addresses Congress."[30]

It was a good day in one other respect as well: in London
Churchill's eldest daughter, Diana, gave birth to his fourth
grandchild, Celia Mary.

With his speech out of the way, it was time for Churchill to
bear down on the problems that the British and American
Chiefs of Staff had been working on since his arrival; foremost,
of course, was the sequel to Operation Husky. Before grap-
pling with that issue, however, the Prime Minister thought it
would be wise to dispel some of the misconceptions about
British postwar policy then current in many high American
circles. On Saturday, the twenty-second, accordingly, he hosted
a luncheon at the British Embassy for Vice President Wallace,
Senate Foreign Relations Committee Chairman Tom Connally,
Secretary of War Stimson, Secretary of the Interior Ickes, and
Under-Secretary of State Sumner Welles. During this luncheon
some very probing questions received some very candid
answers, but, when the meeting broke up, the U.S. officials
were somewhat reassured that the war was not being fought
for the aggrandizement of the British Empire. In concluding
his remarks, moreover, Churchill had had an opportunity to
invoke his fundamental gospel about the postwar era. ". . . I
said that I could see small hope for the world unless the
United States and the British Commonwealth worked together in fraternal association. . . . I should like the citizens of

each . . . to be able to come and settle and trade with freedom and equal rights in the territories of the other. . . . There might even be some common form of citizenship. . . ."[31]

The remainder of the weekend of the twenty-second was spent studying staff reports for the most part, and on Monday, the twenty-fourth, a plenary meeting of the joint staffs was held with the President and the Prime Minister in attendance. It did not go well from Churchill's point of view. He could not get a definite undertaking to capitalize on Husky by crossing the Strait of Messina. After the meeting he unburdened himself to Wilson: "The President is not willing to put pressure on Marshall. . . . It is most discouraging. I only crossed the Atlantic for this purpose."[32] Not even Hopkins could hold out much hope, however. "If you wish to carry your point," he told Churchill, "you will have to stay here another week, and even then there is no certainty."[33]

The Prime Minister was very distressed. Somehow he had to convince Roosevelt that an invasion of mainland Italy was the only sensible course, but in order to convince Roosevelt he had first to convince Marshall, and Marshall had grave doubts about the wisdom of such a venture. His thoughts were focused more on Sardinia—and northern France. Churchill believed that he could win him round, but he was leaving in less than two days, and during that time both he and Marshall would be far too busy to confer privately to any appreciable extent. There was only one thing the Prime Minister could do, and on the morning of the twenty-fifth he did it. "I . . . appealed personally to the President to let General Marshall come to Algiers with me."*[34] Roosevelt took the request under advisement, reserving his final decision for the wind-up session of Trident in the evening. Fortunately, Churchill had plenty to keep his mind occupied while he awaited the verdict.

One of the things that occupied him was a repeat performance of his December 1941 joint press conference with FDR. Once again the scene was the Executive Office of the White House. Roosevelt made a brief introductory statement. As the *Times* reported it, ". . . the President referred to Mr. Churchill

* He was going to Algiers to confer with Eisenhower.

as an old friend of himself and of the newsmen. He said that he did not have to tell his visitor how glad they were to have him back again, since he could tell that was their sentiment by reading the newspapers or looking into the face of any American he might encounter."[35] The floor was then opened to questions, and a good time was had by all.

QUESTION: Mr. Prime Minister, could you say anything about how well satisfied you are with the way things are going on the fighting fronts?

ANSWER: I am very much more satisfied than I was when I was here last. (laughter) It was [here] that the President handed me the telegram of the surrender of Tobruk. As I may have mentioned to him, I don't think there was . . . any Englishman in the United States so unhappy as I was that day since Burgoyne surrendered at Saratoga. (loud laughter)

QUESTION: Mr. Prime Minister, what do you think of the dissolution of the Comintern? [Stalin had made this concession to Allied unity on May 22.]

ANSWER: Well, I like it. (laughter) I like it.

QUESTION: Mr. Prime Minister, do you care to say anything about Mussolini and Italy? Is there any hint or news that you can bring us on that?

ANSWER: You know as much as I do about that. I think they are a softer proposition than Germany. . . . All we can do is apply those physical stimuli (laughter) which in default of moral sanctions are sometimes capable of inducing a better state of mind in recalcitrant individuals and recalcitrant nations. (more laughter)

QUESTION: Mr. Prime Minister, there is a great deal more confidence in the Allied commanders in the field than there was a year ago. Would you care to comment on that?

ANSWER: Well, they have had a chance to come into action on reasonable terms. Indeed, on advantageous terms, because we struck with superior forces at the right spot. We—as your Confederate General used to say —got there firstest with the mostest. (laughter)

QUESTION: Mr. Prime Minister, would you undertake to make a prediction on the progress of the war for the rest

of this year? I have in mind . . . this statement you
and the President made at Casablanca, on new and
heavier blows against all of the Axis members in
1943.

ANSWER: Well, I think that seems to be a very sound prediction, and couched in terms which are unexceptionable
from the point of view of military security. (laughter)

There was a chorus of thank-yous as the conference ended,
and Winston thanked the reporters in return. Then Roosevelt
interposed a final word designed to mask the fact that Churchill was leaving the next day: "May I say one word, please?
Don't get the idea that the conferences are concluded. They
are not. They are continuing." "We have a lot of ground to
cover," the Prime Minister chimed in.[36]

Although the question of Marshall still weighed heavily on
Churchill's mind, the President would give no hint of his decision. Finally, at the last Trident session that evening, he put
an end to the suspense. "The Prime Minister," he said, "would
shortly have an opportunity of talking to the Commander-in-
Chief in North Africa on 'post-Husky' policy, and had suggested that it would be of great value if General Marshall
could go there too. I have accordingly spoken to General
Marshall and asked whether he could defer his visit to the
Southwest Pacific in order to fall in with the Prime Minister's
request. General Marshall said that he was perfectly willing
to do this."[37] Churchill fairly purred. He and Marshall left the
next morning and had "some very agreeable talks"[38] en route.

Sicily was invaded on July 10.

All resistance on the island ended on August 16.

The Italian mainland was invaded on September 3.

CHAPTER ELEVEN

Quadrant and Harvard

"AGREEABLE" as the Churchill-Marshall talks may have been, they were not as instrumental in securing the invasion of mainland Italy as the events precipitated by the Allied landings in Sicily. The speed with which the American Seventh and British Eighth armies dislodged the island's defenders, coupled with a July 19 bombing raid on Rome's railway and airport facilities, brought the war home to the Italian people with a tooth-jarring bang. The Fascist Grand Council hastened to repudiate Mussolini's leadership, and on July 25, "for his own protection," he was placed under arrest. "At this moment you are the most hated man in Italy," King Victor Emmanuel told him sadly, and then called on Marshal Pietro Badoglio to form a new government.

Even before Mussolini actually fell, the softness of the Italian proposition had become increasingly apparent, and the need to capitalize on it with follow-ups to Husky had grown ever more obvious as well. Roosevelt and Churchill found themselves hard pressed to stay ahead of each day's new developments, and barely a month after Trident they began to concert plans for another high-level conference. On July 16 Churchill wrote, "Events in Husky are moving so fast and the degeneration of Italian resistance is so marked that decisions about the Toe, Ball, and Heel . . . will almost certainly have to be taken before we meet. We shall, however, need . . . to settle the larger issues which the brilliant victories of our forces are thrusting upon us about Italy as a whole. Mid-August will only just be in time for this work. . . ."[1]

The place eventually chosen for the meeting was Quebec; the date, August 17; the code name, Quadrant.

Accompanied by his wife, his daughter Mary, and the usual complement of military and diplomatic advisers, Churchill arrived in Canada on August 9 aboard the *Queen Mary*. On the eleventh he and his daughter (a subaltern in the Auxiliary Territorial Service, seconded from her anti-aircraft battery near London to serve as her father's aide-de-camp) departed by train for Hyde Park. Winston shifted their route somewhat to the west so that Mary could have a look at Niagara Falls, and reporters there asked him if the cascading waters looked the same as on his previous visits. "Well," he answered, "the principle seems the same. The water keeps falling over."[2]

Father and daughter arrived at Hyde Park on the evening of the twelfth and stayed two days, much to Inspector Thompson's anguish. "By God, I will take Chequers in the blitz to a Roosevelt weekend-with-the-children," he wrote. "Anyone could walk right into Hyde Park. . . . It was becoming a sightseer's shrine. Searchlights were rigged in tree-boughs, poles, ridges, roofs. The place looked like a *stalag* after a break at midnight. Daytimes it was a sort of bucolic Brighton with all . . . [the Roosevelt grandchildren] determined that every grownup was Santa Claus."[3] Insulated by his eminence, Churchill barely noticed the pandemonium in which his unfortunate bodyguard was submerged. The heat of high summer in the Hudson Valley made a much deeper impression, however. "It was indeed so hot that I got up one night because I was unable to sleep and hardly able to breathe and went outside to sit on a bluff overlooking the . . . River. Here I watched the dawn."[4]

A perspiring Prime Minister and a badly disheveled Scotland Yard Inspector fled from the Roosevelt estate on August 14 and hurried back to the cool and quiet of the Quebec Citadel. FDR arrived there on the seventeenth, the day after the fall of Sicily. On the nineteenth, Quadrant was officially convened. According to Churchill, this gathering of Allied planners was essentially "a series of technical staff conferences," and in fact there were only two plenary sessions at which both the President and the Prime Minister were in attendance. At the first the top priority of the combined bomber offensive against Germany was reconfirmed, and Bolero–Sledgehammer–Round-up* was officially and finally reconstituted under the heading Overlord and given a target date of May 1, 1944. At the second plenary meeting Roosevelt and Churchill approved long-range plans for the prosecution of the war against Japan.

Even as Quadrant was in session, secret negotiations for Italy's surrender were progressing at a feverish pace, and by the end of the conference on August 24, representatives of Badoglio and Eisenhower were very close to agreement. Churchill went off to the lodge of Canadian wood-pulp magnate Frank Clarke at the Lake of Snows, seventy-five miles north of the Citadel, to rest a bit and prepare a radio address to the Canadian people, but both he and Roosevelt, who was back in the United States, kept close tabs on the Italian situation. The Prime Minister gave his speech on the evening of August 31 and then immediately set off for Washington by train. On his arrival at the White House the next day, he was greeted with the news that Badoglio had agreed to the Allied terms.

Everything in Italy now hung in the balance: an armistice might be announced at any moment; the Strait of Messina was to be crossed on September 3; Operation Avalanche (the landings at Salerno) was scheduled for the ninth; so was a naval descent on the harbor at Taranto. Churchill had no desire to be on or over the Atlantic while all these momentous developments were hanging fire. Accordingly, "I deliberately prolonged my stay in the United States in order to be in close contact with our American friends at the critical moment. . . ."5

In the absence of formally scheduled staff talks and, indeed, of any of the impedimenta of a full-dress inter-Allied consultation, Churchill and Roosevelt more or less went about their own business and followed their own personal routines while waiting for the Italian situation to crystallize. It was almost as if Churchill were back in London, except that whenever he and the President had something to discuss they dis-

* Round-up was the plan for the liberation of France in 1943.

cussed it face to face rather than by telegram. "They just talk whenever it is convenient," a White House spokesman told the press,[6] and apart from the absence of Hopkins, who, on the verge of a total physical collapse, had been ordered into Bethesda Naval Hospital, the casual comings and goings along the second-floor corridor resumed pretty much where they had left off three months before. Roosevelt continued to stay up past his bedtime and Churchill continued to prowl around far into the wee hours. One morning at around 2:00 A.M. he erupted into the Map Room to have a look at some newly compiled charts. Neither his switching on the light nor his progress around the room disturbed the slumber of the naval officer on duty, who lay snoring blissfully on a cot. At length the Prime Minister's rummagings and rumblings caused the young lieutenant to awaken. He leapt to his feet in great embarrassment and stood uneasily at attention while Churchill scrutinized one map after another. After many long minutes of silent concentration Winston turned and headed for the door. Passing the anxiously perspiring duty officer on his way out, he favored him with one of his best Churchillian scowls. "Taut watch you keep there, son," he said, and his figure receded into the dim light of the upstairs hall.[7]

Churchill probably did more prowling around than usual during this visit, because his schedule was comparatively uncrowded, which invariably made him restless, and because he was very much on tenterhooks about the success of Avalanche, which was primarily his responsibility. On September 3 the first hard news started coming in from Italy, and it was encouraging. Reggio Calabria had been taken easily, and resistance throughout the Italian toe was light to negligible. Even better news was soon forthcoming. From Eisenhower's headquarters came a telegram signed by General Alexander: THE SHORT ARMISTICE TERMS WERE SIGNED THIS AFTERNOON, ON THE FOURTH ANNIVERSARY OF THE WAR, BETWEEN GENERAL BEDELL SMITH, REPRESENTING GENERAL EISENHOWER, AND GENERAL CASTELLANO, REPRESENTING MARSHAL BADOGLIO. . . .[8] Feeling somewhat relieved by these tidings, Churchill went down to the old diplomatic reception room of the White House to purchase the first one-hundred-dollar bond of America's Third War Loan drive from Henry Morgenthau, Roosevelt's Secretary of the Treasury. "Mr. Morgenthau," he said after the certificate had been presented to him, "I am very glad indeed to come here today and it is a great pleasure to receive from your hand this first war bond of your great new victory loan. . . . This bond which you have given me—provided you make sure the legal details are satisfactorily arranged—I shall hand over to my wife for Mrs. Churchill's Russian Relief Fund. This brings us all together on this joyous occasion."[9]

With the bond safely consigned to Clementine's custody, Churchill went off to the Statler Hotel for an off-the-record luncheon with the Washington press corps. His host was Barnet Nover of the Denver *Post*, who welcomed him as "one of the ablest practitioners of our craft,"[10] and for two hours after being introduced, Winston fielded questions with all his customary verve. Then it was back to the White House for more consultations and more suspense.

Avalanche and the uncertainties over the impending Italian surrender continued to weigh heavily on Churchill during the next two days, and it was in a decidedly stormy mood that he set off for Harvard University on the night of September 5 to receive a degree as an honorary Doctor of Laws and give a speech on Anglo-American unity. The prospect of a major address aggravated his already considerable tensions, and his staff gave him as wide a berth as possible as the train sped on its way up to Boston. "One might think, from his irritability, that the P.M. had the bug," Wilson wrote en route. "For some reason, which I have not yet fathomed, he is taking the speech he is to make at Harvard very seriously."[11]

Wilson finally fathomed the reason when he—and a worldwide radio audience—heard what Churchill had to say. The scene was Sanders Theater, part of Harvard's memorial to the Civil War dead. Accompanied by University President James B. Conant and wearing the robes of an Oxford D.C.L. (borrowed from somebody at Princeton, of all places), Winston entered at the stroke of noon. Wilson, seated in the audience alongside Clementine and Mary, was pained to note that, beneath his majestically flowing robes of brilliant scarlet, the

Prime Minister was sporting a pair of "rather inadequate grey flannel trousers."[12] No one else seemed to notice this sartorial gaffe, however, and the Sheriff of Middlesex County promptly began the ceremonies by striking the scabbard of his sword of office three times on the floor of the stage. There was a prayer and a hymn. Then Governor Leverett Saltonstall spoke a few words of welcome to the honored guest, "a man who knows the worth of that freedom for which he is fighting." After another hymn President Conant conferred the degree. The citation read: "Winston Spencer Churchill, Doctor of Laws. An historian who has written a glorious page of British history; a statesman and warrior whose tenacity and courage turned back the tide of tyranny in freedom's darkest hour."[13]

To loud and prolonged applause the historian-statesman-warrior rose and undertook to begin a new chapter in British-American relations:

Twice in my lifetime the long arm of destiny has reached across the ocean and involved the entire life and manhood of the United States in a deadly struggle. There was no use saying: "We don't want it; we won't have it; our forebears left Europe to avoid those quarrels; we have founded a new world which had no contact with the old"—there was no use in that. The long arm reaches out remorselessly and every one's existence, environment and outlook undergoes a swift and irresistible change. . . .

The price of greatness is responsibility . . . one cannot rise to be in many ways the leading community in the civilized world without being involved in its problems, without being convulsed by its agonies and inspired by its causes. If this has been proved in the past, as it has been, it will become indisputable in the future.

The people of the United States cannot escape world responsibility . . . to the youth of America, as to the youth of all the Britains, I say, you cannot stop; there's no halting place at this point. We have now reached a point in the journey where . . . it must be world anarchy or world order.

Throughout all this ordeal and struggle . . . you will find in the British Commonwealth and Empire good comrades to whom you are united by other ties besides those of state policy and public need. To a large extent they are the ties of blood and history. Naturally, I, a child of both worlds, am conscious of these. Law, language, literature—these are considerable factors. Common conceptions of what is right and decent, marked regard for fair play, especially to the weak and poor. A stern sentiment of impartial justice and above all the love of personal freedom, or as Kipling put it, "Leave to live by no man's leave underneath the law." These are common conceptions on both sides of the ocean among the English-speaking people. We hold these conceptions as strongly as you do. . . . The great Bismarck—for there were once great men in Germany—is said to have observed toward the close of his life that the most potent factor in human society at the end of the nineteenth century was the fact that the British and American peoples spoke the same language. . . . This gift of a common tongue is a priceless inheritance, and it may well some day become the foundation of a common citizenship. . . . If we are together nothing is impossible. If we are divided all will fail. I therefore preach continually the doctrine of the fraternal association of our peoples. . . .

Wrote Wilson, "That was as near as he dared go to proposing a closer union after the war. Winston told me . . . that a little time ago he could not have gone so far. I do not doubt that he tried 'common citizenship' on the President before he launched it. . . ."*[14]

Judging by the ovation that greeted Churchill's remarks, the idea of Anglo-American partnership was by no means repugnant to his listeners. Clementine told reporters that she felt his speech had been "one of the best he ever made," and then dutifully echoed his theme: "I felt it was most moving under the circumstances . . . particularly his appeal for the comradeship of our two nations."[15]

After the ceremony Churchill was escorted to Harvard Yard, where he delivered an impromptu talk to the thousands of Army and Navy ROTC cadets for whom there had been no room in Sanders Theater. When he finished speaking, they returned his V-sign salute with a robust roar of appreciation which, according to one almost deafened witness, "must have done him good."[16]

Back in Washington Winston resumed his vigil in anticipation of the Italian surrender and Avalanche. Eisenhower announced the former on the eighth, but immediately the

* Sherwood confirms that he did so. See *Roosevelt and Hopkins*, p. 750.

Germans began turning Italy into an occupied country and made ready to contest the landing of Allied forces wherever they might appear. Clearly, Avalanche was not going to be a walkover, and Churchill's anxieties increased.

On September 10, however, as the fighting on the Salerno beachhead raged, Churchill was accorded a unique and probably never-to-be-repeated honor. FDR, having decided to await developments at Hyde Park, placed the Prime Minister of Great Britain in charge of the residence of the President of the United States. "Please treat the White House as your home," he told Winston and Clementine. "Invite anyone you like to meals, and do not hesitate to summon any of my advisers. . . ."¹⁷ Thus for two days in the midst of war 1600 Pennsylvania Avenue became 10 Downing Street West. Churchill even convened a meeting of the Combined Chiefs with Harriman and Hopkins—now somewhat recovered—in the White House Council Room, and the historical significance of the occasion stirred him deeply. "It was an honour to me to preside over this conference . . . and it seemed to be an event in Anglo-American history."¹⁸

Before leaving for Hyde Park on the tenth, Roosevelt had at last yielded to the temptation to tweak his British house guest ever so gently about the question of India: he invited Mrs. Ogden Mills Reid to lunch. This formidable matron, sister to Chicago's Colonel McCormick and Vice-President in her own right of the New York *Herald Tribune*, could not have been accused of rabid Anglophilia, and her foremost complaint against the British Empire was what she considered to be its inhuman suppression of the Indian millions. With the arrival of the dessert course her pent-up indignation could be contained no longer, and she demanded heatedly of the Prime Minister: "What do you intend to do about those wretched Indians?" "Madam," Churchill replied loftily, "to which Indians do you refer? Do you by any chance refer to the second greatest nation on earth which under benign and beneficent British rule has multiplied and prospered exceedingly, or do you mean the unfortunate Indians of the North American continent which under your administration are practically extinct?" Mrs. Reid had no response to this; indeed, she was rendered speechless. And as for Roosevelt, he was laughing so hard that Commander Thompson feared he might have a seizure.[19]

On the evening of September 11 the British occupation of the White House was peacefully terminated and the Churchills entrained for Hyde Park. Dispatches from Eisenhower's headquarters were reporting strong German counterattacks, and it appeared that the tide might be turning against the Allies. "These things always seem to happen when I am with the President," Churchill lamented, remembering Tobruk.[20]

The Prime Minister's train arrived at the Hudson River embankment below Hyde Park at 9:30 on the morning of the twelfth and FDR was waiting to drive him up to the estate. It was rather early for Winston to be out and about, however, so Roosevelt took Clementine first and then returned to collect him. As it happened, this September 12 was the Churchills' thirty-fifth wedding anniversary, and the President took them to the Dutchess Hill Cottage for lunch to celebrate and then hosted them himself for dinner. At 10:00 that evening he drove them back down to the New York Central tracks and waved them on their way to Halifax, Nova Scotia, and the battle cruiser *Renown*. Though still gravely preoccupied about Avalanche, Churchill was also tremendously touched by FDR's thoughtfulness, hospitality, and, yes, patience. This visit to America had been essentially extemporaneous, and it had lasted nearly two weeks. Throughout it all, however, Roosevelt had been gracious and accommodating, more so than any unexpected guest had any right to expect, especially when that guest arrived with a goodly fraction of his family. As Winston's train hurtled northward, therefore, he took out a moment to send the President his personal and heartfelt thanks. "You know how I treasure the friendship with which you have honoured me," he wrote, "and how profoundly I feel that we might together do something really fine and lasting for our two countries and, through them, for the future of all."[21]

CHAPTER TWELVE

Victory and Defeat

WHEN CHURCHILL CHARACTERIZED the closing phases of World War II as tragic as well as triumphant he had in mind the whole series of miscalculations which condemned a ravaged world to continuing, though diminished, strife long after the Axis had been liquidated. Of course to a certain extent such strife was inevitable. The complex latticework of international accommodation had been totally disarranged by the years of conflict; new movements had arisen; old allegiances had been blasted away; everywhere nations and peoples were forced to make rapid and drastic reassessments of their circumstances. Despite the unavoidable turmoil, however, the Allied Big Three were in a better position to reshape the world in accordance with some coherent formula than any group of men since the Congress of Vienna. With their enemies obliterated, their freedom of action unimpeded by treaties or secret understandings, and their breadth of jurisdiction truly global in its sweep, Russia, America, and Britain were uniquely situated to dictate the course of history, and there is no question but that the pivotal figure in the Allied triumvirate was Franklin Roosevelt.

The process of blaming—and praising—famous men is one that should not be undertaken except with circumspection. Churchill, for example, observed the rule of never criticizing from hindsight the actions of a responsible official unless he himself had gone on record in opposition to the man at the time in question. The historian, with no such personal corrective to guide him, must consult less clear-cut criteria when he comes to pass judgment. He must ask himself whether, amidst all the clamor of conflicting demands, obligations, and principles, and amidst all the stresses and fatigues of ultimate responsibility, a statesman may fairly be censured for disregarding facts and conditions whose significance proved critical in the light of subsequent developments. If, as is often the case, the discernment of the true scale of events required a degree of prescience on the statesman's part, then it is fatuous to criticize him for mistaking his aim. It is hard enough to comprehend the present without attempting to divine the future as well. But an absence of foresight is not the same as myopia, and if a condition is manifest to a statesman's contemporaries and they go to great lengths to make their perceptions known to him, then he may properly be judged guilty of impolicy if he consistently fails to give due weight to their counsels. Such an indictment comes lodged against Franklin Roosevelt for his refusal throughout the war years to acknowledge constantly accumulating evidence that in Stalin he was dealing with a man whose basic moral orientation was hopelessly at variance with his own. Churchill, who was predisposed by temperament to suspect that this was so all along, subordinated his suspicions to the dictates of military expediency up until the last year of the war. From August 1944 onward, however, he was ever more vigilantly on his guard, and he sought with mounting anxiety to convert Roosevelt to his views.

The President was not to be convinced. Like Wilson before him, he was caught up in a great-hearted but dangerously inopportune crusade to enthrone Good Will and Fair Play alongside Power and Fear as arbiters of international behavior. He would not believe that Stalin regarded such considerations as irrelevant to the conduct of human affairs or that Churchill's forebodings were anything more than the grumblings of an aging anti-Bolshevik. Then too, he was tired; tired, as it turned out, unto death. And Winston was so importunate, so unrelenting in the adduction of one argument after another to support his every position that after a while one grew weary of attempting to debate with him. "He always out-argues me," was the way Lord Fisher had put it in 1915 in explaining his decision to resign as First Sea Lord, and Fisher's discomfiture was by no means atypical. Churchill always bombarded his interlocutors with so many facts, figures, and impassioned phrases that eventually they were reduced to the expedient of saying simply that he had not convinced them. Not only was this irritating from the point of view of their *amour-propre*, it also provoked Winston to press on, more tenacious than ever, with demands to know in which particulars his arguments were unpersuasive. Roosevelt, who had stood this constant badgering in good humor for three hectic years, found his patience wearing thin in 1944–45, and Churchill's obliviousness to the impact he had on the people around him did nothing to ameliorate the situation. Oftentimes it is not enough to be right; one must also take into account the reasons why others are wrong, especially if one wishes to convert them. But the capacity for discerning the emotional biases which usually underlie errors in political judgment was foreign to Churchill's nature, and the more urgently he urged vigilance with respect to Stalin's intentions, the less Roosevelt paid him heed.

Both Churchill and Roosevelt understood, of course, that Russia, which had been cruelly mutilated by Germany twice within the space of thirty years, was not going to be content with anything less than a *cordon sanitaire* of its own once the fighting in Europe was ended. Where they differed was in their estimate of just how broad a cordon the Russians would usurp and of just how ruthless they would be about regimenting the countries within it. Contrary to popular opinion, it was not the agreements made at Teheran and Yalta which decided these questions, nor was it at these high-level gatherings that Eastern Europe was "lost." The worst charge to be made against Churchill and Roosevelt in connection with the two Big Three meetings they attended together is that they were far too casual about trusting themselves to living accommodations where everything they said could be listened to and recorded by the Soviet Secret Police. It is staggering to realize today that FDR stayed in the Russian Embassy at Teheran and that both he and Churchill placed themselves unreservedly in Soviet hands in the Crimea. Some day in the far future the USSR may acknowledge the existence and publish the results of its eavesdroppings in 1943 and 1945, and then we will certainly get a new perspective on Allied policy. At the time, however, neither Stalin nor Molotov could have learned much that they did not already know, except perhaps that Churchill and FDR were sincere about what they said at the conference table. Such sincerity could only have mystified the two Russians.

No, it was not at Teheran and Yalta that the fate of Eastern Europe was sealed, and the concessions Roosevelt made at these meetings are not the ones for which he must be held accountable before the bar of history—where all of his very great positive achievements must also be considered. Eastern Europe was lost on the battlefield as the Soviet Nemesis marched toward Berlin, and to see why much of it need not have been we must go back briefly to the autumn of 1939.

The reader will remember that the Soviet Union overran eastern Poland two weeks after Germany attacked from the west. This action was more in the nature of a peaceful occupation than an invasion, for Poland and Russia were not at war and virtually all Polish forces were engaged in the struggle against the Nazis. When the fighting ended, some hundreds of thousands of Polish soldiers chose to give themselves up to Russian rather than German supervision, but, pursuant to the terms of the Nazi-Soviet Pact, Stalin handed most of them over to Hitler's minions for service in forced-labor battalions. According to the Geneva Convention officers could not be compelled to engage in manual labor, forced or otherwise, and perhaps ten thousand of them remained under Russian control in three camps situated in a forest along the Dnieper River called Katyn. Along with members of the underground, these men, liberals and intellectuals mostly, were the nucleus of any free and democratic—or bourgeois, if you like—Poland that might emerge from the war, but for six months the Polish government-in-exile was able to obtain only sporadic reports about their conditions of captivity. Then, after April 1940, nothing.

When Hitler struck east in June 1941 all Polish internees in Soviet hands were hastily liberated and enrolled in a new Polish army to fight the Hun—all, that is, except the officers from the Katyn area. Inquiries from the government-in-exile elicited little or nothing as to their whereabouts, and for almost two years their fate remained a mystery. Then, in April 1943, the Germans announced the discovery of mass graves where the camps had once stood. Stalin heatedly denied responsibility of course, but both the facts and the logic of the situation told against him, on top of which the Polish émigrés had corroborative evidence of their own which implicated him conclusively. This episode—if not the slaughter of the Kulaks and the hecatomb of the Purges—should have served as a clear warning to Roosevelt that he might not have the true measure of the man he was seeking to "handle," and the events that were to occur in the summer of 1944 should certainly have confirmed his disillusionment.

On July 29, 1944 Moscow Radio called on the people of German-occupied Warsaw to launch a general uprising in connection with the arrival of Soviet troops on the city's outskirts, and less than three days later the insurrection began. Almost immediately the Russian drive toward the city stopped dead, and Hitler, enraged, ordered the insurgents crushed with every resource of *schrecklichkeit* he could command. No fewer than eight German divisions, two of them SS, descended on the Polish capital, and all throughout August and early September the most vicious street- and sewer-fighting imaginable convulsed the city while Stalin's armies stood idle ten miles from its center. Roosevelt and Churchill made repeated appeals to the Marshal at least to permit British and American planes to fly in supplies, but they received only the stoniest refusals in response. It was not until September 10 that the Red Army sluggishly resumed its advances, but even then its attacks were not pressed with any vigor. Early in October the hopelessly lacerated Polish underground gave up.

The lesson of Warsaw and Katyn was clear: whatever lip service Stalin might pay to the concepts of democracy and self-determination in Eastern Europe, he was determined to carve out for himself a huge slice of territory from the Baltic to the Adriatic and unmercifully subjugate the peoples living there. The conclusion to be drawn from this lesson was clearer still: Anglo-American armies should meet Soviet armies as far east as possible—and then stay put until the Yalta and Teheran accords were implemented in keeping with the letter and spirit of their provisions. It was Roosevelt's great failure that he did not grasp this, and Churchill, now decidedly the junior partner in the alliance, was powerless to save the situation. It was al-

most like 1938 all over again. "I could at this stage only warn
and plead," he wrote of the eve of victory. "I moved amid
cheering crowds . . . with an aching heart and a mind op-
pressed by forebodings."[1] The crowning insult came early
in April 1945 when Stalin, imputing to Roosevelt and Churchill precisely the sort of treachery he would have engaged
in himself had the roles been reversed, accused his allies of
negotiating secretly with the German High Command in order
to facilitate a maximum eastward advance. FDR was stung to
real anger by this slur, and in a fiery telegram to Stalin he
termed the charges "vile misrepresentations" of his actions
that caused him "bitter resentment."[2] He was by now, however, a desperately sick man, and the flame of his indignation
quickly flickered out. On April 11, still optimistic, he sent his
last message to Churchill: "I would minimize the general Soviet problem as much as possible, because these problems, in
one form or another, seem to arise every day, and most of them
straighten out. . . . We must be firm, however, and our course
thus far is correct."[3]

The next day Franklin Roosevelt was dead.

For Churchill, the last two years of the war were spent in a
frenetic sort of perpetual motion necessitated in part by matters of state and in part by an urge to sublimate his frustration
over the Roosevelt-Stalin entente. Two months after returning from Quadrant he set off for Teheran and there celebrated
"the most memorable of my birthdays" with the American
President and the Soviet Premier. At dinner on November 30
Roosevelt presented him with a bowl from the Kashan region
of Iran (purchased at the local U.S. Army PX), and the next
morning Churchill formally expressed his gratitude in a note
which concluded: "I cannot thank you enough for all your
friendship and support in the years in which we have worked
together...."*[4]

---

* Shortly after arriving back in Washington Roosevelt discovered that this
friendship and support had hitherto unsuspected roots in consanguinity.
"Dear Clemmie and Winston," he wrote on January 4, "I find the enclosed clipping [from the Salt Lake City *Deseret News*] on my return
home . . . the last sentence shows that Winston is a sixth cousin, twice

One of the major topics of discussion at Teheran had been Overlord, and for the first five months of 1944 this mammoth undertaking was Churchill's main preoccupation. As D-Day approached, however, he found himself embroiled in a heated dispute with both Eisenhower and King George VI over his expressed intention to watch the landings personally from aboard the cruiser *Belfast*. "A man who has to play an effective part in taking . . . grave and terrible decisions of war," he wrote, "may need the refreshment of adventure. He may need also the comfort that when sending so many others to their death he may share in a small way their risks."[5] The King was vehemently opposed to his going, though, and at last Winston had to content himself with a visit to the Normandy beaches on June 12. He was not to be totally balked in his determination to observe a major amphibious assault at first hand, however. August 15 found him aboard the destroyer HMS *Kimberly* no more than seven thousand yards from the Riviera coastline which British, French, and American forces were storming in Anvil-Dragoon, the companion operation to Overlord.

Two weeks after returning from the Mediterranean Churchill embarked on the *Queen Mary* for his last wartime crossing of the Atlantic, and on September 11 he met Roosevelt at Octagon, the second Quebec Conference. The major issues discussed at the Citadel were British participation in the war against Japan in the Pacific and the treatment to be accorded Germany when the fighting ended in Europe. After the conference concluded, Winston paid a brief visit to Hyde Park, where he and FDR, as usual, stayed up talking far into the night. Hopkins was present also, but to Churchill's dismay no longer one of the President's inner circle. His health had proved too precarious and his unpopularity with many segments of the press, the State Department, and Congress was too pronounced to permit Roosevelt the continued luxury of his close companionship. He and Churchill were still on the best

removed" (*F.D.R.: His Personal Letters*, p. 1480). Actually, Churchill and FDR were seventh cousins once removed (see page 48), their common ancestors being Henry and Helena Glover, seventeenth-century residents of New Haven, Connecticut.

of terms, though, and it was with real emotion that they bade each other farewell on the evening of September 19 as Winston set off for New York to rejoin the *Queen Mary* for the voyage home.

Now began a series of journeys for Churchill which was to continue virtually nonstop until Roosevelt's death and the dissolution of the National Coalition compelled him to concentrate on developments back in England. In October he flew to Moscow to grapple person-to-person with Stalin one last time. In November he flew to liberated Paris for a triumphal procession with De Gaulle down the Champs Elysees and then went southward for a look at the fighting front. In December he was in Athens to help quell an incipient civil war between Communist and non-Communist factions there, and in January he visited Belgium and northern France in the wake of the Battle of the Bulge. February 1945 was the month of Yalta, and in March, after brief stops in Brussels and the Netherlands, Churchill crossed the Rhine barely twenty-four hours behind the leading elements of Eisenhower's armies.

The passing of the President of course affected Churchill very deeply, and in his eulogy in the House of Commons he told his colleagues how much his lively correspondence and face-to-face meetings ("in all about one hundred and twenty days of close personal contact") with Roosevelt had meant to him: "I conceived an admiration for him as a statesman, a man of affairs, and a war leader. I felt the utmost confidence in his upright, inspiring character and outlook, and a personal regard—affection, I must say—for him beyond my power to express today...."[6]

Now an unknown factor, Harry Truman, sat in the Oval Office, and it was with him that Churchill undertook to deal with the collapse of the Third Reich and the apparition of Soviet power in Central Europe.

Truman was soon to be confronted with an unknown factor himself, however, in the person of Clement Attlee, for less than three weeks after V-E Day the coalition government in Great Britain broke up and Churchill was obliged to form a caretaker administration pending the outcome of a general election. Winston counted on his personal popularity—which had never once fallen below 75 percent in the Gallup polls during the war—to help keep the Conservative party in power. The Labourites, for their part, feared that his self-confidence might be all too well founded and went to great lengths to tell the electorate, "You can't vote for Churchill unless you live in Woodford."* The Tories, on the other hand, seemed at first to be somewhat careless about the vote-getting value of their greatest political asset. "I notice in the newspaper," Churchill wrote waspishly to a high party functionary, "that the Central Office or Party Chiefs have issued instructions that no one over seventy should be tolerated as a candidate at the forthcoming election. I naturally wish to know at the earliest moment whether this ban applies to me."[7] Several dozen top-ranking Tories promptly fell over themselves in their haste to smooth the Prime Minister's ruffled feathers.

The Conservatives had greater problems to contend with than their chief vote-getter's pique, however. Ten years had passed since the British electorate had last had an opportunity to express itself, and the world had turned several somersaults in that momentous decade. All the Tories could show for their efforts as an independent majority through 1940 was the disaster of appeasement and a badly botched war effort. Still more detrimental to their ambitions, though, was a profound shift in the social and political orientation of the average British voter, a shift which was now about to manifest itself in a most emphatic manner.

Churchill was at Potsdam with Truman and Stalin when the results began to come in on July 25, and he immediately flew home to be on hand for the nation's verdict on his leadership —for it was in those terms that he conceived of the election. It came as a violent shock. After "five years and three months of world war, at the end of which time all our enemies [had] surrendered unconditionally or [were] about to do so, I was immediately dismissed by the British Electorate from all further conduct of their affairs."[8]

Stunned and hurt, the new leader of His Majesty's loyal op-

* Woodford was a subdivision of Churchill's former Epping constituency which, due to population growth, now merited more than a single MP.

position went away to Lake Como and the French Riviera to recover his battered spirits. ". . . The verdict of the electors had been so overwhelmingly expressed that I did not wish to remain even for an hour responsible for their affairs,"[9] he wrote from the depths of his disappointment.

But with painting and sunshine, the sting of what he believed to be his countrymen's rejection of him began not to prick quite so sharply. Even though he had indeed traversed his allotted threescore years and ten, he was still not ready to acquiesce in any permanent exclusion from the seat of power. He was in opposition, so he would oppose, and meanwhile he would speak his mind on all the many unresolved issues that were the legacy of the second global conflict of the century. His battle for continued political predominance had been lost, but the war in which he had played so signal a role had been won. Now he turned his thoughts to the nourishment and preservation of the fragile peace.

Part Three

COUNSELOR
AND
COMPATRIOT

CHAPTER THIRTEEN

Iron Curtain

✕ THE FACT that the last twenty years of Churchill's life are often considered anticlimactic is a good measure of his accomplishments during the first seventy. For just about anyone else in the world a Prime Ministry, a Nobel Prize, and ten volumes of historical prose would stand forth as the impressive record of a lifetime. For Churchill, however, the achievement of these summits in the space of less than two decades is somehow regarded as disappointing. He was like Horatius in the years after the Etruscans' defeat: greatly honored, widely hailed, but with no more bridges to defend.

There were bridges still standing, of course, and Horatii still required to defend them, but the responsibility was no longer in European hands. The most that the Old World democracies could offer their New World protector in the early postwar years was good counsel, and in January 1946 the Old World's leading democrat set off across the Atlantic carrying with him a good supply of it. "I think I can be of some use over there," he told Wilson; "they will take things from me."[1]

Late in 1945, when Churchill's plans to come to America were made public, Franc Lewis ("Bullet") McCluer, the president of a small Presbyterian college in Fulton, Missouri, called Westminster, contacted Brigadier General Harry Vaughan (class of '16), military aide to the president of a large nonsectarian republic in North America. McCluer told Vaughan that Westminster needed an eminent speaker—"of international reputation," according to the terms of the endowment—to deliver the annual Green Foundation lecture early in March.[2] Vaughan, the faithful alumnus, promptly got McCluer an appointment with fellow Missourian Harry Truman, who proved to be very sympathetic to Westminster's cause. He not only agreed to forward the college's speaking invitation to Chartwell under the aegis of the Presidential Seal, he also scribbled across the bottom of it, "This is a very fine old* college in my state. I will be very glad to go out with you and introduce you. I hope you can come."[3]

Thus the stage was set for what was to become "Fulton's Finest Hour."

Before that hour struck, however, Churchill had much more recuperating to do from the stresses of wartime leadership, and even he acknowledged it. "I want sun, solitude, serenity, and something to eat," he confided to Wilson, "and perhaps something to drink."[4] On January 14, accordingly, he and Clementine arrived in New York aboard the *Queen Elizabeth* en route to the Miami Beach estate of his erstwhile host at the Lake of Snows, Colonel Frank Clarke (see page 194). Waiting for him at Pier 90 on Fiftieth Street was one of the largest press contingents ever to cover a New York event, not to mention a good-sized crowd of well-wishers endeavoring with improvised "credentials" to convince police guards that they were the journalistic representatives of such diverse institutions as the Columbia Business School, the Harvard Club, and Lord & Taylor's Charge Account Department.[5] Baruch was on hand as well, along with several high-ranking military officials.

At 9:30 P.M. Winston and Clementine descended the gangplank to the sounds of cheers and applause. Churchill flashed the V sign and remarked, "I thank you for this very private reception."[6] He and his wife were then ushered into a large heated waiting room, and a proper press conference began:

Q.   Are you available for any syndicate offers?
A.   I am always prepared to accept any offer.
Q.   Will you comment on the socialist program of the Labor Party?
A.   I never criticize the government of my country abroad. I very rarely leave off criticizing it at home.

---

* Old by Missouri standards: Westminster was founded in 1851.

Q. Do you expect to eat much in America?
A. After rationing I hope to make up for lost time; I cannot say for lost weight.
Q. What is your reaction to the British White Paper fixing a quota for Jewish immigration into Palestine?
A. I am opposed to it. As you know, I am a Zionist from the very beginning of this great experiment.
Q. What is your reaction to the fact that you will be living in Florida near Al Capone?
A. Oh, you refer to the former distinguished resident of Chicago. I had not addressed myself to the problem.
Q. How do you feel about sharing the secret of the atomic bomb?
A. I think it would be a great mistake to share it until there have been arrangements made for the control of such a dread agency.
Q. Is it true that you are writing your memoirs?
A. No. And I don't know that I shall write them, or whether if I write them they will ever be published while I am still alive. But you don't know when I may jot down a few things that might be of interest.
Q. Are you taking a train tonight?
A. I am *leaving* on a train which is *going out.*

And indeed he was. With the reporters satisfied, he posed for a last few photographs and then announced cheerfully, "I'm off for Alabam'—or thereabouts." The next stop on his itinerary was Pennsylvania Station, and the next stop after that, Miami Beach.[7]

The Churchills arrived in Florida on the morning of January 16 after a train journey pleasantly punctuated at every major station by the plaudits of friendly crowds. They settled in to Colonel Clarke's house on North Bay Road and formally faced reporters one last time before starting their vacation in earnest. Nothing much new emerged from this second press conference, but from Clementine's answer to the question "What should women do to contribute to world peace?" the reader may get an idea of just how long ago 1946 really is. "If you are young, get married and have babies," she said. "If you are old, I don't know. Keep out of the way, I suppose."[8]

Winston now broke out his paints while his wife gratefully broke open some of the two dozen freshly laid eggs that were delivered to the Clarke estate every other morning, compliments of the Miami Beach Rotary Club. (Eggs were among the most severely rationed commodities in Great Britain at this time.) After a day of sniffing around, Churchill selected a view of Di-Lido Island on the Venetian Way for his first canvas, and for a week or so thereafter he worked contentedly, painting pictures that were even brighter and more colorful than the sunlit landscapes which inspired them.

On January 25 a letter arrived from Harry Hopkins in New York. "Only being laid up in the hospital prevented me from meeting you at the boat the other day," he wrote. "All I can say about myself at the moment is that I am getting excellent care. . . . Do give my love to Clemmie. . . ."[9]

This was the last letter Hopkins ever wrote. On January 29 he died. "A strong, bright, fierce flame has burned out a frail body," Churchill mournfully observed. "Few know better than I the services he rendered to the world cause. To dynamic, compulsive, and persuasive force he added humor and charm in an exceptional degree. We do well to salute his memory. . . ."[10]

Saddened, the Churchills continued their vacation. They visited Cuba for a week, watched Eddie Arcaro boot home a winner at Hialeah, and, presumably, ate a large number of eggs. Winston also began to rough out the lineaments of the speech he would make at Fulton, and on February 10 he journeyed by air to Washington to discuss what he would say with President Truman. It was now becoming apparent to observant people that this speech was going to be something out of the ordinary. Speculation began to mount as to what the subject would be, and as Churchill boarded his plane for the return flight to Miami on February 12, reporters tried to pump him about it. "Did you discuss Russian relations with the President?" they inquired. "No comment," was Churchill's reply, and with a grin he added, "I think 'no comment' is a splendid expression. I am using it again and again. I got it from Sumner Welles during his tour of Europe."[11]

The winds of rumor and conjecture blew harder once Winston was back in Florida, especially after Secretary of State James Byrnes made what was officially termed a "friendly social call" on him there.[12] Even after the Byrnes visit, though, the subject of the speech remained undisclosed.

On February 26, with his vacation drawing to a close, Churchill made his first formal public appearance. Before a crowd of eighteen thousand people at the Orange Bowl he accepted an honorary Doctor of Laws degree from the University of Miami. "I have enjoyed my stay in your genial sunshine," he told his audience, "and it has done me a lot of good. . . . I am surprised," he continued,

that in my later life I should have become so experienced in taking degrees when, as a schoolboy, I was so bad at passing examinations. In fact one might almost say that no one ever passed so few examinations and received so many degrees. From this a superficial thinker might argue that the way to get the most degrees is to fail the most examinations. This would, however, be a conclusion unedifying in the academic atmosphere in which I now preen myself, and I therefore hasten to draw another moral with which I am sure we shall all be in accord: namely, that no boy or girl should ever be disheartened by lack of success in his youth but should diligently persevere and make up for lost time. There at least is a sentiment in which I am sure the faculty and the public, the scholars and the dunces will all be cordially united. . . .

Although the tone was playful, the scarring memories were apparently still vivid.

The moment had come to bid Miami Beach adieu. On the evening of March 1 the Churchills attended a farewell dinner in their honor at the Surf Club and then boarded a private railway car for the trip to Washington. The pleasure portion of this trip to the United States was over. Now it was time to get down to business.

Winston and Clementine, together with their daughter Sarah, arrived in Washington on Sunday, the third, and were met at Union Station by Randolph, who, fittingly enough, was in the United States on a lecture tour. The reunited family took up residence at the British Embassy, and after a drive around the city in brisk sunny weather redolent of approaching spring, Winston applied himself with a will to his Westminster address. Next morning he joined Truman aboard a ten-car Presidential Special and headed west.

For the first several hours out of Washington the Briton and the Missourian discussed together the Civil War countryside that was passing outside the window. Winston related the Barbara Frietchie incident of 1943, and even put on a repeat performance of his recitation. His mind was primarily on his speech, however, and for most of the day he shut himself up in his Pullman bedroom, revising, rephrasing, and rehearsing. He emerged at dinnertime reasonably satisfied, and spent the rest of the evening in relaxed badinage with his host. "I have only one complaint to make of the American people," he told Truman: "you stop drinking with your meals." The President supplied some appropriate rejoinder about how that custom enabled the United States to save enough money on wine and spirits to lend large amounts to Great Britain—as it was about to do now, for example, Congress willing.* Churchill counterpunched with "The great American pastime these days seems to be twisting the loan's tail." Mr. Truman retired to his bed.[13]

It was not, perhaps, coincidental that March 5, 1946, witnessed not only the ceremonies at Fulton but also the delivery of two United States notes of protest to the Soviet Union, one in reference to the unauthorized Russian presence in Iran and the other in reference to the Red Army's confiscatory occupation policies in Manchuria. Both the protests and the address Churchill gave marked a crucial, though studiously unacknowledged, shift in western diplomacy vis-à-vis Stalin, such a crucial shift, in fact, that the Truman administration thought it advisable to maintain the pretense that the President did not know what his British guest was going to say.

The special train carrying the two men pulled into Jefferson City at 11:20 A.M., and, after a brief motorcade through the town, Truman and Churchill were driven the twenty-five miles to Fulton. Lunch followed at the home of Bullet McCluer, and then came, in a very real sense, the moment of truth.

---

* A loan of $3,750 million had been negotiated by John Maynard Keynes and was, at the time of the Fulton speech, being debated on Capitol Hill.

Truman's introduction was characteristically short and to the point, and he concluded it with "I know [Mr. Churchill] will have something constructive to say." There was loud applause. Then Winston started to speak.

He began with a disclaimer: "Let me . . . make it clear that I have no official mission of any kind and that I speak only for myself." He continued by stating that the paramount task facing the world was the prevention of another global war and that the United Nations was the key to the accomplishment of that task. He added, however, that neither peace nor the UN could be preserved in the absence of a "special relationship" of fraternal association between the British Commonwealth and the United States, and he expressed again his hope that the future would see the English-speaking peoples united by a common citizenship.

All this was essentially prologue, and after elaborating on such themes for several minutes, he turned his attention to what Harry Hopkins would have referred to as "the root of the matter."

. . . It is my duty to place before you certain facts about the present situation in Europe.

From Stettin in the Baltic to Trieste in the Adriatic an iron curtain has descended across the continent. Behind that line lie all the capitals of central and eastern Europe. Warsaw, Berlin, Prague, Vienna, Budapest, Belgrade, Bucharest, and Sofia, all these famous cities and the populations around them lie in what I must call the Soviet sphere, and all are subject, in one form or another, not only to Soviet influence but to a very high and in some cases increasing measure of control from Moscow. . . .

An attempt is being made by the Russians in Berlin to build up a quasi-Communist party in their zone of occupied Germany by showing special favour to groups of left-wing German leaders. At the end of the fighting last June the American and British armies withdrew westward, in accordance with an earlier agreement, to a depth at some points of 150 miles upon a front of nearly 400 miles, in order to allow our Russian allies to occupy this vast expanse of territory which the western democracies had conquered.

If now the Soviet Government tries, by separate action, to build up a pro-Communist Germany in their areas, this will cause new serious difficulties in the American and British zones, and will give the defeated Germans the power of putting themselves up to auction between the Soviets and the western democracies. Whatever conclusions may be drawn from these facts—and facts they are—this is certainly not the liberated Europe we fought to build up. Nor is it one which contains the essentials of permanent peace. . . .

On the other hand, ladies and gentlemen, I repulse the idea that a new war is inevitable; still more that it is imminent. It is because I am sure that our fortunes are still . . . in our own hands, and that we hold the power to save the future, that I feel the duty to speak out now that I have the occasion and opportunity to do so.

I do not believe that Soviet Russia desires war. What they desire is the fruits of war and the indefinite expansion of their power and doctrines. . . .

From what I have seen of our Russian friends and allies during the war, I am convinced that there is nothing they admire so much as strength, and there is nothing 'for which they have less respect than weakness, especially military weakness.

For that . . . reason the old doctrine of a balance of power is unsound. We can not afford, if we can help it, to work on narrow margins, offering temptations to a trial of strength.

If the western democracies stand together in strict adherence to the principles of the United Nations Charter, their influence for furthering those principles will be immense and no one is likely to molest them. If, however, they become divided or falter in their duty, and if these all-important years are allowed to slip away, then indeed catastrophe may overwhelm us all. . . .

Last time I saw it all coming and cried aloud to my own fellow countrymen and to the world, but no one paid any attention. Up till the year 1933 or even 1935 Germany might have been saved from the awful fate which has overtaken her and we might all have been spared the miseries that Hitler let loose upon mankind.

There never was a war in history easier to prevent by timely action than the one which has just desolated such great areas of the globe. It could have been prevented, in my belief, without the firing of a single shot, and Germany might be powerful, prosperous and honoured today, but no one would listen and one by one we were all sucked into the awful whirlpool.

We surely, ladies and gentlemen, I put it to you . . . surely we must not let that happen again. This can only be achieved by reaching now, in 1946 . . . a good understanding on all points with Russia under the general authority of the United Nations Organization and by the maintenance of that good understanding through many peaceful years by the world instrument, supported by the whole strength of the English-speaking world and all its connections. . . .

If the population of the English-speaking Commonwealth be added to that of the United States, with all such cooperation implies in the air, on the sea, all over the globe, and in science and in industry, and in moral force, there will be no quivering, precarious balance of power to offer its temptation to ambition or adventure. On the contrary, there will be an overwhelming assurance of security.

If we adhere faithfully to the Charter of the United Nations and walk forward in sedate and sober strength, seeking no one's land or treasure, seeking to lay no arbitrary control upon the thoughts of men, if all British moral and material forces and convictions are joined with your own in fraternal association, the high roads of the future will be clear, not only for us but for all, not only for our time but for a century to come.

Thus was the concept of the Iron Curtain born—or perhaps "baptized" is the more precise term, since the phrase was hardly new in diplomatic parlance. Churchill himself had used it in a letter to Truman ten months earlier,[14] and credit for originating the expression back in 1942 goes to, of all people, Hitler's Finance Minister, Schwerin von Krosigk.

Whatever its provenance, "Iron Curtain" was now in the language to stay, and the speech that put it there was now part of history. Rarely—no, never before—had a single public address generated such a typhoon of responses. Here was the former leader of one of the Big Three Powers sharing a platform with the current leader of another barely six months after the Axis had been conquered and declaring that the third represented a threat to world order. In Congress three senators got together to announce that they considered the speech "shocking."[15] A New York periodical, *P.M.*, called it an "ideological declaration of war against Russia."[16] Under-Secretary of State Dean Acheson hastily reconsidered a commitment to attend a dinner in Churchill's honor at the Waldorf-Astoria. And in Moscow Joseph Stalin termed his former ally a "warmonger" and a "firebrand of war."

The positive reactions were just as intense as the negative ones. "A great speech by a great man," said one congressman,

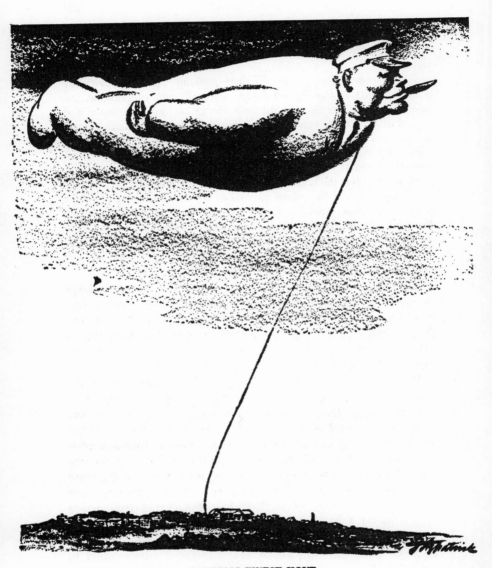

FULTON'S FINEST HOUR

This cartoon by Fitzpatrick appeared in the St. Louis *Post Dispatch* on the day Churchill delivered his "Iron Curtain" speech at Fulton, Missouri—March 5, 1946.

"a realistic speech by a realistic man."[17] "Brilliant," said the *Wall Street Journal*, with a "hard core of indisputable fact." Finally there was the New York *Times*'s appraisal: "Mr. Churchill came with a message of such interest and importance to our country, to his, and to the world at large that he converted his presence at Fulton into a historic event and in doing so established new bonds between the Westminster that is the heart of Britain and the many Westminsters from one shore of this land to the other."[18]

Truman and Churchill left Fulton together on the evening of March 5 and reboarded their special train at Jefferson City. They parted company next morning in Columbus, where the President was due to make a speech. Winston continued on to Washington, arriving on the morning of the seventh. Guests at the British Embassy for dinner on the evening of his return were Mr. and Mrs. Acheson. The Under-Secretary had not yet cancelled his plans to attend the Waldorf dinner, so the occasion was a pleasant one. Mrs. Acheson, it turned out, was one of the former Prime Minister's most ardent admirers. Even better, she was a fellow painter of considerable accomplishment and skill. Greatly pleased by her outspoken praise of his Fulton address, Winston insisted she give him an equally candid critique of his paintings, expecting no doubt a further helping of encomia. What he got, however, was the frank opinion "Your palette is keyed too high," and a debate of some pungency ensued. Acheson remembered that when the guests got up from the table Churchill's cigar was going like "a steam locomotive on a stiff grade." He didn't much like being disagreed with, but he did greatly admire people who staunchly defended their own points of view. "A woman of conviction, your wife," he said to the Under-Secretary, and henceforth regarded her as one of his favorite people.[19]

On Friday, the eighth, Churchill journeyed down to Richmond to address the Virginia Joint Assembly. Smarting a bit from the furious controversy his Westminster speech had stirred up, he rhetorically inquired of the legislators, "Do you not think you are running some risk in inviting me to give you my faithful counsel on this occasion? You have not asked to see what I am going to say. I might easily, for instance, blurt out a lot of things people know in their hearts are true but are a bit shy of saying in public, and this might cause a regular commotion and get you all into trouble." Judging by their laughter, the members of the Assembly were willing to take the risk, and judging by the rest of Churchill's speech, he did not repent of a single syllable he had uttered at Westminster College. "Peace will not be preserved by pious sentiments," he concluded. "It will not be preserved by casting aside in dangerous times the panoply of warlike strength. . . . Great Heart must have his sword and armour to guard the pilgrims on their way. . . ."

After the applause had died down, Army Chief of Staff Eisenhower delivered a tribute to the speaker: "It is my earnest conviction that only history can measure the true value . . . of the service he has rendered to all of us. . . ."

The General accompanied Churchill down to Colonial Williamsburg. There the authenticity of the setting was unexpectedly heightened by a bit of real-life drama. The two men had just climbed into an open eighteenth-century carriage for a tour of the town when photographers' flashbulbs caused the horses pulling it to rear violently in their traces. Eisenhower grabbed Winston's arm protectively while Winston himself settled his hat more firmly on his head and clamped down on his cigar. The horses were eventually restrained and the tour proceeded—on foot. "I'm afraid we've let you down," said host John D. Rockefeller III. "Don't mind, old boy," replied his unruffled guest. "I'm having a lot of fun."[20]

Back in Washington on Saturday, Churchill met in the office of Secretary of War Patterson with many of the senior military chiefs he had dealt with during the war. He recalled his first view of the nascent American army at Fort Jackson in 1942 and described its rapid evolution into battle-worthy cadres numbering in the millions as "an achievement which the soldiers of every other country will always study with admiration and with envy."[21]

After a restful Sunday at the British Embassy, Sarah, Clementine, and Winston made ready to depart for New York. Churchill made a farewell call on Truman at the White House and then went over to the State Department to say good-bye to Secretary Byrnes. After this meeting Clementine tried to hurry him along, as he was late for a luncheon of the Overseas Press Club. "You've no right to keep people waiting," she scolded as he dawdled over his papers. "You are wrong, my dear," he responded. "I am in the position of a condemned man. If he takes his time over his breakfast before he is led to his execution and is urged to hurry, he can truthfully and properly say, 'You are obliged to wait for me because without me there would be no ceremony!' "[22]

The reporters forgave him his unpunctuality, and after a couple of hours of give-and-take with them he gathered up his wife and daughter and set off by train for New York.

The Churchills arrived at Pennsylvania Station shortly before 9:00 P.M. on March 11, and were driven directly to the Waldorf, where they again took up residence after an interval of fourteen "not entirely uneventful" years. Baruch stopped by to make sure they were comfortably settled and also, perhaps, to forestall his friend from grabbing a taxi and setting off in search of his apartment. All was well, and Churchill prudently stayed all night in his suite.

March 12 was a special day: it marked the eleventh month since FDR's death and the last pilgrimage of a former colleague to his Hudson River home. Together with Eleanor Roosevelt, Churchill walked to the site of the President's grave. Once there, he stood apart, bareheaded and silent, lost in memories of his departed friend. Bright sunshine played on the simple stone of white marble, and a sharp breeze ruffled the pine boughs surrounding it. A fresh wreath of carnations and rhododendron leaves lay where Churchill had set it down. Only two jinking swallows and the wind tinged the silence. After several minutes Winston turned away, eyes brimming. As he walked from the grave site, hat in hand, someone heard him sigh to himself very softly, "Lord, how I loved that man."

From Hyde Park Churchill traveled on to Albany for a meeting with Governor Dewey. He stayed the night in the Executive Mansion and returned next morning to New York, where the big news was the presence of Russian tanks and planes within twenty miles of Teheran. Many people felt the situation was dismally reminiscent of 1938, and Stalin added to the gloomy sense of *déjà vu* by declaring in a *Pravda* interview, "If Winston Churchill and his friends start a war against Russia now as they did after World War I, they will be beaten, just as they were beaten twenty-six years ago."

Meanwhile, New York City's official greeter and master of ceremonies, Grover Whelan, had other, not altogether unrelated, problems to contend with. He was responsible for organizing the city's tribute to Churchill (scheduled a bit clumsily for the Ides of March) and both Irishmen and Communists were disenchanted by the prospect. "Honorable Sir," said one letter Whelan received. "Surely a man with the good old Irish name of Whelan would not be anxious to give the glad hand to a Churchill, considering he springs from one of the most anti-Irish cliques evolved in modern England."[23] A further problem was that the Mayor, whose name happened to be O'Dwyer, was becoming a bit anxious about honoring a famous link to the Black-and-Tans. When he heard that the CIO might stage a protest during the Waldorf dinner, therefore, he quickly informed his harassed official greeter that he would under no circumstances cross a picket line.

Of course the gruesome irony about all this ruckus was that Churchill had been one of the most instrumental factors in bringing about an Irish settlement in the years before and after World War I. As a Liberal he had been a staunch advocate of Irish independence since 1905, and as Secretary of State for the Colonies in 1922 he had helped negotiate the Ulster compromise which made that independence possible. It was Churchill's father who had taken a somewhat refractory attitude on the Irish question, but sixty years later it was Winston himself who got the blame. After almost half a century in politics, however, he had developed a pretty thick skin, and on the eve of the ceremonies in his honor he imperturbably displayed —and imbibed—good spirits at a dinner given for him by Henry Luce at the Union Club.

Meteorologically speaking, March 15, 1946, was an unqualified misery: chill, gray, with drizzle and with rain. Adding to the general murk were the reports in the morning papers of Acheson's defection, along with a statement by James Roosevelt that Churchill "presented [only] the British point of view" at Westminster.[24]

Whelen arrived at Churchill's suite at 10:30 A.M. and told him of the foul weather. Winston thereupon produced, appropriately enough, an ulster weighing a good twenty pounds and professed himself ready to face the elements. Downstairs he asked that the top of the convertible touring car he was to ride in be lowered: "I'd like to see the people."[25] It was and he did.

And the people saw Churchill. The motorcade moved down Park Avenue to Twenty-third Street and then crossed to the West Side Highway for the trip to the Battery. Despite the rain, large crowds lined the streets downtown as the procession moved up Whitehall Street and Lower Broadway toward City Hall Plaza. Averaging out the estimates of Irish and non-Irish policemen, about four hundred thousand people turned out, not to mention many tens of thousands who looked on from office and hotel windows. In the Council Chamber at City Hall, Mayor O'Dwyer presented Churchill with New York's gold medal for distinguished service. Then it was back into the weather and uptown for a luncheon at the Metropolitan Club. After being introduced there by Fiorello La Guardia, Churchill acknowledged that the day's events had not unfolded under ideal conditions. "I've seen New York wet," he said. "I've seen it dry in other days, and I hope that you won't think me ungracious if I say that in both cases the result was not entirely in accord with human perfection."[26]

That was probably the least controversial public statement he ever made.

Beginning around 5:30 P.M., the first of what were eventually to be about a thousand pickets recruited from the ranks of New York's CIO and Communist party began to gather outside the Waldorf. By six a full-fledged demonstration was in progress, noisy enough to be heard all the way up in Churchill's suite on the twenty-eighth floor. There were chants: "G.I. Joe is home to stay; Winnie Winnie Go Away"; songs— this, for example, to the tune of "London Bridge," "The English people turned him down, turned him down, turned him down. The English people turned him down. *So Do We!*" and even epigrams: "The sun never sets on the British Empire because God doesn't trust Churchill."[27] When Winston heard that he was really amused. "It's the first time I've ever heard Communists call upon God for assistance," he told Whelan, and then went over to the window and called out, "Let's hear it again."[28]

By eight o'clock almost all the guests had arrived (except the Mayor, of course) and the CIO pickets began to disperse. His Honor scurried into the Grand Ballroom around 8:30, a bit late for the first course of Fumet of Gumbo Chervil, but in plenty of time for the ceremonial portions of the evening. It was well past 10:30, in fact, before Churchill, having been introduced in turn by Ambassador Winant, Governor Dewey, and Mayor O'Dwyer himself, finally got up to speak.

Restaurants and bars without radios were suddenly short of clientele that night, while those with radios enjoyed a temporary boom. Movie theaters emptied, and one restaurant manager said the whole atmosphere reminded him of 1941.[29]

In the Grand Ballroom, meanwhile, a capacity crowd of 1,624 paying guests faced the three-tiered dais where eighteen ambassadors and fifty assorted VIPs, including a former Assistant Secretary of State named Nelson Rockefeller, waited, like most of the nation, to hear what the old lion had to say.

"I think I must regard this wonderful gathering, the like of which I have never seen surpassed, as the culmination of my rest cure in the United States," he began. "When I spoke at Fulton ten days ago I felt it was necessary to speak in arresting terms about the present plight of the world." He paused. Had he reconsidered his position on Russia? Did he regret the force with which he had expressed himself at Westminster College? Slowly, and carefully enunciating each syllable, Winston gave his answer: "I do not wish to withdraw or modify a single word." This was said as much to Stalin as to the audience at the Waldorf, and it brought to mind Joan of Arc's famous retort to the bullying Duke de la Tremouille: "Thou'rt answered, old Gruff-and-Grum."

Churchill found the crowd's reaction highly gratifying, and

he sailed on through his speech to a sonorously optimistic conclusion: "We in the British Commonwealth will stand at your side in powerful and faithful friendship . . . and together I am sure we shall succeed in lifting from the face of man the curse of war and the darker curse of tyranny. . . ." It was a proud end to a long and strenuous day, and the next morning the *Times* noted, "No other man has a shorter or straighter road to the confidence, the respect and the affection of the American people."[30]

Churchill's U.S. odyssey was now drawing to a close. On Monday, the eighteenth, he received yet another honorary degree, this one from Columbia. Although 1,700 students voted to protest his Fulton address, "only" about 250 of them actually picketed the ceremonies. In his acceptance speech Winston adopted a somewhat lighter tone than he had been using since March 5 and suggested to "our Communist friends" that they study "the admirable modern works on the life and the soul of the white ant.* That will show them not only a great deal about their past, but will give a very fair indication of their future."

On Tuesday evening Baruch took him and Clementine to the old Hudson Theater on Forty-fourth Street to see the Lindsay-Crouse hit comedy *State of the Union*. One of the high points of the show came in Act II when the hero read out a humorous newspaper headline. The headline would change from day to day depending on current events, and on March 19 it was: AFTER STRENUOUS TWO WEEKS CHURCHILL FINALLY RELAXES IN NEW YORK SEEING PLAYS.[31]

March 20 was the last day of the visit. Winston paid a call on Cardinal Spellman and was shown around St. Patrick's Cathedral, but that was his only engagement. Shortly before midnight he and Clementine, accompanied by Baruch and Colonel Clarke, returned to Pier 90, where the *Queen Elizabeth* had deposited them over two months before. There they stepped aboard the *Queen Mary*, which would now carry

* Presumably the studies written by Jean Henri Fabre and Julian Huxley. A white ant is a termite.

them away. To an interviewer outside his stateroom Churchill confided, "I have enjoyed [my vacation in the United States] very much. I came here for a rest cure and now I am going home to have a rest after the rest cure."[32]

He wasn't going to have much of a rest though. He was still Leader of the Opposition, and Parliament was in session. In addition, the special case he carried with him, compliments of the Soundscriber Corporation of New Haven, Connecticut, indicated that resting would be a low-priority activity for the next several years, even in the absence of political obligations. "You don't know when I may jot down a few things that might be of interest," was how he had put it the night the *Queen Elizabeth* had arrived. Now, on the morning the *Queen Mary* was to depart, he might have said, "You don't know when I may dictate some." Inside the Soundscriber case were two electronic disk-recorders. The means for transcribing a definitive history of World War II were on their way to Great Britain along with the historian who was now about to recount it.

CHAPTER FOURTEEN

Mid-Century Convocation

ONE MUST GO BACK to Julius Caesar to find another man of Churchill's stature who was as proficient at writing history as at making it. And although the Second World War is generally ranked below The World Crisis as Churchill's most accomplished historical effort, the unique vantage point from which it is written renders it far and away the most significant labor he ever undertook. It is comparable in its importance to Napoleon's accounts of his campaigns or to Caesar's *Commentaries*, without being even remotely as self-serving. That the over-all quality of the work declines somewhat from volume to volume is hardly surprising, given the complications caused by a stroke and the author's advancing age (see Chapter 15). What is remarkable, on the other hand, is that the decline is so minimal and the general level of discourse so high. The first two volumes, *The Gathering Storm* and *Their Finest Hour*, were completed in 1947 and 1948 respectively, before the deterioration of Churchill's health began; they set a standard of excellence by which the succeeding volumes have been judged, and it is not in absolute but only in these relative terms that the later books suffer.

Churchill got to work on his memoirs soon after his return from America, and as he wrote he had the satisfaction of seeing that, for once, his warnings were not going to be disregarded. A year and a week after his Fulton speech the Truman Doctrine was promulgated, guaranteeing American support to "free peoples who are resisting attempted subjugation by armed minorities or by outside pressures." With this declaration the United States assumed responsibility for backing the existing regimes in Greece and Turkey against Communist insurgency, thereby relieving the British, who were financially unable to bear the burden any longer. Then, exactly fifteen months after Fulton, the new American Secretary of State, George Marshall, proposed a plan for European recovery at Harvard University. His ideas were received with enthusiasm on the Continent, and in less than a year the machinery for the plan's implementation was running smoothly.

Stalin reacted quickly to these initiatives. In February 1948 he engineered a Communist takeover in Czechoslovakia, and in June he closed off surface access to the city of Berlin from the west. While a massive airlift kept the German capital alive, Americans and western Europeans made haste to concert plans for mutual defense, and by the early spring of 1949 the North Atlantic Treaty was ready in Washington to be signed.

Thus, in the space of three years, the vigilance and military readiness for which Churchill had argued at Fulton were accomplished facts. And when an invitation came from the Massachusetts Institute of Technology to address their Mid-Century Convocation on the Social Implications of Science on the very eve of the signing of the NATO pact, Winston felt this would be the perfect occasion to review the international situation and to assess the changes that had taken place since 1946.

As on their previous visit the Churchills arrived in America aboard the *Queen Elizabeth*, accompanied this time by daughter Mary and son-in-law Christopher Soames. As on their 1931 visit they were met by the press at Quarantine rather than at dockside, but whereas eighteen years before, only a few dozen reporters and photographers had stormed their ship, on Wednesday morning, March 23, 1949, they were confronted by nearly two hundred: "the largest press group that ever went out to meet an incoming vessel," according to New York port officials.[1]

Winston was affable but evasive during fifteen minutes of questions in the *Queen Elizabeth's* theater. He declared himself "a whole-hearted supporter of the Atlantic Pact," which was hardly news, and he reaffirmed his misgivings about Russia and its iron curtain dependencies, which was hardly necessary.[2] During the rest of the conference he contented himself with feints and parries. A general election was looming on the horizon in Great Britain, and he could not afford to be as free and easy as in 1946. Thus when one reporter asked him about the life of the average Englishman in postwar times, all that was forthcoming by way of reply was: "It is too large a topic which might lead you into controversy, which you know we try to avoid—except on proper occasions."[3] Plainly this occasion was not a proper one.

Baruch was on hand to greet the *Queen Elizabeth* when it docked, and he deftly bundled the Churchills into his car for the trip to his East Sixty-sixth Street apartment, where they would be staying. Pickets on Twelfth Avenue representing such organizations as the National Council of American-Soviet Friendship and the Kings County American Labor Party flashed placards and shouted slogans as the Baruch limousine sped by, but all they got for their trouble was a big smile and a V sign.

After a quiet evening with his American host, Churchill set off by train for Washington on Thursday morning. A large and enthusiastic crowd met him at Union Station, and at the British Embassy the entire staff turned out to line the driveway in his honor. Touched, Winston asked that his car be stopped at the Embassy gate on Massachusetts Avenue and then walked up to the Ambassador's residence between two lines of cheering British subjects. A reception followed his arrival, and in the evening he was Truman's guest at an informal formal—or vice versa—dinner at Blair House. Marshall, now retired as Secretary of State, was present for the occasion as was his successor, Dean Acheson, now forgiven for his Waldorf-Astoria *démarche*. To Churchill's delight, Mrs. Acheson was there as well, and so were Margaret Truman, Vice President Barkley, Chief Justice Vinson, and the British Ambassador, Sir Oliver Franks.

On Friday morning Churchill spent an hour reminiscing in private with Marshall and then went to Blair House to thank

Truman for his hospitality and to say good-bye. Before taking leave of the President for the return journey to New York, Winston presented him with red Morocco-bound copies of *The Life of Marlborough* and *Their Finest Hour*. (He had sent *The Gathering Storm* to him in 1948.)

Churchill's train arrived at Pennsylvania Station shortly after 5:00 P.M., but the car with Churchill in it did not; it had been detached shortly before five and brought to a special siding. Thus he was able to evade reporters and speed directly to Baruch's apartment. There he hurriedly dressed for a large dinner Henry Luce was giving in his honor that evening at the Ritz-Carlton Hotel. The press did manage to waylay one of his staff, but unfortunately for them he proved to be the soul of discretion. Asked to confirm the fact that his chief had consumed a full bottle of brandy on the trip down to Washington, all the aide would say was "Don't you know Mr. Churchill is a teetotaler?"[4]

✳ This is probably as good a point as any to consider the fantasticated subject of Winston's drinking and the even more fanciful notion that he was in some way an alcoholic. Of course, he liked to drink. Like most supercharged people, he required a fairly constant degree of sedation to keep him from spinning out of control. He had, moreover, a turbulent cauldron of repressed childhood emotions to contend with, and while many of these could be sublimated in work, others required additional muting if recurring bouts with the dreaded "black dog" were to be avoided. Given these factors, Churchill found he could best maintain his psychological equilibrium by drinking steadily, *but not heavily*, throughout the day. In other words, he consumed prodigious amounts over the course of a morning, afternoon, and night, but rather less per hour than the average guest at the average cocktail party. At the same time he was also a formidable trencherman, and the net result was that he invariably metabolized alcohol faster than he imbibed it. No one, not even his closest friends, ever saw him heavily intoxicated, and, indeed, drunkenness was rather a deep-seated taboo with him. "I had been brought up and trained to have the utmost contempt for people who got drunk," he wrote in *My Early Life*,[5] and although he never carried this training to the point of intolerance where others' foibles were concerned, he was ruthlessly strict in applying it to himself.

Thus, I think, it is proper to conclude that Winston Churchill was "normal" on alcohol; that it served to stabilize him and kept him functioning at top efficiency. And if it be said that this conclusion inevitably entails a verdict that he was technically an alcoholic, then it would seem to follow that technical alcoholism is a condition that ought to be encouraged.

Despite the presence of fifteen hundred American Labor Party picketers outside, Luce's Ritz-Carlton dinner went very well—except from the point of view of one unfortunate guest. This was a chubby middle-aged gentleman who, all unwary, stepped out of his limousine at the Madison Avenue entrance wearing a black homburg and smoking a cigar. Churchill and Baruch could hear the loud boos that greeted the poor fellow as they entered the hotel on the deserted Forty-sixth Street side.[6]

Winston had dinner with Governor Dewey on Saturday night and then took all day Sunday off. On Monday he met with Eleanor Roosevelt and had dinner with the New York *Times* editorial board at the newspaper's headquarters on Forty-third Street. On Tuesday he attended a luncheon given by the American Committee on a United Europe and was Luce's guest at the Union Club in the evening. Also on Tuesday he met with American Zionist leaders to discuss Israel's future and the recent successful conclusion of the first Arab-Israeli war.* He assured them of his continuing support. "Remember," he said, "I was for a free and independent Israel all through the dark years when many of my most distinguished countrymen took a different view. So do not imagine for a moment that I have the slightest idea of deserting you now in your hour of glory."[7]

---

* Israel and Egypt had concluded an armistice on February 24; Israel and Lebanon on March 23. An armistice with Jordan was imminent and in fact was signed on April 3.

In Washington meanwhile, during a Congressional debate on Truman's proposed $5.5 billion authorization for the Marshall Plan, Republican Senator Langer of North Dakota charged that Churchill "took up arms for Spain" in Cuba during the Spanish-American War. He left his few drowsy listeners to divine for themselves the relevance of that accusation to European economic recovery. When Winston heard about it, however, he was irate, and he shot off a telegram to his friend Tom Connally, Chairman of the Foreign Relations Committee. Connally read out his rebuttal on the Senate floor on Wednesday evening. As a veteran of the Spanish-American War himself, moreover, the Senator from Texas was able to corroborate Churchill's claim that the United States and Spain had not been engaged in hostilities in 1895. As everyone seemed to agree, furthermore, that they had not been so engaged in 1946 either, it appeared that Winston's undisputed absence from Cuba during the other seventy-two years of his life constituted an air-tight alibi.

Once again a politician swept up in the blast of his own oratory had come a cropper by failing to do his homework.[8]

As Connally was refining Senator Langer's concept of chronology, Winston was seated in Louis Sherry's Restaurant on Park Avenue participating in a farewell dinner being given for him and Clementine by Baruch on the eve of their departure for MIT. Shortly after midnight the dinner broke up and "Bernie" accompanied his house guests down to Grand Central Station and their waiting train.

On his arrival at Boston's South Station Thursday morning, Winston was greeted by a throng of some six thousand people shouting "Good Old Winnie" and similar friendly salutations.[9] He proceeded directly to the local Ritz-Carlton Hotel to put the finishing touches on his speech and worked steadily through the day, pausing only once, to have tea with President and Mrs. Conant of Harvard. That evening fourteen thousand MIT alumni and guests began their descent on the Boston Garden while the final preparations for a nationwide radio and television hookup—larger even than the one that had carried Truman's recent inauguration—were carefully carried out. By 8:45 the huge auditorium was packed and all the cameras and microphones were ready. Churchill appeared on the platform at 9:00 and received a two-minute standing ovation. Baruch introduced him, and then, sporting the insigne of the Distinguished Service Medal that Pershing had pinned on him in 1919, Winston delivered his message.

"Ladies and gentlemen," he began, "I frankly confess that I feel somewhat overawed in addressing this vast scientific and learned audience on the subjects which your panels are discussing. I have no technical and no university education, and have just had to pick up a few things as I went along."

After getting his laughter, he proceeded to survey the enormous changes that science and technology had wrought in world affairs since 1900 and noted how imperfectly man had kept pace with them in terms of moral and intellectual refinement: "His brain got no better, but it buzzed the more. The scale of events around him assumed gigantic proportions while he remained about the same size." Churchill then reviewed the two world wars and the efforts that had followed each of them to set up some kind of international organization and maintain peace. He referred to his Fulton speech and to the steps America and Western Europe had taken to contain Soviet expansionism since he made it: ". . . The relations of Communist Russia with the other Great Powers of the world are without precedent in history. Measures and counter-measures have been taken on many occasions which in any previous period could only have meant or accompanied armed conflict. The situation has been well described by distinguished Americans as the 'cold war.' And the question is asked, 'Are we winning the cold war?' . . ."

On the minus side in reply to this question was "the collapse of China under Communist attack and intrigue." On the plus side, however, there were the heartening developments in Europe. All in all he was hopeful. He felt the West's determination to stand firm was equal to the threat posed by Stalin's rapacity. "We seek nothing from Russia but good will and fair play. If, however, there is to be a war of nerves, let us make sure that our nerves are strong and are fortified by the deepest convictions of our hearts. . . ."

With that said, he rolled onward to his peroration:

This is a hard experience in the life of the world. After our great victory, which we believed would decide the struggle for freedom for our time at least, we thought we had deserved better of fortune. But unities and associations are being established by many nations throughout the free world with a speed and reality which would not have been achieved perhaps for generations.

Of all these unities the one most precious to me is, to use an expression I used first at Harvard six years ago . . . the fraternal association of the British Commonwealth of Nations and the United States. . . .

Let us then move forward together in discharge of our mission and our duty, fearing God and nothing else.

He got an even bigger ovation at the end of his speech than he had gotten when he stood up to deliver it, and he professed himself much gratified, especially because this had been the first mass-televised address he had ever made. "It's amazing," he remarked to Clementine, "to think that every expression on my face was being viewed by millions. I hope the raw material was as good as the method of distribution."[10]

The next day MIT, rightly supposing that yet another honorary degree would be superfluous, conferred on Churchill an honorary lectureship. Winston thanked the officers of the institute for inviting him to speak and summed up his two-day sojourn as their guest: "I carry away from this gathering sentiments which will enable me for the rest of my life to view with a totally different light the Boston Tea Party, of which I have heard in my early days."[11] He and Clementine then returned to South Station and caught the midnight train for New York.

The Churchills arrived at Grand Central shortly after 6:00 A.M. on Saturday, April 2, and shortly before nine they left their compartment and were accompanied by Baruch to the Hudson River berth of the *Queen Mary*. The press got one last crack at Winston on board the Cunard liner. Asked if a Pacific Pact modeled on the NATO arrangement should be considered, he gave an answer worth remembering in light of later years' developments: "It ought to be looked into, but we must be careful not to spread our resources too thin." In general, though, he responded to questions in a spirit of fun well in keeping with his cherubic grin and dark blue siren suit. "I wore this once to the Kremlin," he told his interlocutors. "It didn't go so well; pushing democracy too far."[12]

The *Queen Mary* sailed that afternoon, and another Churchill visit to America was over. Said the New York *Times* in a warm valedictory: "The people of this country have . . . known him in his impulsive and adventurous youth, in the midstream struggles of his great career, and now as an elder statesman. His physical strength has diminished, but the pungency of his thinking and speaking has not. The man who acted so splendidly has given us also splendid, resounding words. It hardly matters now whether he calls himself a liberal or a conservative. He has spoken and acted for human liberty at the moments of its greatest crises. He so speaks and acts now. With each visit he is increasingly welcome here. May he come soon again."[13]

CHAPTER FIFTEEN

The Sun Starts to Set

IN 1942 CHURCHILL had declared, "I have not become the King's first minister in order to preside over the liquidation of the British Empire," and in 1945 the verdict of the British electorate saved him from being forced to do so. By 1952 he was the King's First Minister once again, and what saved him this time was the fact that there was virtually no British Empire left to liquidate. In the short space of seven years the biggest, though conspicuously not the strongest, of the victorious Big Three powers had shrunk from nearly a quarter of the world's territory and a third of the world's population to a fiftieth and a twentieth respectively of its former size. India was gone, Burma was gone, and the last vestiges of control in the Middle East were going fast. Like some muffled churchbell in the darkness, the words of Kipling's prophecy were now ringing true:

> Far-called, our navies melt away;
> On dune and headland sinks the fire:
> Lo, all our pomp of yesterday
> Is one with Nineveh and Tyre.

All that was left of the glory of Great Britain was a lingering memory and a small island off the coast of Western Europe, a small island whose economic viability without its empire was very much open to doubt. It could not feed itself nor could it furnish its industries with many needed raw materials. Its industries, in turn, did not sell enough of their products abroad to compensate for the remorseless flow of imports.

Thus it was forced to exist on the debit side of the ledger—and on the receiving end of American generosity—to the tune of some $7 billion since 1945. Thus also from the purely personal point of view, Churchill's return to power toward the end of 1951 could not have come at a more unpropitious time. As supremely well suited as his temperament had been to England's determination to resist in 1940, so was it supremely ill suited to the retrenchments and withdrawals incumbent upon the nation eleven years further on. It was not that he did a bad job; despite a stroke in 1949 and the strain of two election campaigns in 1950 and '51, he was still more than capable when it came to running a government. He did a good job, in fact—but it was a job that would have been better left undone. For instead of grappling in earnest with Britain's economic problems (from which, even in his days at the Exchequer, he drew precious little inspiration) he dedicated most of his energies to maintaining his country's image among the ranks of the great powers. And while the force of his personality and the renown of his name staved off the inevitable for a few years, the reprieve he won for the *grandeur* of the British Empire was to prove a very costly one when the sun finally set on it.

As always from Churchill's point of view the key to preserving Britain's greatness lay in close collaboration with the United States. It is not surprising, therefore, that one of his first acts after being returned to office in the autumn of 1951 was to prepare the ground for his eleventh* visit to America. Anglo-American relations were somewhat strained after the Attlee-Bevin years. Although the two countries were co-operating in Korea, they had fallen out of step on the issue of recognizing the People's Republic of China. In Iran, moreover, the seizure of British oil companies by the government of Mohammed Mossadegh had found Washington unwilling to associate itself with London's official protests, and much bad feeling had been the result. Of course, Churchill had not by any means been enthusiastic about the Labour government's foreign policy, so the task of fence-mending came more or less

* Or twelfth if the visit to Hyde Park in 1944 is counted.

naturally to him. On New Year's Eve, 1951, scarcely two months after his return to power, he stepped aboard the *Queen Mary* at Southampton, resolved to re-establish the "special relationship" he and Roosevelt had initiated between the English-speaking powers.

On the far shore of the Atlantic, meanwhile, a not altogether unrestrained welcome appeared to be in the offing. On the frivolous side there was the telegram sent by our old friend Senator Langer to the vicar of Boston's Old North Church requesting that two lanterns be hung in the belfry to warn of the British approach.[1] Far more serious, however, were the reports emanating from Washington that "the welcome mat is definitely not out." "Hardly a day goes by," wrote the correspondent of the London *Times*, "without one department or another providing a little about something it expects Mr. Churchill to demand and which he is not going to get, about some stiff questions he is going to be asked, or some policy that is going to be thrust down his throat."[2] And according to *Newsweek* both Truman and Acheson were making "no secret of their wish that Churchill would stay away...."[3] After a while the rumors of the hostile reception awaiting the Prime Minister started coming so thick and fast that Truman felt obliged to repudiate them publicly himself. During a press conference on the afternoon of January 2 he said that he did not know where "such foolish reports" originated and added that Churchill would be given "as warm a reception as possible."[4] Despite this Presidential disclaimer the rumors persisted, largely because they were based on a fairly respectable foundation of fact. It was not that Churchill personally was unwelcome; it was just that, in his eagerness to iron out any wrinkles in the fabric of Anglo-American relations, he had chosen (as in 1941) an awkward moment to pay a visit. As Acheson had told Eden in London a month earlier, Truman would be weighted down with both his State of the Union and Budget messages early in January. As the Secretary of State noted privately, moreover, in terms of the time and energy invariably demanded by official visits, "Mr. Churchill's usually topped the list."[5]

On the high seas Winston read the accounts of rumors and

denials of rumors with understandable dismay. "When I have come to America before," he confided to Wilson, "it has been as an equal.... They have become so great and we are now so small. Poor England! ..."[6]

But not, as it turned out, Poor Churchill!, for it was quickly apparent on his arrival that he at least had not shrunk in American eyes. As the *Queen Mary* glided into the Upper Bay on January 5, the Prime Minister heard scores of steam whistles ashore and afloat let go with a piercing welcome. Fireboats sprayed streams of water into the air as he transferred to the Coast Guard cutter *Navesink*, and on his arrival at the Brooklyn Army Base he was greeted with applause, cheers, and even military honors. He was delighted, and he delighted newsmen in turn by beginning a brief press conference with the statement that he would be glad to answer any questions with explanations why he could not answer them.[7] In a more serious vein he told the reporters, "... you must not expect too much from these conferences. It will be a question of creating that friendly attitude and getting ourselves a little above that paper level on which there is so much correspondence, to make easier the discussion of all the difficult matters that will arise in the next two or three years. Though I hope it will not be so long before I'll be here again."[8]

From the army base Churchill was driven to Floyd Bennett Field, where the Presidential plane *Independence* was waiting to carry him to Washington. He arrived in the capital shortly after noon, and there to greet him as he descended to the tarmac was the full complement of President, Cabinet, Diplomatic Corps, and Joint Chiefs of Staff. James Reston of the *Times* noted that Truman "was obviously delighted" to see the Prime Minister again,[9] and the President confirmed the impression in a brief plane-side speech of greeting: "I can't tell you when I have had more pleasure than I have this morning in welcoming you as a visitor to the United States of America."[10] Churchill responded in kind, and Truman then whisked him off to Blair House for a steak and strawberry shortcake lunch. Reporters, meanwhile, whisked themselves off to file their stories and try to describe to their editors the mysterious object that Winston was carrying around on his head that day. The New York *Times* and *Time* magazine correspondents ended up calling it a "sawed-off stovepipe." The British Information Service called it a "high bowler." The British Embassy called it a "billycock," and London hatters, on being consulted, labeled it a "hard crown" or a "Cambridge." When all the returns were in, the most memorable, if not exactly the most illuminating, description was that of a New York haberdasher, who declared: "It's not a cut-down tall hat, it's a high-crowned low-crowned hat."[11]

Whatever it was, Churchill had discarded it in favor of a more readily identifiable nautical cap by the time he stepped aboard the Presidential yacht *Williamsburg* in the evening. There, during dinner and after, the first high-level discussions of the visit took place. The conversation ranged widely—the European defense community, the Middle East, Russia, Korea —and all in all, thanks in part to a plenitude of champagne, the occasion passed off very nicely. "The Prime Minister loved every minute of the evening," Acheson recollected,[12] and in fact when Churchill got back to the British Embassy around midnight Wilson observed that he was, almost literally, bubbling over. "Oh, I enjoyed it so much," he rhapsodized; "we talked as equals."[13] Certainly, for someone who was not supposed to be particularly welcome, he had been made to feel very welcome indeed, and the New York *Times* may have summed it up best in an editorial the following morning when it said: "There never was a time when Winston Churchill could come to the United States and not find the red carpet rolled out for him."[14]

Though January 6 was a Sunday the discussions between Britons and Americans continued. A daytime meeting at the Pentagon and an evening meeting at the British Embassy took place without Truman, who had to work on his State of the Union address. While the atmosphere continued cordial, Acheson occasionally became somewhat impatient with his opposite number, Anthony Eden, because of what he regarded as his too-facile approach to problems that had long since proven themselves to be nearly intractable.[15] The Secretary of

State was more in tune with Churchill, who, Reston reported, gave "the conversations a scope and a lift that were absent in the Truman-Attlee talks" of 1951.[16]

At the White House on Monday, Churchill and Truman discussed military and economic problems. It was indicative of Winston's cast of mind that the subject that exercised him most around this time was the essentially minor question of whether an Englishman or an American would be given operational naval command of the Atlantic. In his eyes the last remnant of Britain's Imperial prestige was bound up with this issue and he brushed aside all efforts by his subordinates to get him to accept a compromise.[17] Finally the subject had to be deferred for a week or so while less controversial topics were discussed, but despite this impasse the tone of the talks continued friendly.

Truman was Churchill's guest for dinner at the British Embassy in the evening, toasted him as "the great man of the age,"[18] and played selections from Chopin for him on the piano. On a personal level, at any rate, the trip thus far had done nothing but good.

On the eighth a full day of conferences concluded the formal phase of Winston's visit, and a communiqué was issued outlining the most important points on which agreement had been reached. Among these were (1) Anglo-American support for, but not participation in, the European defense community (support given reluctantly by Churchill. Acheson: ". . . at heart he did not approve of" a multinational European army, regarding it as, in his words, "a sludgy amalgam"[19]); (2) support for the principle of a freer exchange of atomic energy information as agreed on at Quebec and Hyde Park in 1943, but neglected by the Attlee government and restricted by Congress in 1946; (3) support for streamlining and strengthening NATO's organizational structure with respect to both political and military functions; (4) acceptance of the need to make strategic raw materials—steel from the United States, tin and aluminum from the British Commonwealth—more easily procurable by each from the other.

These areas of agreement were encouraging, but no one deluded himself that all areas of disagreement had been smoothed over. As Reston summarized it: "The two leaders did not remove the difficulties and differences that have harassed Anglo-American relations for the past two years so much as they defined what the differences were and set their aides to work on them in a good and hopeful atmosphere."[20]

One difference that was not resolved, for example, was whether the U.S. Garand .303 rifle or the British .280 should be used by the NATO armies. In an effort to break the deadlock General "Pug" Ismay, Secretary of State for Commonwealth Affairs, asked, "Isn't there some bastard Anglo-American type of fitting that could be adapted?" But his suggestion only earned him a gentle Prime Ministerial reproof: "Oh, Lord Ismay, I must ask you to guard your language. I am an Anglo-American type, you know."[21]

On Wednesday, the ninth, Churchill sat in the Presidential box in the gallery of the House of Representatives and listened to Harry Truman speak in sober terms on the state of the Union. He then caught The Executive to New York, arriving at Pennsylvania Station shortly after six. Baruch was on hand to greet him and once again serve as his host, and no sooner was Winston settled at 4 East Sixty-sixth Street than a couple of dozen members of the American Irish Minutemen showed up and began to picket the building.

Churchill spent a quiet evening with Baruch and Wilson and a quiet day on the tenth catching up on his dictation and correspondence. He received a visit from the Duke of Windsor and lunched with executives of *Life* magazine and the New York *Times*. Afterwards, over coffee and brandy, he launched into a spur-of-the-moment tribute to the United States for the contributions it had made to Britain's and Europe's welfare, concluding with "I marvel at America's altruism, her sublime disinterestedness." Wilson, who had heard so many of his patient's postprandial speeches that he sometimes yielded to inattention, was suddenly brought up short when he glanced at the head of the table. "All at once I realized Winston was in tears, his eyes were red, his voice faltered. He was deeply moved. . . ."[22]

Visitors to the Baruch apartment in the evening included

Sarah Churchill and her second husband and Joyce and Raymond Hall of Kansas City, whose mark on greeting cards was soon to be rendered more prestigious by a new series featuring Churchill-painted landscapes. After dinner Baruch accompanied his house guest down to Grand Central Station and bid him *bon voyage* as he boarded the Twentieth Century Limited for Montreal.

Canada was almost restful for the Prime Minister. His beloved friend Field Marshal Alexander was Governor-General, and the population as a whole was even more wildly affectionate than in America. The Canadian Premier, Stephen St. Laurent, gave him a sumptuous dinner, and the speech Churchill delivered toward the end of the affair was received with the greatest enthusiasm. After basking for five days in the glow of this unrestrained adulation Winston was fortified in spirit, and he headed back to Washington ready to step once again before Congress.

Almost ready, at any rate, for he was suffering from a degree of *trac* nearly comparable to that of a Broadway ingénue on opening night. "The speech has become an obsession," Wilson noted; "it has hung over him, like a dark cloud, since the day we left England."[23] All through January 16 he labored over what he was going to say, pausing only in the afternoon to be inducted into the Society of the Cincinnati, a patriotic organization made up of men whose ancestors had fought in the American Revolution—on the American side, that is. Churchill qualified for membership, thanks to his great-great-grandfather Lieutenant Reuben Murray of Connecticut, who had marched with General Washington. In accepting the blue and white ribbon of the Order, Winston remarked, "When the events took place which this society commemorates, I may say I was on both sides in the war between us and we."[24] Then he hastened back to the British Embassy and reimmersed himself in his Congressional address.

Thursday, January 17, was the day of reckoning. "This is the third time it has been my fortune to address the Congress of the United States upon our joint affairs," he began. "I am honoured, indeed, by these experiences which I believe are unique for one who is not an American citizen."

His audience appeared friendly and he moved rapidly to dispose of the most sensitive issue he had to discuss. "I have not come here to ask you for money—" he said, and then paused to let the baldness of the disclaimer register. After a moment of stunned silence it did, and laughter and loud applause dispelled the last of Winston's anxieties about his reception—"to ask you for money to make life more comfortable or easier for us in Britain," he was careful to qualify after the commotion had died down. "I have come here not to ask for gold but for steel; not for favors but equipment." The assembled legislators, excepting always Senator Langer, seemed to appreciate the distinction.

Winston sailed on, concluding once again with the wisdom of the great German of his youth: "Bismarck once said that the supreme fact of the Nineteenth Century was that Britain and the United States spoke the same language. Let us make sure that the supreme fact of the Twentieth Century is that they tread the same path."

With that the ordeal was over. Whatever the men on Capitol Hill might do when it actually came down to voting on the question of steel and equipment for England, there was no question about their feelings of high esteem for England's spokesman. As a correspondent of the New York *Times* observed, "Congress gave to Prime Minister Churchill today a more affectionate reception than ever it has given in late years to the President of the United States himself."[25] There was frosting on the cake, moreover, when Churchill found General of the Army George C. Marshall waiting to congratulate him at the British Embassy.

There was now only one last item of business left to clear up before leaving Washington: the Atlantic Command. On the morning of the eighteenth the British and American Chiefs of Staff came speedily to an agreement whereby an American admiral would have over-all authority while a British admiral would command the approaches to the British Isles out to the one-hundred-fathom line. Well pleased with themselves, the soldiers and sailors retired for luncheon, but shortly before the full-dress meeting with Churchill and Truman in the afternoon, the First Sea Lord, Sir Roderick Robert McGrigor, returned to his colleagues ashen-faced and gasped out, "Hurricane warnings along the Potomac!" Winston had read their proposed communiqué, ripped it in two, and thrown the pieces into the air.[26]

Soon after McGrigor's weather bulletin the President and the Prime Minister walked in, and Truman asked Churchill if he had any comments to make. It was like asking the hurricane if it had any winds. Acheson remembered, "We then listened to what I think was the most eloquent and moving speech I have ever heard. . . . For centuries England had kept alight the flame of freedom. . . . The major burden now . . . had passed to us. But Britain could and would still do her part, and she asked to do it, a right she had earned, in that element which was peculiarly hers . . . 'upon that Western sea whose floor is white with the bones of Englishmen.' . . ."[27]

As Winston spoke a note came surreptitiously across the table to Acheson from British Ambassador Sir Oliver Franks: "Be very very careful." The Secretary of State took the admonition to heart, and tactfully suggested a recess when Churchill had done declaiming. While the President and the Prime Minister talked of other matters, the remaining conferees huddled together anxiously in council. It was the Attlee government that had committed Britain to this naval arrangement, Acheson pointed out, and it was a mistake to try to force Churchill to agree to it—and it wasn't even necessary. The Prime Minister would never want to obstruct the *operation* of an Atlantic Command even though he disagreed with its *organization*. So let the Command go forward operationally as agreed on while permitting Churchill to express his organizational disagreement as a matter of record.

As Eden was now back in London, Franks accepted the plan for the British side. The conferees then hastily drew up a new communiqué and rejoined their waiting chiefs. Acheson read the draft aloud, concluding with the key words "the Prime Minister, while not withdrawing his objections, expressed his readiness to allow the appointment of a Supreme Commander to go forward. . . . He reserved the right to bring forward modifications for the consideration of NATO, if he so desired, at a later stage." There followed a period of silence which, according to the Secretary of State, "began to be unendurable." Then Churchill banged his hand down on the table and declared, "I accept every word of it." Amidst audible sighs of relief Truman said that he accepted it too and directed that the draft communiqué be given out immediately. When asked if his press secretaries ought to review it first for language, he replied, "I don't think so. The Prime Minister and I have both been over it, and one of us, at least, uses fair English."[28] Which "one of us" he did not choose to specify.

Thus the second Battle of the Atlantic ended to everyone's satisfaction, and Winston headed off to New York again, tired, as the saying goes, but happy. On board the crack Senator of the Pennsylvania Railroad he let his thoughts flow freely. "This visit to America has been a gamble. But it has come off, I think. It will do a lot of good. We have taken up old friendships and made new ones. I like Truman fearfully."[29]

This last comment, though sincere, is a bit misleading, since Harry Truman was much the least favorite of the three Presidents Churchill dealt with extensively. Winston had worshiped Roosevelt like a father and came to love Eisenhower like a son; Truman he only "liked fearfully," and the reasons are not far to seek. Truman was all business, no nonsense, straight from the shoulder—plain speaking, in short. Churchill on the other hand was a baroque figure—a digressor, dilator, raconteur, speechifier, and self-indulger. Whereas Roosevelt would look on with amusement and delight and Eisenhower with awe and esteem, Harry Truman would just sit politely until the geysers subsided and then go right back to the business at hand. Though Winston liked him fearfully, and though he in turn had nothing but admiration for the Prime Minister, there was missing between them that chemical spark of affection which draws forth personal relationships from official ones. This was to neither man's discredit certainly, but it was sad in a way because each, I think, would have liked to like the other more.

Churchill arrived in New York nursing a bad cold on Saturday afternoon, January 19. On the twentieth Wilson ordered him to bed. A City Hall reception had to be canceled, but Mayor Impellitteri came to the Baruch apartment anyway to present Winston with the City's Medal of Honor. Late on the evening of the twenty-second, wearing his ulster, a homburg, and a muffler over his black silk pajamas, the Prime Minister was driven over to the West Side and the waiting *Queen Mary*. At 1:10 A.M. the Cunard liner sailed.

Thus ended what was in many ways the most solidly successful journey Churchill ever made to the United States. He had sailed into an atmosphere chilly with rumors of hostility toward both himself and his country, but by the time he sailed away he had ignited a veritable bonfire of good feeling. As *Newsweek* summarized it, "Not since the war had relations between Britain and the United States been put on such a friendly cooperative basis."[30] And as Wilson summarized it, marveling at the hardiness of the perennial prodigy he was watching over, "... in Washington he is still a man apart. They can see, of course, that he is very old and rather deaf. But they still believe in him and in him alone among British politicians. There is something in this man which they do not find in other men...."[31]

CHAPTER SIXTEEN

The Ocean Widens

BARELY TEN DAYS after Churchill returned from America George VI died in his sleep. Profoundly affected by the loss of the monarch with whom he had traversed the years of conflict, Winston drew out of his grieving a strong echo of his voice of 1940: "During these last months the King walked with death, as if death was a companion, an acquaintance, whom he recognized and did not fear. In the end death came as a friend. And after a happy day of sunshine and sport, and after a good night to those who loved him best, he fell asleep, as every man or woman who strives to fear God and nothing else in the world may hope to do. I, whose youth was passed in the august, unchallenged and tranquil glories of the Victorian era may well feel a thrill in invoking, once more, the prayer and the anthem: 'God Save the Queen.'"

Thus, for Churchill, the wheel had come full circle; the tumult and the shouting had died, the captains and the kings had departed: Edward VII, George V, Edward VIII, George VI—half a century of British kings bounded by the great historic names of Victoria and Elizabeth; six rulers whose reigns stretch from 1837 to probably the twenty-first century—and Winston Leonard Spencer Churchill had served them all.

The passing of the King made Churchill feel his years. Shortly after his speech to the nation he suffered a spell of aphasia, and it was clear to Wilson and Winston's Principal Private Secretary, Jock Colville, that his burden of leadership had somehow to be lightened. He gave them no co-operation, however, and tired as he was he carried on. A minor stroke in the summer increased Wilson's and Colville's anxieties but did nothing to make Churchill more malleable, and as it turned out he surprised both of them with his powers of recuperation. By November he was back in form, reinvigorated perhaps by the news of Eisenhower's election in America. Suddenly a vacation trip to Jamaica planned for January took on a new significance for him: he would stop in the United States "on the way"* and re-establish personal relations with Ike even before the inauguration. From London on December 28 he cabled Baruch, who had accepted the role of trusted intermediary, HOPE TO TALK TO OUR FRIEND AFTERNOON OR EVENING FIFTH AND . . . SHOULD HOPE TO SEE HIM AGAIN SEVENTH STOP BUT I LEAVE THIS TO YOU AS I DON'T WANT TO BURDEN HIM. . . .[1]

On the fifth the New York *Times* heralded his return to America: "One could hardly say anything more obvious than that Winston Churchill, who arrives in New York this morning, is heartily welcome. . . ."[2] The *Queen Mary* docked shortly after 8:00 A.M. at Pier 90 on Fiftieth Street and Winston met the press about an hour later. "It has been a year exactly since I was here last," he announced. "I hope you've had a good year. We haven't had a bad one, and I'm glad to report our general state of health on the other side of the ocean is at least as good as it was last year. Nothing like being modest." With this pleasantry out of the way he started fielding questions: there was "nothing extraordinary" about his conferring with General Eisenhower; there were worse things than stalemate in Korea —"Checkmate is worse, I believe"; the real center of gravity of world politics was the iron curtain—"Maybe I'm biased by being rather nearer to it"; Roosevelt's promise of a free exchange of atomic energy information had still not been redeemed; "trade, not aid" was "the wise policy"; and finally, on the possible widening of the Korean conflict: "Certainly we think it would be a great pity for the United States and the United Nations army to wander all about this vast China. We think that it would be a great pity to make an indefinite extension of the war. . . ."[3]

* "On the way" was the phrase used in the official announcement issued from 10 Downing Street on December 26 (New York *Times*, December 27, 1952, p. 3, col. 2).

With the reporters satisfied, Baruch escorted Winston to East Sixty-sixth Street for the inevitable brief encounter with Irish-American pickets downstairs and the inevitable warm hospitality upstairs. Eleanor Roosevelt came for lunch and Eisenhower arrived for an hour's chat around five in the evening. Newsmen were intrigued to note that he carried a large sheaf of papers with him when he left the Baruch apartment, but subsequent inquiry turned up the disappointing fact that they did not concern any grave and secret matters of state but were merely advance proofs of *Triumph and Tragedy*.[4]

The President-elect returned for dinner at eight and stayed till eleven discussing the spectrum of world problems. Churchill did most of the talking, naturally, and Eisenhower did most of the listening, but as even Winston knew, that did not mean the General had no opinions of his own.

He expressed them next day to Colville at his temporary offices in the Commodore Hotel: the Prime Minister must not press for too open Anglo-American collaboration, he said, lest other nations be offended. The "special relationship" was fine in principle, but it should not be flaunted.[5] Eisenhower also expressed his vexation over Winston's "wander all about this vast China" remark. He and his aides had gone to such lengths, both publicly and privately, to dissociate themselves from such a policy that it seemed to him that the Prime Minister ought to have left well enough alone.[6]

Eisenhower made these comments to Colville on the sixth rather than to Churchill face to face on the fifth, knowing that, transmitted indirectly, they would not carry as much of a sting. Colville was no less alive to the issue of his chief's sensitivity where Presidential, or even pre-Presidential, disapproval was concerned, so he smoothed down the General's statements as much as he could consistent with conveying their import. He wisely waited, moreover, until Secretary of State-designate Dulles and Ambassador to England-designate Winthrop Aldrich had concluded an after-dinner conference with the Prime Minister before presenting the bitter pill. As he had expected, Churchill was decidedly upset.

Uncharacteristically—except perhaps where American Presidents were concerned—Winston repressed his feelings during his afternoon meeting with Eisenhower on the seventh. When Dewey and Dulles sought in the evening to dissuade him from returning to the United States for economic talks in February, however, they caught the full blast of his pent-up aggravation. He "was furious" and "spoke so harshly" that as the two shaken Republicans took their leave, Colville "felt obliged to explain rather lamely that a sharp debate was Churchill's idea of a pleasant evening." In fact, of course, as Colville noted privately, the problem was that, as Winston was beginning to realize to his "bitter disappointment . . . he was welcomed and revered in America much more as Winston Churchill than as the Prime Minister of the United Kingdom."[7]

It may not have been much of a consolation, but Churchill had had an example of the welcome and the reverence at noon that day. Accompanied by Mayor and Mrs. Impellitteri, his daughter Sarah, who was working as a television actress in New York at the time, Borough President Cashmore, and Baruch, he had journeyed to 426 Henry Street in Brooklyn, where, it was then believed, his mother had been born in 1850. Actually Jennie Jerome had been born not far away, at 8 Amity Street, in 1854, almost exactly ninety-nine years before Winston's visit,*[8] but as is the case with most such sentimental pilgrimages, it was the thought that counted on this occasion. Official Brooklyn historian James Kelly hovered constantly near Churchill's ear, adducing datum after datum to disprove the vile canard that Jennie had been born in Rochester. Meanwhile Mr. and Mrs. Joseph Romeo and their four children, the incumbent residents of 426 Henry Street, looked on in respectful silence. "Very nice house," Churchill said to them as he made ready to leave. Outside several hundred people, including most of the student body of Junior High School 29, waited eagerly to get a glimpse of the man who was rapidly becoming—if he had not already become—a living legend in his mother's homeland. There were newsmen waiting too, and one of them pressed forward as Winston emerged: "How does this house compare with your own birthplace of Blen-

---

* She was born January 9, 1854; his visit was January 7, 1953.

heim Palace?" he asked. Churchill chewed on his cigar a moment, cogitated, and then replied diplomatically, "I am equally proud of both."[9]

On Thursday, the eighth, Winston flew down to Washington in the *Independence* to, as he put it, "pay his respects" to Harry Truman. He spent an hour with the President and Acheson at the White House in the afternoon and pressed his host to come to England for a visit after Eisenhower's inauguration. "Rather wistfully," according to Acheson, Truman said he would love to go but had to be careful not to do anything that might be misconstrued. Churchill chuckled. "I've been being misconstrued for fifty years and no one has really found me out yet."[10]

Winston left the Executive Mansion for his Embassy at 5:30. The meeting had been "very pleasant," he told reporters, "and that isn't off the record."[11] Back on British territory he presided over a reception for Congressional VIPs, among them the young (forty-four) junior Senator from Texas who had been tabbed to become Minority Leader in the 83rd Congress. (Lyndon Johnson's newly elected Senate colleague Jack Kennedy, meanwhile, was busily at work moving out of his old suite at the House Office Building.)

Thursday evening at nine, Churchill gave a dinner in the President's honor at the Embassy. At the outset he and Truman made several valiant attempts to call each other by their first names, but the effort proved too great for them and after awhile they reverted to the much more comfortable "Mr. President" and "Mr. Prime Minister."[12]

The dinner was relaxed and lighthearted with much joking and poking fun. Acheson and Defense Secretary Robert Lovett asked Churchill to judge whether Truman's "merits as a statesman were overbalanced by his demerits as a pianist." They accused him of logrolling when he decided in the President's favor, but their objections were overruled.[13]

On Friday morning the *Independence* carried Winston off to join Clementine in Jamaica. After two weeks of sun, they returned together by air to New York and went directly from Idlewild Airport to Pier 90 and the *Queen Mary*.

Churchill had considerable cause to reflect as the ship headed out of New York Harbor, and on balance he could not have taken much comfort from his impromptu preinauguration visit to the United States. For the first time in all his years of power he had detected, in the incoming administration, not a coldness exactly, but a subtle, just perceptible drop in warmth. It was not by any means that Dulles and Eisenhower seemed to regard England as just another foreign country; it was that they no longer seemed to view her as an intimate confidant. All things considered, there was no escaping the conclusion that, like the mist-shrouded towers of lower Manhattan, Winston's dream of close association between the British and American peoples was fading perceptibly into the winter gloom.

CHAPTER SEVENTEEN

A Last Hurrah

THE ENSUING MONTHS did little to retard the continental drifting apart of British and American foreign policies. The death of Stalin in March 1953, for example, aroused in Churchill the hope that Russia might profitably be approached about a relaxation of East-West tensions, but the United States, having been a bit slow to grasp the nature of Soviet duplicity in the late 1940s, was now in the throes of a truly Pauline conversion to the anti-Communist Word. Domestically Senator Joseph McCarthy was purging "subversives" with Inquisitional zeal; internationally John Foster Dulles was threatening on a more or less weekly basis to chastise iron curtain aggressiveness with the massively retaliatory wrath of the righteous Bomb. "This fellow preaches like a Methodist minister," a frustrated Winston complained to Wilson, "and his bloody text is always the same."[1]

Quite apart from any specific differences of opinion, there was the general problem of U.S. impatience with the mechanics of collective security. The French were frittering away any prospect of a European army while failing conspicuously to hold the anti-Communist fort in Indo-China. The Italians were so busy changing governments that their foreign policy hardly even got formulated. The West Germans were clamoring for recognition and rearmament on the one hand and for reunification and neutrality on the other. And the British? Well, the British had recognized Red China, seemed decidedly halfhearted about joining the crusade to "roll back" Communism around the world, and on top of everything else kept insisting that they had a vested interest in America's most closely guarded atomic secrets. Many State Department officials were increasingly of the opinion—those few, at any rate, who, given McCarthy, still dared to have opinions— that since the United States was nine or ten times as powerful as the whole passel of European shadowboxers and since, in addition, it was footing nine-tenths of the cost of protecting them, the time had come for the polite fiction of "a common defense policy" to be dropped and the plain fact of American authority to be acknowledged.

Much, though by no means all, of the distress Churchill experienced in connection with these developments in Washington was offset after his return from America in January by his absorption in the preparations for Elizabeth II's coronation. Here at least was one area where the glory of Great Britain could unabashedly be re-evoked, and the Queen had made the occasion all the sweeter by bestowing upon Winston in April the most coveted honor available to a British subject— the Order of the Garter. Henceforth, and in the best possible sense, he was to be *Sir* Winston, in the company of such men as Wellington, England's kings and princes, and his own illustrious ancestor the first Duke of Marlborough.

The innumerable official functions connected with the coronation taxed Churchill to the utmost, and in early June, several weeks after the ceremonies took place, he suffered his third stroke. Again, it was not a major one, but it makes little sense to call any stroke minor when a man is seventy-eight. His recuperative powers did not desert him, however, and as the summer wore on he made up most of the ground he had lost.

On the world scene, meanwhile, great changes were taking place. On July 27, after more than two arduous years of truce negotiations, a Korean armistice at last was signed. On August 20, however, the Soviet Union announced that it had exploded a hydrogen bomb, and as summer wound down into autumn a resurgently healthy Winston began pressing Eisenhower for a meeting to discuss these and other new developments. The President finally consented to come to Bermuda in December, but in order to keep the "special relationship" out of the limelight he insisted that the French be invited as well. This pleased Churchill not at all, but there was nothing he could do but accede to Eisenhower's wishes.

Bermuda did not accomplish a great deal, but from Winston's point of view it was enough that he got a few hours alone with Ike. He was feeling reasonably sanguine in any case at the time because in October, within six months of the Garter, his writings had won him an even more coveted Nobel Prize.

Despite Bermuda and Churchill's best efforts Anglo-American relations continued to fray at the edges during the first months of 1954. Once again it seemed to Winston that the only way to arrest the deterioration was for him and Eisenhower to iron out their differences face to face. Yet another time he asked a U.S. President for a meeting, and yet another time he was invited to come to America, his journey to commence soon after his official installation as a Knight of the Garter at Windsor Castle in June. The auspices were not favorable, though. "No one, save Winston, seems to think that much will come out of this visit," Wilson wrote in his diary. "There will be some straight talk, and Winston will be disappointed. ..."2

Churchill and Eden left London aboard the BOAC Boeing Stratocruiser *Canopus* on Thursday night, June 24, and arrived at Washington National Airport on Friday morning. On hand to greet them were Secretary Dulles and Vice President Nixon, not to mention the by now customary army of reporters. "We have come to talk over a few family matters," Winston told them, "and to try to make sure there are no misunderstandings."3

Churchill was given his old suite at the White House while Eden was quartered in the Lincoln Room. Talks began immediately and continued through lunch and the afternoon. Despite all the gloomy predictions, moreover, they proceeded with perfect harmony. "The day has been an incredible success," said Winston as he dressed for dinner. "It is astounding how well things have gone. Whatever cropped up, we seemed at once to agree on the principle which ought to guide us in seeking a solution."4

Saturday went just as well as Friday. In addition to the talks with Dulles and Eisenhower, Winston met at lunch with about two dozen Congressional leaders. "To jaw-jaw is always better than to war-war," he told them, and as always his remarks got a blazingly warm reception. Once again, however, there was that disturbing dichotomy Colville had noted in 1953 between the strong surge of response evoked by Winston Churchill the man and the strong lack of response evoked by Winston Churchill the Prime Minister. House Ways and Means Committee Chairman John Taber of New York was a perfect example: "I was charmed," he said, "but not where my pocketbook is."[5]

Eisenhower hosted dinner at the White House on Saturday evening, but, even though Baruch was among the guests, Winston excused himself at the unprecedentedly early hour of eleven o'clock. The six hours of sleep he had lost on the flight over from England were now catching up with him. Whereas in the morning he had been soaring with enthusiasm ("I do not feel at all tired. There is something in the magnetism of this great portion of the earth's surface which always makes me feel buoyant"), now, he admitted, he was "all in." On Sunday morning, however, after a long night's sleep, it was "I am not at all tired" once again.[6]

It was just as well that he was not at all tired, because Sunday was to be a very full day of talks on the Middle East and Southeast Asia. Monday too was to be strenuous, the highlight being what James Reston estimated to be "the largest news conference in the history of this capital."[7] More than one thousand reporters and columnists gathered for lunch at the Statler Hotel to witness what most of them suspected would be Churchill's last official encounter with the American press. Reston found him "weary and slow of speech,"[8] and so he was. "I'm sure you will consider," Winston said, "that you must be generous, as you always are, and tenderhearted to an aged guest. . . ."[9] But he didn't require too much indulgence, for no matter how aged, weary, and slow of speech he was, he was still good copy. Asked what "the temperature" of the friendship between the United States and Britain was, he replied after some deliberation, "Normal!" Asked if he saw any prospects for an Arab-Israeli peace, he reiterated his support for the Jewish state: "I am a Zionist. Let me make that clear. I was one of the original ones after the Balfour Declaration. . . . I think it a most wonderful thing that this community should have established itself so effectively . . . and should have afforded a refuge to millions of their co-religionists who had suffered so fearfully under the Hitler, and not only the Hitler, persecution."[10]

Another questioner wanted to know if "larger Conservative and Republican majorities" in Parliament and Congress respectively might improve Anglo-American relations. Churchill answered that he was not going to choose between Republicans and Democrats: "I want the lot!"[11]

It was on the subject of East-West relations that Winston had the most to say, and it was on this subject, of course, that he and Dulles were in sharpest disagreement.

I am of the opinion that we ought to have a try at peaceful coexistence, a real good try for it. . . . I am very much in favor of patient, cool, friendly examination of what the Russian intentions are. . . . You may some day hear that I have done something or other which looks as if I were going to become a Communist, but I assure you that I have been all my life . . . fighting this. . . . I even remember making a speech at Fulton six years ago [sic] at which I didn't get a very warm welcome because it was so anti-Russian and anti-Communist. . . . But I am not anti-Russian; I am violently anti-Communist. But I do beg you to make sure that no stone is left unturned in this period to give them a chance to grasp the prospects. . . .[12]

As Reston observed, "It was a paradoxical situation": a man with Churchill's record "standing on a hotel platform in Washington explaining that really he wasn't pro-Communist."[13] Paradoxical it certainly was, but more than that it was indicative of the fact that even at seventy-nine Winston could still shake off the encumbrances of the past and turn a fresh eye on the world situation. Peaceful coexistence was not in 1954 an idea whose time had come; it may not even be timely today, but on the major-power level at least it is certainly the direction in which the world has been moving for the last dozen years. That Winston Churchill, the old anti-Bolshevik, should have been among the first to advocate it says something about the quality of his vision in the realm of international affairs.

Tuesday, June 29, was a day for taking leave. Eisenhower bade Churchill farewell at the White House in the morning, and, after lunch at the British Embassy with Dean Acheson, Winston was accompanied to the airport and seen off by Dulles and Nixon. He spent a night and a day in Canada and then flew back very late on June 30 to board the *Queen Elizabeth* in New York.

Certainly this, Churchill's last official visit to the United States, had not been the catastrophe that everyone, excepting him, had been anticipating. It may have been, as *Time* put it, "nearly useless" in terms of concrete understandings and basic reassessments of policy,[14] but there had been another dimension, a personal one, and in that domain Winston, simply by crossing the ocean, had given Anglo-American relations a much needed dose of invigoration. He was old, true, and tired, and his country was undeniably in decline, but as Jock Colville said in summing up the over-all worth of the journey, "the United States never succeeded in resisting the personality of Winston Churchill."[15]

CHAPTER EIGHTEEN

Old Comrades

SOCRATES' DICTUM that the life that is unexamined is not worth living has a slightly antic ring to it in this age of obsessive self-analysis. Certainly, the rich, varied, colorful—and decidedly unexamined—life of Winston Churchill might well be cited as a refutation of the statement, and certainly Churchill himself would have taken violent exception to it. In December 1942, for example, he sent the Lord President of the Council, Sir John Anderson, a minute which is most indicative of his attitude: "On August 4, 1942," he wrote, "the War Cabinet set up a Ministerial committee to . . . supervise the work of an expert committee on the use made of psychologists and psychiatrists in the Fighting Services. . . . I am sure it would be sensible to restrict as much as possible the work of these gentlemen, who are capable of doing an immense amount of harm with what may very easily degenerate into charlatanry. . . . There are no doubt easily recognisable cases which may benefit from treatment of this kind, but it is very wrong to disturb large numbers of healthy, normal men and women by asking the kind of odd questions in which the psychiatrists specialise. There are quite enough hangers-on and camp-followers already."[1]

Clearly, and understandably, Winston had an enormous stake in keeping his gaze averted from the dark places of the soul, and thanks to his incomparable intellect and drive he managed for eight decades to walk blindfolded around the rim of an emotional volcano without falling in. To be sure, he tripped and stumbled a couple of times, but he never went over the brink. On April 5, 1955, however, he retired as Prime Minister and quite suddenly found himself bereft of that life-long centrifugal impulsion of all-consuming ambition and work which had kept him well clear of the abyss.

And so he fell.

In his case it was not living the unexamined life that was the problem, but ending it. Much of his last decade was spent sitting disconsolately by the fire and watching as the flames too slowly consumed the hours. Often he would ask whoever was sitting with him what time it was, and then, only a few minutes later, he would ask again. On learning that not even a quarter of an hour had passed he would sigh "Oh Lor'" and look back into the embers.[2]

By retiring when he did, Churchill condemned himself to ten desolate years of imprisonment in the crumbling citadel of his flesh, a life sentence of waiting in the company of the surly "black dog," of waiting without hope of reprieve—waiting, as we shall see, for the right moment to die.

In the great world outside, meanwhile, the cause of Anglo-American unity suffered perhaps its worst setback since the War of 1812. Between October 29 and October 31, 1956, Britain, France, and Israel, endowed jointly and severally with a sense of timing calculated to give the *coup de grâce* to empires, attacked Egyptian forces on the Suez Canal less than a week before a U.S. Presidential election. John Foster Dulles quickly joined his voice to the global outcry of condemnation, and from the councils and cabinet rooms of the divided Tory government came bitter mutterings of *"Et tu, Brute."* Churchill wrote privately to Eisenhower pleading that Suez not be allowed to undermine British-American ties and the President responded in generally reassuring, but not overly specific, terms.

Three months after the crisis an ailing Anthony Eden was replaced as Prime Minister by Harold Macmillan, which meant, among other things, that England was once again being led by a man whose mother had been a citizen of the United States. This fact, along with Macmillan's long and friendly collaboration with Eisenhower in the Mediterranean theater during the war, provided the framework for a trans-

Atlantic *rapprochement*. But a reconciliation, alas, is rarely as intense as a love affair, and after Suez the special relationship between Washington and London was nothing much more than a husk.

The special relationship between the United States and Churchill, however, grew steadily more passionate. Now that Winston was more or less out of politics—even though still a Member of Parliament—Americans could give free rein to their affection for him without any doubts or misgivings. Winston for his part still loved the United States as much as ever and still cherished his fast-fading dream of Anglo-American fraternity. In 1959, accordingly, despite his years and infirmities, he resolved to set foot on his mother's native soil one last time.

During the last week of April Bernard Baruch in New York received two letters from Churchill's home in London. The first, beginning "My dear Bernie," was from Winston himself and was full of plans and proposals connected with his forthcoming visit. The second, beginning "Dear Mr. Baruch," was from Winston's private secretary, Anthony Montague Browne. "I should tell you for your strictly private information," it read, "that Sir Winston has not been very well, and we were in doubt as to whether he should go. However, he is determined to visit America again, so that is that! I know that you will safeguard him from fatigue as much as possible."[3] (Apparently Baruch, who at eighty-eight was four years Churchill's senior, did not need to be safeguarded from fatigue himself.)

Charles Wilson was also "in doubt" as to whether Winston should go to the United States and told him he was "mad to take the risk" of a trans-Atlantic airplane journey. As a good doctor, however, he did not disregard the psychological factors —"his mind is made up. Anything, I fancy, to break the purgatory of these interminable days"—and in the end he agreed, "under duress," to his patient's departure.[4]

Thus it was that on May 4, 1959, the man who had charged the dervishes at Omdurman boarded a BOAC Comet and crossed the ocean under jet propulsion. He transferred to the Presidential plane *Columbine III* at Idlewild Airport in New

York and flew on to Washington, where a Presidential welcome lay in store.

"Well, my friend, you're back again," said Eisenhower as Winston labored painfully down the ramp. Churchill took a moment to collect himself, then replied, "I am indeed glad to see you."[5] The two men made their way to a bank of microphones where the President made a formal speech of greeting. Churchill responded: "Mr. President, ladies and gentlemen, I am most happy once again to set foot in the United States—my mother's country I always think of it and feel it. I have come here on a quiet visit to see some of my old comrades of wartime days. . . ."[6]

Winston was established in his old suite at the White House, the suite in which he and Eisenhower had first met in 1942. Dinner in the evening with just the President and his family was a simple affair, simple and rather sad, for it was well past midnight London time and Churchill was feeling the effects both of his years and of the as yet undiagnosed malaise of jet-lag. The change in him since 1954, moreover, was starkly dramatic, and during the meal Eisenhower observed sorrowfully to his daughter-in-law, Barbara, "I only wish you had known him in his prime."[7]

On the fifth, however, after a solid night's sleep, Winston felt somewhat more lively, and the President took him over to Walter Reed Army Hospital to visit two of the "old comrades." John Foster Dulles was dying of cancer (he had less than three weeks to live, in fact) and George Catlett Marshall had been totally paralyzed by a stroke. Both men bore their afflictions with dignity, but for Eisenhower, who was still distressed over the deterioration in Churchill's general condition, the occasion was a bruisingly melancholy one. One correspondent observed that "at times during the afternoon . . . [the President] was plainly choked up,"[8] and Churchill too, although not so fully alive to the pathos of the situation, was visibly moved.

A stag dinner at the White House in the evening provided a welcome change of mood. A dozen of the World War II admirals and generals who had worked under Winston and Ike on Torch, Husky, Avalanche, and Overlord listened to their two former chiefs re-evoke the stirring days of courage and reward.

On Wednesday, the sixth, Eisenhower took Churchill to have a look at his Gettysburg farm. They traveled by helicopter from Washington, which gave Winston a chance to inspect the Civil War battlefield from the air en route. Back on the ground they boarded an electric golf cart and toured the fields and pastures, Winston resplendent in a ten- or even twelve-gallon western hat. Now and then they would dismount for a closer look at one of the President's Black Angus cows, and newsmen would swarm around. "Twice, with but a glance," the New York *Times* correspondent remembered, "the President seemed to ask reporters to forebear when his guest evidently was unaware of their repeated entreaties for his 'impressions.' "[9]

This gesture brought back memories of other occasions: Eisenhower gripping Churchill's arm at Colonial Williamsburg in 1946 during the incident with the frightened horses; Eisenhower as President-elect repeating constantly "I don't want you to get pneumonia" as Churchill waited in thirty-four-degree weather to see him off outside Baruch's apartment;[10] and then Eisenhower as President trotting down to Winston's limousine in 1954 and unobtrusively helping him up the five front steps to the White House.[11] There was that protective concern in the General's approach to Churchill, that tender solicitude which grown-up children often show toward their aging parents. And now, in the midst of all his Presidential responsibilities, here he was taking three full days out of his schedule simply to provide a tired "old comrade" with hospitality. Tired as he was, Winston was by no means incognizant of such unfettered loyalty and affection, and he wrote in a shaky hand to Clementine that "Ike" was a "real friend."[12]

To many eyes there was something incongruous about this friendship between the son of a Kansas dairy worker and a scion of the ducal house of Marlborough, but beneath the superficial contrasts the two men had some significant similarities of background. Each had graduated from his country's military academy and, unalike as the two institutions were (think back to Winston's disparaging observations of 1895), the gentleman-soldier tradition was common to both. In addition, both West Point and Sandhurst gave their graduates a military perspective on world affairs, not a narrow one necessarily, but one rooted in a lively appreciation of the role of power.

Eisenhower and Churchill also had adversities in common. In 1921, the same year that Marigold Churchill died in England at the age of three, Doud Dwight Eisenhower died in infancy in the United States.

The 1930s had seen both Churchill and Eisenhower in what seemed like permanent eclipse, the former a "busted flush" who would never be Prime Minister and the latter a twenty-year Lieutenant Colonel serving under a disdainful Douglas MacArthur in the Philippines. With the coming of war, however, both men were rocketed into prominence, and from July 1942 onward they were in contact with each other on an almost daily basis.

No one worked closely with Churchill for three years without coming to admire him enormously for his qualities—or vowing to throttle him for his defects; conversely, no one worked closely with Churchill for three minutes, let alone years, whom he did not admire. Out of admiration grew regard, and out of regard grew friendship. Thus the not particularly articulate Kansas soldier and the hortatory British politician had clasped hands.

Back in Washington on the evening of the sixth, Eisenhower recalled their first meeting and their wartime collaboration at a second White House stag dinner in Churchill's honor. Winston responded mistily to a Presidential toast with his perpetual refrain: "It resounds in my mind, a precious and happy thought . . . the union of the English-speaking peoples. I earnestly hope that an effort will be made, a fresh and further effort forward, to link us together. . . ."[13]

Next morning Churchill left the White House. "I'm sorry it can't be longer," said Mamie Eisenhower as Winston bowed good-bye and tottered down the broad steps.[14] That night at the British Embassy he gave a dinner for the President, and on the afternoon of May 8 he left Washington for the last time.

He was obviously exhausted when Baruch collected him at

La Guardia Airport, and the ageless financier told reporters, "He is not going to see a soul."[15] As usual, though, Winston confounded all prophecies, and on the afternoon of the tenth he went to have tea with Consuelo Vanderbilt Balsan at her apartment at 1 Sutton Place South. Madame Balsan, the former Duchess of Marlborough, was one of the few links remaining to his first visit to New York in 1895, and Churchill rightly assumed that he would not have another opportunity to reminisce with her about that far-off time.

Several hours later he was driven out to Idlewild. A crowd of three or four hundred people cheered and waved as he stepped haltingly onto the ramp of the Comet that was to take him eastward across the Atlantic. He stopped and turned, trying to find the words which would convey his feelings as he bade the United States farewell, searching for the proper valedictory. Finally, stymied, he gave a sort of shrug of resignation and looked around wet-eyed at the crowd. "Ladies and gentlemen," he said at last, "I must now leave you and return to Britain." There was the briefest pause and then a sudden wan smile; the well of inspiration was not completely dry after all. "Britain," he said, "my other country."[16]

CHAPTER NINETEEN

Ave Atque ... Ave

✳WINSTON SAILED INTO NEW YORK HARBOR for the last time on April 12, 1961, the sixteenth anniversary of Roosevelt's death. Above him, early in the day, a Russian named Gagarin had taken man's first flight in space. The planet the cosmonaut had flown around in less than two hours was the same planet Winston had sailed across to New York in 1895; but the world was not the same world—and Churchill at eighty-six was many times removed from Churchill at twenty. "I do not contemplate ever taking a sea voyage for pleasure," he had written in his earlier incarnation; "I shall always look upon journeys by sea as necessary evils—which have to be undergone in the carrying out of any definite plan."[1] Now, however, there was no definite plan to carry out, or even an indefinite one; there was only the need to pass time. He had joined the *Christina* at Gibraltar on March 9, and the hundred-yard-long Onassis yacht had set a meandering course westward, calling at ports in the Caribbean and then turning north up the U.S. Atlantic coast. And so in many respects this cruise did resemble "a sea voyage for pleasure," but from Winston's point of view it was more like a sea voyage to ease pain. Time, as Shaw observed, is a wrecker.

The *Christina* glided past the Statue of Liberty at 10:30 A.M., and the harbor, alerted to Churchill's coming, sent up a piercing salute from steam whistles, foghorns, fireboats, and police launches. Half a dozen helicopters hovered overhead, and at the Battery a crowd of several hundred waved at the sleek white corvette, trying forlornly to convey a feeling not unlike love across a thousand yards of chilly gray water.

"What an extraordinary people the Americans are!"

The yacht tied up at a mid-river buoy off the West Seventy-ninth Street boat basin, almost in the shadow of the West Side Highway, which had been renamed "Winston Churchill Drive" for the duration of the visit. From Manhattan a launch carried luncheon guests out to the *Christina's* mooring. UN Ambassador Adlai Stevenson was among them, and after the meal he returned to dry land pensive and moved. "This is a very great man who has been the conscience of freedom in his time," he told the reporters waiting at the dock, "and who now is in the sunset of life and entitled to the privacy that he has earned in those years of endeavor. I count it a great privilege to talk to him again." Had Mr. Churchill offered any advice on how to deal with the Soviet Union, the Ambassador was asked. "No, no," Stevenson answered with a rueful smile. "I wish he had."[2]

Winston was taken up on deck after lunch and there he watched as the *Queen Mary* was eased from her berth at the Cunard pier and sent on her way to Southampton. The sight must have called up many memories. He then took a long nap, rising toward evening to dress for cocktails and dinner. "Dear old Bernie," now ninety, would soon be coming aboard. That at least was something to look forward to. "I certainly will be glad to see my old friend again," Baruch told the press as he prepared to set off for mid-Hudson. "It will be good to be with him. He's a wonderful young man at eighty-six."[3]

"Their hospitality is a revelation to me...."

While dinner was in progress a steward tapped the shoulder of Anthony Montague Browne. "Please ring operator 18 in Washington," he said; "there is a top priority call."[4] Browne excused himself and went to the telephone in the lounge. In a few minutes he was talking to John Kennedy.

From 1937 to 1941 Joseph P. Kennedy had served as U.S. Ambassador to the Court of St. James's. Thus his second-oldest son, a Harvard history student, had watched Britain's Prime Minister in action at the climax of his career with even greater interest than many Britons, and with no less admiration. In

addition, he had written a book about Munich and appeasement called *Why England Slept*. Now he wanted to talk to
one Englishman who hadn't.

Browne explained that it would take a while to get Winston
to the phone, and the President asked him to call back when
all was arranged. Ten minutes later the call went through.

Kennedy proposed that Churchill come to the White House;
he even offered to send a special plane for him. For Winston
it was "a most pleasant surprise"[5]—but accepting the invitation was out of the question. Quite apart from the logistical
difficulties involved in a journey to Washington, what with
doctors, nurses, valets, and secretaries, there was the considerable strain of moving from yacht to pier to car to plane to
car to White House, a process which would have to be repeated in reverse and in full on a return trip to New York.
Clementine was unwell back in England, moreover, and Winston was anxious to get back to her. So he declined with regret, accepting quietly for "some later time."[6]

*"They make you feel at home and at ease in a way that I have
never before experienced. . . ."*

He had spoken to his first President, William McKinley, in
1900, and now, after Roosevelt, Wilson, Hoover, FDR, Truman, and Eisenhower, he had spoken to his last. Mercifully, he
could not have known as he made his slow, painful way back
to the dining table that John Kennedy would die much as Mc-
Kinley had, and that he, cruelest of ironies, would survive
them both.

The next day was set for Churchill's departure via Pan
American jet, but the weather, as if in sorrow, set up a wailing
lament of wind and rain. Gusts of fifty miles an hour and
better made a transfer off the *Christina* unthinkable, and it
was not until late afternoon that the swells calmed sufficiently
to permit the boat to move to a dockside mooring. Winston
derived one consolation from the twenty-four-hour delay,
however, for shortly after 8:00 P.M., Baruch came aboard, and
together they savored a second last evening.

April 14 dawned blustery and cool. With Onassis' assistance

Churchill left the *Christina* and entered a limousine provided by Commissioner Richard Patterson of the New York Department of Commerce and Public Events. With small British and American flags whipping on the front fenders, the big Cadillac moved uptown and east, toward Baruch's apartment. The financier was waiting downstairs, and as soon as he was settled a police escort guided the limousine out of Manhattan toward Idlewild Airport.

Shortly before 9:30, the small procession arrived at the Pan American terminal. With two canes and Onassis and Baruch to lean on, Winston unsteadily made his way toward the waiting plane. A crowd of some three hundred people was waiting also, and they sent up cheers and applause when Churchill appeared. He looked around, startled at the sudden noise. Then, slowly slowly, he smiled and lifted his hat. There was a lack of focus in his expression, and the few wisps of white hair that the hat had protected now knifed back and forth in the wind. But the gesture, though halting, was still Winston's and the people behind the gate knew its value.

"This is a very great country my dear Jack."

The plane was scheduled to depart at ten, and almost on the minute the doors were shut and the engines of the 707 roared into life. The crowd at the gate watched as the jet taxied and turned onto the active runway. Churchill was leaving, and this time there would be no return.

The engine roar deepened and grew; the plane began to roll. It moved down the runway into the wind, constantly gathering speed as it rolled. At 10:16 A.M. the nose lifted; then, with an inexorable majesty, the wheels lifted too.

Pan American Flight 100 was airborne.

Sir Winston and America said good-bye.

CHAPTER TWENTY

Last Things

"THE SPAN OF MORTALS is short, the end universal; and the tinge of melancholy which accompanies decline and retirement is in itself an anodyne. It is foolish to waste lamentations upon the closing phase of human life. Noble spirits yield themselves willingly to the successively falling shades which carry them to a better world or to oblivion."[1]

Thus Churchill on Marlborough, and Churchill on Churchill as well, except in his case there was one last item of business to attend to, one final mission, which kept him from yielding to the successively falling shades. And he would have liked to yield; clocks ticked no faster than before his American journey, and for the man who has never really come to terms with himself, each day falls like the lash of a whip as he waits for the end.

There were occasional reprieves, to be sure, moments when the blackness modulated into a sort of nacreous gray. Aristotle Onassis stood ready day or night to place both himself and his fabulous yacht, *Christina*, at Churchill's disposal, a gesture of homage by a Greek to the man who had delivered Greece from both German and Russian domination. Many of Winston's final winters, therefore, were spent in pursuit of the sun in the Mediterranean and the South Atlantic. To his eyes the light must have been paler than that he remembered in the Sudan, or near Estcourt, or in the Mamund Valley, or at Meerut; but light was light, and some elixirs never grow stale.

Then there was the light from America. On April 9, 1963, pursuant to an Act of Congress, the son of the worst ambassador America ever sent to Great Britain proclaimed Winston Churchill an honorary citizen of the United States. In so doing, said John F. Kennedy, "I only propose a formal recognition of the place he has long since won in the history of freedom and in the affections of my—and now his—fellow countrymen."² Only one other man, the Marquis de Lafayette, has ever stood high enough in American esteem to be accorded such an honor, and no man will ever deserve it more.

But use every man after his desert, and who shall scape whipping? None of us do, of course: the span is short, the end universal; and as the darkness gathered round Churchill the lash fell especially hard. Sarah, Randolph, and Diana shed the ties of their marriages, and Sarah and Randolph had serious problems with alcohol as well. Then, in October 1963 Diana ended her life with a massive overdose of sleeping pills, her black dog having finally proved too fierce to tame. For Winston the only consolation was that he would not have to contend with his own that much longer.

He celebrated—if that is the proper word—his ninetieth birthday on November 30, 1964, his unsteady smile betraying all the burnt-out innocence of infancy's return. He could barely walk, he could hardly hear, the sparks in the fabulous brain were feeble and few; but the spirit, whatever that may be, still ruled what was left of the organism, and there was that one last mile to go before he slept.

On Saturday evening, January 9, 1965, Winston declined both brandy and cigars after dinner. On Sunday he took to his bed and gradually sank into a coma. On Monday Wilson and a colleague diagnosed another stroke. An official announcement was made on Friday, and on the eighteenth the London *Times* commented, "Life is clearly ebbing away, but how long it will be until the crossing of the bar it is impossible to say."³

The *Times* was mistaken. Churchill knew how long, and so did Jock Colville. When one of the Queen's private secretaries called on Her Majesty's behalf to ask him, he said, "He is not going to die until the twenty-fourth January. He told me once that Lord Randolph . . . had died on 24th January 1895 and that he would die on the same day when the time came."⁴

Lord Randolph had died around eight in the morning.

✝ Shortly after eight A.M. on Sunday, January 24, 1965, his son
Winston ceased to breathe, whether out of unsurpassed filial
devotion or in defiant triumph that he had passed his biblical
threescore years and ten free of the pall of his father's shadow
—or both—we cannot know. One way or another, he now, like
Lincoln, belonged to the ages.

Along about the time that Winston was failing on his second attempt to get into Sandhurst, a comparably unsuccessful
novelist was interested to learn from an opthalmologist friend
that his eyesight "was quite uninteresting . . . because it was
normal. I naturally took this to mean that it was like everybody else's"; Bernard Shaw continued, "but he rejected this
construction as paradoxical, and hastened to explain to me that
I was an exceptional and highly fortunate person optically,
normal sight conferring the power of seeing things accurately,
and being enjoyed by only ten per cent of the population, the
remaining ninety per cent being abnormal. I immediately perceived the explanation of my want of success in fiction. My
mind's eye, like my body's, was 'normal': it saw things differently from other people's eyes, and saw them better."[5]
Churchill was endowed with precisely this "normality" of
vision in the realm of international relations, and his normality, like Shaw's, was so acute that initially it hampered his
progress. People who see clearly sometimes perceive very
bizarre and discomforting things, things the myopic and
astigmatic have tacitly agreed are not there. It takes a good
degree of *savoir-faire* to be both clear-sighted and popular, and
for most of his life Winston was only the first. In an uncanny
fashion he was repeatedly able to see through the dense fog
of details and preconceptions that obscures the affairs of nations and to catch hold of the single salient factor, the key
to the course of events. This capacity—this gift, more exactly
—is closely akin to prophecy, and just as mysterious. It is the
power of discerning the obvious, of seeing that the Emperor's
new clothes don't exist, the power which only once in a million times can survive the process of acculturation we call
"growing up." As Churchill himself said, "The human mind,
except when guided by extraordinary genius, cannot sur-

mount the established conclusions amid which it has been reared."[6] And it is perhaps for that reason that there is so often something childlike, child-*ish* even, in the character of genius. Certainly Churchill, with his petulance, his impatience, his insensitivity to others, was almost a classic case of infantile omnipotence at work, and in his impetuosity, his exuberance, and his unbridled zest for adventure one sees the mark of the child as well.

"The fox knows many things," said the seventh century B.C. satirist Archilocos, "but the hedgehog knows one big thing." Churchill with his "normal" vision was the hedgehog par excellence. Three times in his life he knew One Big Thing that was true about the world. On only the last of the three occasions, however, did he succeed in making his knowledge felt.

His first hedgehog incarnation came during the Great War. The One Big Thing he knew then was that frontal assaults mounted against barbed wire and machine guns were always to the advantage of the defensive. For both pragmatic and humanitarian reasons, therefore, he constantly implored his government colleagues and the supreme military commanders to refrain from the criminally stupid and invariably catastrophic offensives that after four years of fighting left the Entente Powers with ten battle dead for every seven of the Kaiser's, or, if you prefer brute numbers, 2,100,000 young men killed versus 1,450,000—on the western front alone! He did not just implore negatively either. Faced with the challenge of offering an alternative route to a strategic decision, he pointed, with reason, to the Central Powers' southern flank. Though the wisdom of the Dardanelles campaign will be debated as long as history is written, there is no question but that a concerted and sustained Allied offensive at any one of several points in the eastern Mediterranean would have done more to undermine Germany and Austria-Hungary than all the accumulated carnage in France and Flanders. There is also no question that if Churchill's major tactical option, tank warfare, had been developed and employed as he urged it should be, the stalemate on the western front could have been broken. The only things that ultimately saved France and Britain from the consequences of their own military blindness were sea power, the infusion of American strength during the last year of the war (which more than compensated for the loss of Russia), and German generals who proved just about as blockheaded about the value of an offensive strategy as their opposite numbers on the far side of the Somme. Never, I think, in human history has an older generation of men more grievously failed in its duty to a younger one than in 1914–18. Churchill, as usual, summed up the calamity best: "All had to learn and all had to suffer. But it was not those who learned the slowest who were made to suffer most."[7]

Winston's second hedgehog incarnation, of course, was as the voice in the wilderness during the 1930s, and the One Big Thing he knew then was that Hitler represented a radical departure from customary standards of international morality, low as they may have been. It was not just that a revived and resentful Germany was a threat to the United Kingdom or that National Socialism was an ugly totalitarian creed. No, what Churchill recognized more clearly than anyone else in England was not the geopolitical implications of a revanchist Reich but the fact that Adolf Hitler was quintessentially *bad*: a canker, a bacillus, a germ, a force amenable to neither the blandishments of reason nor the constraints of law, a rabid wolf that Neville Chamberlain chose to pet and pet because of the occasional lap-dog noises that came through the foam round its fangs. Churchill referred to Hitler as "this wicked man," and it seems so obvious now that we forget how reluctant people were to acknowledge it forty years ago. "But see what he has done for Germany," they would say, or "Well, you must admit, the Versailles Treaty *is* a scandal." Foxes are uncomfortable with moral absolutes.

Churchill's final hedgehog incarnation lasted from 1944 to 1946. Then the One Big Thing he knew was that, Teherans, Yaltas, and Potsdams notwithstanding, Stalin would take everything in Europe that wasn't nailed down and protected by force. In his Iron Curtain speech he raised the issue of Stalin's *bona fides* in a manner the great democracies could not ignore, and thanks largely to the fact that his track record was so incomparably impressive on the subject of European affairs, the West's leaders finally chose to heed his advice. He knew all the moves on the board, after all, the value of the pieces, the significance of the groupings. Not Metternich, not Richelieu, not Frederick the Great, not even Bismarck himself, ever had a better intuitive understanding of the flow of the Old World power game, and none had ever brought more raw talent to bear on the playing of it.

We have noted the key facet of this talent—the penetrating hedgehog vision. But vision without action is the domain of the onlooker, and if ever there was an unmitigated participant it was Churchill. His capacity for work, for concentration, was staggering; and when one considers the offices he held, the books he wrote, the pictures he painted, the battles he fought in, the lands he visited, the skills he acquired, the speeches he made, and the honors that were granted him, it brings to mind not one life but ten. Then there was his showmanship and his fabled eloquence: the cigar, the V sign, and the awe-inspiring growl. Above all there was his humanity—his human-ness, more correctly. One strives in vain to think of a more unlikely heroic figure. Short, chubby, stoop-shouldered, with the panoply of his emotions marching across his features for everyone to see; this was no lofty diplomatist, no august statesman —this was a real human being, a real person with real feelings and real faults. No wonder everybody called him "Winston"; all the more formal terms of address were somehow wide of the mark. He was "Winston," he was himself, and he would roll right over you unless you too had the courage to be yourself. No pomp, no protocol, no fanfare, ever scared him off. In February 1945, for example, he was to have lunch with King Ibn Saud. ". . . I had been told that neither smoking nor alcoholic beverages were allowed in the Royal Presence. As I was the host at luncheon I raised the matter at once, and said to the interpreter that if it was the religion of His Majesty to deprive himself of smoking and alcohol I must point out that my rule of life prescribed as an absolutely sacred rite smoking cigars and also the drinking of alcohol before, after, and if need be during all meals and in the intervals between them. The King graciously accepted the position. . . ."[8]

That was Winston!

Vision, energy, intellect, eloquence, humanity—our subject begins to sound like a candidate for Congress. But remember, these are proven qualities, not presumptive ones. He had a fierce visceral aversion to bullies, whether nations or individuals; he had tenacity, wisdom, and wit. He had his love for his country, for its Commonwealth, and of course for the United States as well. One thing was needed to tie all these qualities together, however, to make them jell. That thing I can call only "right instinct," or "fundamental decency" if you prefer; the moral dimension. Winston Churchill was a "gentleman" in all the finer senses of the word. Not so much a gentleman in terms of style and deportment—he was a bit too rambunctious on that score—but in terms of honor and integrity. He was not always kind, not always considerate, not always thoughtful of others; but from the principles of honesty, sincerity, and loyalty he never deviated one jot. Deceit, intrigue, treachery, and corruption were all foreign to his nature. He charted his own course, marched to his own drum, and made of his days a memorial to courage.

For such a life, and for the man who lived it, we may be truly thankful.

Acknowledgments

A PROJECT LIKE THIS BOOK is not accomplished without the help of many many people, and, inadequate as the gesture is, I would like at least to mention some of them.

First and foremost, I must thank my father and mother, Robert and Harriet Pilpel, without whose help this effort and a great many others could never possibly have come to fruition. I would like to thank Kay Halle for her encouraging words, and Mr. Robert Hastings for taking time out of a busy schedule. I am in debt to Nancy Bressler of the Princeton University Library, Dennis Curtis at Yale, and Joan Judge in New York. A. H. Raskin at the New York *Times* generously provided special references. Kenneth McCormick and Robert Lantz both gave moral support and excellent advice. The late Morris L. Ernst added to his already long list of kindnesses to me. In England I was greatly assisted by Betty Cash and her late husband, Allan. Mr. Martin Gilbert, Sir Winston's official biographer, gave freely of his time and excellent counsel, as did Dr. Henry Pelling. I am deeply indebted to Arnold Kaplan, who patiently provided material and moral reinforcements over the course of three years, and Sue Hefner of the International Churchill Society was most helpful as well.

To the many other people who gave of their time and talent, but are too numerous to mention by name, I proffer my sincere gratitude.

As is customary with books of this kind, I hereby absolve all the people mentioned above of responsibility for any gaffes which may have escaped my attention as well as for any outright blunders that *Churchill in America* may contain. Much that is good about the book is due to them (the people, not the blunders); all that is bad about it is due to me.

Notes

Whenever possible in the notes I have supplied specific page references for newspaper citations. I crave the reader's indulgence for those citations where the information was not available.

In the case of books, the letters "PB" following a citation indicate that the page reference pertains to the paperback edition of the work.

CHAPTER ONE

1. Winston S. Churchill, *My Early Life*, pp. 74–75.
2. Randolph S. Churchill, *Winston S. Churchill*, vol. 1, p. 253.
3. Ibid., p. 254.
4. Henry Pelling, *Winston Churchill*, p. 20.
5. *My Early Life*, p. 5.
6. *Winston S. Churchill*, vol. 1, p. 35.
7. Maurice Baring, *The Puppet Show of Memory*, quoted in ibid., p. 51.
8. *My Early Life*, pp. 12–13.
9. *Winston S. Churchill*, vol. 1, p. 47.
10. Ibid., p. 79.
11. Ibid., p. 93.
12. *My Early Life*, p. 19.
13. *Winston S. Churchill*, vol. 1, p. 119.
14. Ibid.
15. Ibid., pp. 124–25.
16. Ibid., pp. 188–89.
17. Quoted in ibid., p. 44.
18. *My Early Life*, p. 4.
19. Winston S. Churchill, *Amid These Storms*, pp. 51–52.
20. *My Early Life*, p. 46.
21. Isaiah Berlin, *Mr. Churchill in 1940*, p. 24.
22. Ibid., p. 25.
23. *Winston S. Churchill*, vol. 1, p. 255.
24. Ibid., p. 256.

25. Ibid.
26. Ibid., p. 257.
27. Ibid., companion vol. 1, part 1, p. 596.
28. Ibid., vol. 1, p. 254.
29. *Amid These Storms*, p. 52.
30. *Winston S. Churchill*, companion vol. 1, part 1, p. 596.
31. Ibid., vol. 1, pp. 258–59.
32. Ibid., companion vol. 1, part 1, pp. 596–97.
33. Ibid., p. 597.
34. Ibid., p. 598.
35. Ibid., p. 599.
36. Ibid.
37. Charles Wilson, *Churchill: Taken from the Diaries of Lord Moran*, p. 576.
38. *Winston S. Churchill*, companion vol. 1, part 1, p. 599.
39. Ibid., p. 598.
40. Ibid., p. 600.
41. Ibid., p. 598.
42. Ibid., p. 600.
43. Ibid.
44. Ibid., p. 601.
45. *My Early Life*, p. 79.
46. Ibid.
47. *Winston S. Churchill*, vol. 1, p. 267.
48. *My Early Life*, pp. 83–84.
49. *Winston S. Churchill*, vol. 1, p. 266.
50. Quoted in *Winston S. Churchill*, companion vol. 1, part 1, p. 620.
51. Ibid., p. 622.

CHAPTER TWO
1. *My Early Life*, pp. 59–60.
2. *Amid These Storms*, p. 320.
3. *Mr. Churchill in 1940*, p. 17:
4. *Amid These Storms*, p. 313.
5. *Winston S. Churchill*, vol. 1, p. 278.
6. Ibid.
7. Ibid., p. 346.
8. Ibid., pp. 357–58.
9. Ibid., p. 371.
10. *Daily Mail*, December 2, 1898.
11. Winston S. Churchill, *Savrola*, p. 32.

12. *Winston S. Churchill*, vol. 1, pp. 422–23.
13. Ibid., p. 285.
14. Ibid., p. 411.
15. Elizabeth Longford, *Winston Churchill*, p. 37.
16. *My Early Life*, p. 199.
17. *Winston S. Churchill*, vol. 1, p. 427.
18. Ibid., p. 430.
19. Ibid., pp. 433–34.
20. Ibid., p. 435.
21. *My Early Life*, pp. 250–52.
22. *Winston S. Churchill*, vol. 1, p. 491.

CHAPTER THREE

1. *Winston S. Churchill*, companion vol. 1, part 2, p. 1219.
2. Ibid., vol. 1, p. 523.
3. Ibid., companion vol. 2, part 1, p. xxviii.
4. Ibid., p. xxix.
5. Ibid., companion vol. 1, part 2, p. 1220.
6. Ibid., p. 1223.
7. E. E. Morison, ed., *The Letters of Theodore Roosevelt*, vol. 5, p. 1454, note.
8. Richard Harding Davis, *The Young Winston Churchill*, unpaged.
9. *Winston S. Churchill*, companion vol. 1, part 2, p. 1220.
10. New York *Times*, December 9, 1900, p. 28.
11. Springfield *Republican*, December 21, 1900, p. 4.
12. New York *Tribune*, December 9, 1900, p. 4.
13. Ibid., December 13, 1900, p. 4.
14. New York *Times*, December 16, 1900, p. 20.
15. *The Letters of Theodore Roosevelt*, p. 116.
16. Springfield *Republican*, December 16, 1900.
17. Ibid.
18. C. Eade, ed., *Winston S. Churchill: The War Speeches*, vol. 2, p. 170.
19. Springfield *Republican*, December 16, 1900.
20. New York *Times*, December 13, 1900, p. 2.
21. New York *Tribune*, December 13, 1900, p. 9; and *Winston S. Churchill*, companion vol. 1, part 2, p. 1222.
22. New York *Times*, December 9, 1900, p. 28.
23. Ibid., December 13, 1900, p. 2.
24. New York *Tribune*, December 13, 1900, p. 9.
25. Ibid.

26. *My Early Life*, p. 362.
27. *Winston S. Churchill*, vol. 1, p. 525.
28. *The Young Winston Churchill*.
29. New Haven *Evening Register*, December 13, 1900, p. 1.
30. New Haven *Morning Journal*, December 14, 1900.
31. Ibid.
32. New Haven *Evening Register*, December 14, 1900, p. 3.
33. Ibid.
34. *Winston S. Churchill*, companion vol. 1, part 2, p. 1223.
35. Washington *Post*, December 15, 1900, p. 2.
36. *Winston S. Churchill*, companion vol. 1, part 2, p. 1223.
37. *My Early Life*, p. 362.
38. Baltimore *Sun*, December 17, 1900, p. 7.
39. *Winston S. Churchill*, companion vol. 1, part 2, p. 1223.
40. *My Early Life*, p. 217.
41. Ibid., p. 219.
42. Boston *Herald*, December 18, 1900, p. 1.
43. Ibid.
44. *Winston S. Churchill*, vol. 1, p. 341.
45. *My Early Life*, p. 362.
46. Boston *Herald*, December 18, 1900.
47. Boston *Globe*, December 18, 1900, p. 2.
48. Boston *Herald*, December 18, 1900.
49. Boston *Globe*, December 18, 1900, p. 2.
50. Ibid.
51. Hartford *Courant*, December 20, 1900, p. 10.
52. Springfield *Republican*, December 21, 1900, p. 4.
53. *Winston S. Churchill*, companion vol. 1, part 2, p. 1223.
54. Ibid., vol. 1, p. 527.
55. Ibid.
56. *My Early Life*, p. 372.
57. New York *Times*, December 29, 1900, p. 2.
58. *Winston S. Churchill*, companion vol. 1, part 2, p. 1224.
59. Ibid., p. 1225.
60. Ibid., p. 1228.
61. *Michigan Quarterly Review* 5, no. 2 (1966): 75.
62. Ibid., p. 76.
63. Ibid., pp. 77–78.
64. *Winston S. Churchill*, companion vol. 1, part 2, p. 1229.
65. *My Early Life*, p. 362.
66. Chicago *Tribune*, January 11, 1901, p. 3.
67. Ibid.

68. K. Halle, ed., *Irrepressible Churchill*, p. 42.
69. *Winston S. Churchill*, companion vol. 1, part 2, p. 1231.
70. Ibid.
71. Richard Harrity and R. G. Martin, *Man of the Century: Churchill*, p. 62.
72. *My Early Life*, p. 363.

CHAPTER FOUR

1. *Winston S. Churchill*, vol. 2, p. 73.
2. *My Early Life*, p. 367.
3. *Winston S. Churchill*, companion vol. 2, part 1, p. 350.
4. Ibid.
5. New York *Times*, January 7, 1906, p. 6.
6. *The Letters of Theodore Roosevelt*, vol. 5, p. 408.
7. Ibid., p. 1329.
8. Ibid., p. 1034.
9. Ibid.
10. New York *Times*, August 9, 1906, p. 1.
11. Violet Bonham-Carter, *Winston Churchill: An Intimate Portrait*, pp. 3–4.
12. *The Letters of Theodore Roosevelt*, vol. 6, pp. 1383–85.
13. Ibid., p. 1465.
14. Ibid., p. 1467.
15. *Winston S. Churchill*, vol. 2, p. 241.
16. Ibid., p. 243.
17. Ibid., pp. 243–44.
18. Ibid., p. 253.
19. Ibid., p. 260.
20. Pelling, *Winston Churchill*, p. 129.
21. *Winston Churchill: An Intimate Portrait*, p. 7.
22. Martin Gilbert, ed., *Churchill*, p. 156.
23. *Irrepressible Churchill*, p. 63.
24. Ibid., p. 56.
25. Pelling, *Winston Churchill*, p. 158.
26. Ibid., p. 154.
27. *Winston S. Churchill*, companion vol. 1, part 2, p. 1219.
28. Pelling, *Winston Churchill*, p. 129.
29. *My Early Life*, p. 259.
30. *Amid These Storms*, pp. 69–70.
31. *Irrepressible Churchill*, p. 71.
32. *The Letters of Theodore Roosevelt*, vol. 6, p. 810.
33. *Winston S. Churchill*, vol. 2, p. 694.

34. Martin Gilbert, *Winston S. Churchill*, vol. 3, p. 31.
35. Pelling, *Winston Churchill*, p. 190.
36. *Churchill: Taken from the Diaries of Lord Moran*, p. 179.
37. *Winston S. Churchill*, vol. 3, p. 473.
38. *Amid These Storms*, pp. 307, 247.
39. *Winston S. Churchill*, vol. 3, p. 745.
40. Margaret Coit, *Mr. Baruch*, p. 210.
41. New York *Times*, July 5, 1918, p. 7.
42. Elliott Roosevelt *et al.*, eds., *F.D.R.: His Personal Letters 1905–1928*, p. 392; Frank Friedel, *Franklin Delano Roosevelt: The Apprenticeship*, p. 354.
43. Pelling, *Winston Churchill*, p. 168.
44. *Amid These Storms*, p. 196.
45. Forrest C. Pogue, *George C. Marshall: Ordeal and Hope*, p. 199.
46. *Amid These Storms*, p. 197.
47. *George C. Marshall*, p. 199.
48. George C. Marshall, *Memoirs of My Services in the World War, 1917–18*, p. 217.
49. Pelling, *Winston Churchill*, p. 283.
50. *Amid These Storms*, p. 215.
51. *Irrepressible Churchill*, p. 100.
52. Ibid., p. 101.

CHAPTER FIVE
1. Baruch Papers, Princeton University Library, letter from WSC to BB dated June 29, 1929.
2. Ibid., letter from WSC to BB dated July 10, 1929.
3. New York *Times*, August 18, 1929, sec. 2, p. 1.
4. Randolph S. Churchill, *Twenty-one Years*, p. 82.
5. John Spencer Churchill, *A Churchill Canvas*, p. 85.
6. Ibid.
7. *Twenty-one Years*, p. 82.
8. Ibid., p. 83.
9. Ibid.
10. New York *Times*, September 8, 1929, p. 4.
11. *A Churchill Canvas*, pp. 85–86; *Twenty-one Years*, p. 83.
12. San Francisco *Chronicle*, September 8, 1929.
13. *My Early Life*, p. 288.
14. San Francisco *Chronicle*, September 8, 1929.
15. London *Daily Telegraph*, December 23, 1929, p. 10.
16. *Twenty-one Years*, p. 84.
17. London *Daily Telegraph*, December 30, 1929, p. 10.

18. Ibid.
19. *Twenty-one Years*, p. 85.
20. London *Daily Telegraph*, December 30, 1929, p. 10.
21. Ibid.
22. Ibid., December 23, 1929, p. 10.
23. *Twenty-one Years*, p. 85.
24. Ibid.
25. San Francisco *Chronicle*, September 10, 1929.
26. *Twenty-one Years*, pp. 85–86.
27. San Francisco *Chronicle*, September 12, 1929.
28. London *Daily Telegraph*, December 30, 1929, p. 10.
29. Ibid., December 23, 1929, p. 10.
30. Ibid.
31. Ibid.
32. Baruch Papers.
33. Ibid.
34. *Twenty-one Years*, p. 86.
35. Ibid., p. 87.
36. Fred L. Guiles, *The Intimate Biography of Marion Davies*, PB p. 283.
37. Baruch Papers.
38. *A Churchill Canvas*, p. 89.
39. Ibid.
40. Ibid., p. 90.
41. London *Daily Telegraph*, December 30, 1929, p. 10.
42. *Twenty-one Years*, p. 88.
43. Ibid.
44. *A Churchill Canvas*, p. 91.
45. Ibid., p. 92.
46. New York *Times*, September 23, 1929, p. 30.
47. *A Churchill Canvas*, p. 92.
48. *Twenty-one Years*, p. 90.
49. Ibid.
50. San Francisco *Chronicle*, September 28, 1929.
51. *A Churchill Canvas*, pp. 93–94.
52. Ibid., p. 95.
53. *Twenty-one Years*, pp. 92–93.
54. *A Churchill Canvas*, p. 96.
55. New York *Times*, October 9, 1929, p. 3.
56. London *Daily Telegraph*, November 18, 1929, p. 10.
57. New York *Times*, October 13, 1929, p. 2.
58. Baruch Papers, letter from WSC to BB dated July 28, 1929.
59. London *Daily Telegraph*, February 3, 1930, p. 8.

60. Herbert Hoover, *The Memoirs of Herbert Hoover*, vol. 1, p. 162.
61. London *Daily Telegraph*, December 16, 1929, p. 10.
62. Ibid.
63. Ibid., December 9, 1929, p. 10.
64. Ibid.
65. Ibid.

CHAPTER SIX

1. Pelling, *Winston Churchill*, p. 346.
2. Baruch Papers, letter from WSC to BB dated July 30, 1931.
3. New York *Times*, December 5, 1931, p. 20.
4. Walter H. Thompson, *Assignment: Churchill*, p. 103.
5. Ibid., pp. 103–04.
6. Boston *Evening Transcript*, March 11, 1932, p. 15.
7. *Assignment: Churchill*, p. 105.
8. Ibid.
9. New York *Times*, December 12, 1931, p. 15.
10. *Assignment: Churchill*, pp. 106–07.
11. London *Daily Mail*, January 4, 1932.
12. Ibid., January 5, 1932.
13. *Assignment: Churchill*, p. 106.
14. London *Daily Mail*, January 5, 1932.
15. Ibid., January 4, 1932.
16. New York *Times*, December 21, 1931, p. 23; Jack Fishman, *My Darling Clementine*, pp. 76–77.
17. New York *Times*, December 22, 1931, p. 3.
18. Phyllis Moir, *I Was Winston Churchill's Private Secretary*, p. 29.
19. Ibid., pp. 30–32.
20. Ibid., p. 32.
21. New York *Times*, December 31, 1931, p. 4.
22. Ibid.
23. Baruch Papers, letter from WSC to BB dated January 18, 1932.
24. *I Was Winston Churchill's Private Secretary*, pp. 34–36.
25. New York *Times*, January 26, 1932, p. 2.
26. Ibid., January 29, 1932, p. 5.
27. Hartford *Courant*, February 1, 1932, p. 2.
28. Chicago *Tribune*, February 3, 1932.
29. Ibid.
30. Kay Halle, ed., *Winston Churchill on America and Britain*, p. 86.
31. Ibid., p. 87.
32. *Assignment: Churchill*, p. 114.

33. Chicago *Tribune*, February 8, 1932.
34. *My Darling Clementine*, p. 73.
35. *Assignment: Churchill*, p. 114. In his essay "Guarding Church-ill" in Charles Eade, ed., *Churchill by His Contemporaries*, Thompson states (p. 251) that the Indian proved to be unarmed. Perhaps he was intent on strangulation.
36. *My Darling Clementine*, p. 78.
37. New York *Times*, February 10, 1932, p. 41.
38. *I Was Winston Churchill's Private Secretary*, pp. 82–83.
39. *Winston Churchill on America and Britain*, p. 266.
40. Washington *Post*, February 13, 1932, p. 18.
41. New Orleans *Times-Picayune*, February 21, 1932, p. 9.
42. *Winston Churchill on America and Britain*, pp. 266–67.
43. Washington *Post*, February 14, 1932, p. 6.
44. Winston S. Churchill, *The Gathering Storm*, The Second World War, vol. 1, PB p. 78.
45. *Winston Churchill on America and Britain*, p. 265.
46. Atlanta *Constitution*, February 18, 1932.
47. Ibid., February 23, 1932, p. 17.
48. Ibid., February 24, 1932.
49. Boston *Evening Transcript*, March 10, 1932, p. 4.
50. New York *Times*, March 12, 1932, p. 16.

CHAPTER SEVEN

1. Robert Rhodes James, *Churchill: A Study in Failure*, PB p. 379.
2. Speech to the Council of the West Essex Unionist Association, February 23, 1931.
3. *Churchill: A Study in Failure*, PB p. 275.
4. Ibid., PB p. 364.
5. *The Gathering Storm*, PB p. 72.
6. Ibid., PB p. 231.
7. Speech, March 24, 1938.
8. Speech, October 5, 1938.
9. *The Gathering Storm*, PB p. 365.
10. Francis Lowenheim, Harold D. Langley, and Manfred Jonas, eds., *Roosevelt and Churchill: Their Secret Wartime Correspondence*, p. 89.
11. Robert E. Sherwood, *Roosevelt and Hopkins*, p. 126.
12. *The Gathering Storm*, PB p. 392.
13. House of Commons, November 11, 1942.
14. Winston S. Churchill, *The Hinge of Fate*, The Second World War, vol. 4, PB p. 78.
15. *The Gathering Storm*, PB pp. 679, 681, 682.

16. Charles Eade, ed., *The War Speeches of Winston S. Churchill,* vol. 1, p. 137.
17. The Chamberlain-Halifax-Churchill meeting is described in *The Gathering Storm,* PB p. 592.
18. Ibid., PB p. 596.
19. Winston S. Churchill, *Great Contemporaries,* PB pp. 246, 256.
20. *The War Speeches of Winston S. Churchill,* vol. 1, pp. 18, 195–96, 255–56, 240, 206–07.
21. *Roosevelt and Churchill: Their Secret Wartime Correspondence,* p. 104.
22. Ibid., p. 119.
23. *Roosevelt and Hopkins,* p. 225.
24. *Roosevelt and Churchill: Their Secret Wartime Correspondence,* p. 127. The poem quoted from is "The Building of the Ship," by Longfellow.
25. *The War Speeches of Winston S. Churchill,* vol. 1, p. 352.
26. *Roosevelt and Churchill: Their Secret Wartime Correspondence,* p. 131.
27. William L. Shirer, *The Rise and Fall of the Third Reich,* PB p. 1080.
28. Ibid., PB p. 1081.
29. *The War Speeches of Winston S. Churchill,* vol. 1, pp. 452–53.
30. *Roosevelt and Hopkins,* p. 351.
31. Ibid., p. 350.
32. *The Gathering Storm,* PB p. 392.
33. Winston S. Churchill, *The Grand Alliance,* The Second World War, vol. 3, PB p. 365.
34. *Roosevelt and Churchill: Their Secret Wartime Correspondence,* p. 162.
35. *The Grand Alliance,* PB pp. 509–10.
36. Ibid., PB pp. 511–12.

CHAPTER EIGHT

1. *Roosevelt and Hopkins,* p. 435.
2. *The Grand Alliance,* PB pp. 159–60.
3. *Roosevelt and Hopkins,* p. 441.
4. *The Rise and Fall of the Third Reich,* PB pp. 1167–73.
5. *The Grand Alliance,* p. 540.
6. Arthur Bryant, *The Turn of the Tide,* p. 225.
7. *Roosevelt and Churchill: Their Secret Wartime Correspondence,* p. 170.
8. Ibid., p. 171.

9. Eleanor Roosevelt, "Churchill as a Guest," in *Churchill by His Contemporaries,* pp. 186–87.
10. New York *Times,* December 23, 1941, p. 1.
11. Ibid., p. 5.
12. *The Grand Alliance,* PB p. 558.
13. *Churchill: Taken from the Diaries of Lord Moran,* p. 11.
14. *Assignment: Churchill,* p. 248.
15. *Roosevelt and Hopkins,* pp. 442–43.
16. Ibid., p. 236.
17. *The Grand Alliance,* PB p. 559.
18. *Roosevelt and Hopkins,* p. 442.
19. *Churchill: Taken from the Diaries of Lord Moran,* p. 12.
20. New York *Times,* December 24, 1941, Editorial Page.
21. *Roosevelt and Hopkins,* p. 445.
22. Ibid., p. 444.
23. *Complete Presidential Press Conferences of Franklin Delano Roosevelt,* Conference no. 794, pp. 383, 385.
24. Ibid., p. 386.
25. Ibid., p. 387–89.
26. New York *Times,* December 24, 1941, p. 4.
27. Ibid., Editorial Page.
28. *Churchill: Taken from the Diaries of Lord Moran,* p. 14.
29. Ibid.
30. *Assignment: Churchill,* p. 250.
31. *FDR: His Personal Letters,* p. 1260.
32. *Churchill: Taken from the Diaries of Lord Moran,* p. 15.
33. *The Grand Alliance,* PB p. 565.
34. *Churchill: Taken from the Diaries of Lord Moran,* p. 16.
35. *Assignment: Churchill,* p. 254.
36. *Churchill: Taken from the Diaries of Lord Moran,* p. 16.
37. *Assignment: Churchill,* p. 256.
38. New York *Times,* December 27, 1941, p. 4.
39. *Churchill: Taken from the Diaries of Lord Moran,* p. 16.
40. *The Grand Alliance,* PB p. 566.
41. Ibid., PB p. 567.
42. Ibid., PB p. 581.
43. *Churchill: Taken from the Diaries of Lord Moran,* p. 17.
44. Ibid., p. 18.
45. Ibid.
46. Ibid., p. 19.
47. New York *Times,* December 30, 1941, p. 3.
48. Ibid., January 2, 1942, p. 5.

49. Ibid.
50. *The Grand Alliance*, PB p. 582; New York *Times*, January 2, 1942, p. 4.
51. New York *Times*, ibid.
52. Ibid.
53. *The Grand Alliance*, PB p. 575; New York *Times*, January 3, 1942, p. 4.
54. *The Grand Alliance*, PB p. 581.
55. Eleanor Roosevelt, "Churchill at the White House," *The Atlantic Monthly*, March 1965, p. 78.
56. Ibid., p. 79.
57. Ibid., p. 78.
58. Gerald Pawle, *The War and Colonel Warden*, p. 142.
59. New York *Times*, January 4, 1942, p. 5.
60. *Roosevelt and Hopkins*, p. 444.
61. *Churchill: Taken from the Diaries of Lord Moran*, p. 22.
62. *Assignment: Churchill*, pp. 258–59.
63. Ibid., p. 260.
64. *The Grand Alliance*, PB p. 582.
65. *Assignment: Churchill*, p. 261.
66. *The Grand Alliance*, PB p. 586.
67. Ibid., PB p. 587.
68. Ibid., PB p. 593.
69. *Newsweek*, January 27, 1947, p. 32.
70. *Roosevelt and Hopkins*, p. 478.
71. Ibid., p. 443.

CHAPTER NINE
1. *The Hinge of Fate*, PB p. 62.
2. *Roosevelt and Churchill: Their Secret Wartime Correspondence*, p. 179.
3. *The Hinge of Fate*, PB p. 181.
4. *Roosevelt and Churchill: Their Secret Wartime Correspondence*, p. 192.
5. *The Hinge of Fate*, PB p. 190.
6. Ibid., PB p. 191.
7. *Roosevelt and Hopkins*, p. 531.
8. *Roosevelt and Churchill: Their Secret Wartime Correspondence*, p. 201.
9. *The Grand Alliance*, PB p. 567.
10. *Roosevelt and Churchill: Their Secret Wartime Correspondence*, p. 201.

11. Ibid., pp. 217–18.

12. Ibid., p. 220.

13. *The War and Colonel Warden*, p. 167.

14. *The Hinge of Fate*, PB p. 327.

15. Ibid., PB pp. 327–28; *The War and Colonel Warden*, pp. 167–68.

16. *The Hinge of Fate*, PB p. 330.

17. William D. Hassett, *Off the Record with FDR, 1942–1945*, p. 67.

18. New York *Times*, June 19, 1942, pp. 1, 2.

19. Ibid., Editorial Page.

20. *The Hinge of Fate*, PB p. 332.

21. Ibid., PB p. 333.

22. Ibid.

23. *Roosevelt and Hopkins*, p. 592.

24. *The Hinge of Fate*, PB p. 334.

25. Ibid., PB pp. 335–36.

26. Ibid., PB p. 334.

27. Dwight D. Eisenhower, *Crusade in Europe*, p. 51.

28. New York *Times*, June 23, 1942, p. 1.

29. Ibid.

30. *Churchill: Taken from the Diaries of Lord Moran*, p. 42.

31. Ibid., p. 43.

32. *The Hinge of Fate*, PB p. 336.

33. Ibid., PB p. 339.

CHAPTER TEN

1. *The Hinge of Fate*, PB p. 354.

2. Ibid., PB pp. 394–95.

3. *Roosevelt and Churchill: Their Secret Wartime Correspondence*, p. 228.

4. *The Hinge of Fate*, PB p. 424.

5. *Roosevelt and Hopkins*, p. 617.

6. *The Hinge of Fate*, PB p. 427.

7. Ibid., PB p. 437.

8. Ibid., PB pp. 470–71.

9. Ibid., PB p. 524.

10. Harold Macmillan, *The Blast of War*, p. 243.

11. *The Hinge of Fate*, PB p. 633.

12. Ibid., PB p. 643.

13. *F.D.R.: His Personal Letters*, pp. 1415–16.

14. *The Hinge of Fate*, PB pp. 680–81.

15. Ibid., PB p. 689.
16. Ibid., PB p. 690.
17. New York *Times*, May 12, 1943, p. 24.
18. *The Hinge of Fate*, PB p. 679.
19. Ibid., PB pp. 691–92.
20. *Churchill: Taken from the Diaries of Lord Moran*, p. 101.
21. *The Hinge of Fate*, PB p. 692.
22. Ibid., PB p. 693.
23. Ibid.
24. New York *Times*, May 16, 1943, Section II, p. 8.
25. Cf. minute to General Ismay dated January 25, 1944, *Closing the Ring*, The Second World War, vol. 5, PB p. 601; and minute to the Foreign Secretary, *Triumph and Tragedy*, The Second World War, vol. 6, PB p. 592.
26. *The Hinge of Fate*, PB p. 693.
27. New York *Times*, May 20, 1943, p. 3.
28. *Churchill: Taken from the Diaries of Lord Moran*, p. 103.
29. *The Hinge of Fate*, PB p. 694.
30. *Churchill: Taken from the Diaries of Lord Moran*, p. 103; *Roosevelt and Hopkins*, p. 729; New York *Times*, May 20, 1943, p. 3.
31. *The Hinge of Fate*, PB p. 700.
32. *Churchill: Taken from the Diaries of Lord Moran*, p. 107.
33. *The Hinge of Fate*, PB p. 704.
34. Ibid.
35. New York *Times*, May 26, 1943, p. 8.
36. *Complete Presidential Press Conferences of Franklin Delano Roosevelt*, Conference no. 899, pp. 340–354.
37. *The Hinge of Fate*, PB p. 704.
38. Ibid., PB p. 708.

CHAPTER ELEVEN

1. *Roosevelt and Churchill: Their Secret Wartime Correspondence*, p. 355.
2. *Closing the Ring*, PB p. 70.
3. *Assignment: Churchill*, p. 280.
4. *Closing the Ring*, PB p. 70.
5. Ibid., PB p. 106.
6. New York *Times*, September 3, 1943, p. 4.
7. *The Atlantic Monthly*, March 1965, p. 79. See also William Rigdon, *White House Sailor*.
8. *Closing the Ring*, PB pp. 95–96.

9. New York *Times*, September 4, 1943, pp. 1, 6.
10. *Sir Winston Churchill: Memorial Addresses and Tributes in the Congress of the United States*, p. 170.
11. *Churchill: Taken from the Diaries of Lord Moran*, p. 124.
12. Ibid.
13. New York *Times*, September 7, 1943, p. 14.
14. *Churchill: Taken from the Diaries of Lord Moran*, p. 125.
15. New York *Times*, September 7, 1943, p. 14.
16. *The Atlantic Monthly*, March 1965, p. 49.
17. *My Darling Clementine*, pp. 208–09.
18. *Closing the Ring*, PB p. 119.
19. *The War and Colonel Warden*, p. 247. See also speech by Admiral of the Fleet Earl Mountbatten of Burma delivered at the University of Berne, Switzerland, March 4, 1970.
20. *Churchill: Taken from the Diaries of Lord Moran*, p. 126.
21. *Roosevelt and Churchill: Their Secret Wartime Correspondence*, pp. 367–68.

CHAPTER TWELVE

1. *Triumph and Tragedy*, PB p. 391.
2. *Roosevelt and Churchill: Their Secret Wartime Correspondence*, p. 704.
3. Ibid., p. 709.
4. A facsimile of this letter appears in *Man of the Century*, p. 213.
5. *Closing the Ring*, PB p. 536.
6. *Triumph and Tragedy*, PB p. 405.
7. Ibid., p. 635.
8. *The Gathering Storm*, PB p. 596.
9. *Triumph and Tragedy*, PB p. 577.

CHAPTER THIRTEEN

1. *Churchill: Taken from the Diaries of Lord Moran*, p. 328.
2. *Time*, February 11, 1946, p. 90.
3. The Editors of *Life*, *The Unforgettable Winston Churchill*, p. 119.
4. *Churchill: Taken from the Diaries of Lord Moran*, p. 328.
5. *The New Yorker*, January 26, 1946, p. 18.
6. Ibid., p. 19.
7. Press conference excerpts from ibid.; New York *Times*, January 15, 1946, p. 13; and *Newsweek*, January 23, 1946, p. 24.
8. New York *Times*, January 17, 1946, p. 26.
9. *Roosevelt and Hopkins*, p. 930.

10. New York *Times*, January 30, 1946.
11. Ibid., February 13, 1946.
12. Ibid., February 18, 1946, p. 8.
13. *Newsweek*, March 18, 1946, p. 30.
14. See *Triumph and Tragedy*, PB p. 489.
15. New York *Times*, March 7, 1946, p. 1.
16. Quoted in *Time*, March 18, 1946, p. 19.
17. New York *Times*, March 7, 1946, p. 5.
18. Ibid., March 6, 1946, p. 26.
19. Dean Acheson, *Sketches from Life of Men I Have Known*, pp. 62–63.
20. New York *Times*, March 9, 1946, p. 3; *Time*, March 18, 1946, pp. 18–19.
21. *The Hinge of Fate*, PB pp. 336–37; *Time*, March 25, 1946, p. 25.
22. New York *Times*, March 13, 1946.
23. Grover Whelan, *Mr. New York*, p. 263.
24. New York *Times*, March 15, 1946.
25. *Mr. New York*, p. 266.
26. Ibid., p. 269; New York *Times*, March 16, 1946, p. 3.
27. New York *Times*, March 16, 1946, p. 3.
28. *Mr. New York*, p. 270.
29. New York *Times*, March 16, 1946, p. 2.
30. Ibid., p. 12.
31. Ibid., March 20, 1946.
32. Ibid., March 22, 1946, p. 3.

CHAPTER FOURTEEN

1. New York *Times*, March 24, 1949, p. 6.
2. Ibid., p. 1.
3. Ibid., p. 6.
4. Ibid., March 26, 1949.
5. *My Early Life*, p. 127.
6. New York *Times*, March 26, 1949.
7. *Irrepressible Churchill*, p. 90.
8. UPI dispatch, March 30, 1949; New York *Times*, March 31, 1949, p. 2.
9. New York *Times*, April 1, 1949, p. 10.
10. *My Darling Clementine*, pp. 326–27.
11. New York *Times*, April 2, 1949.
12. Ibid., April 3, 1949.
13. Ibid., Section IV, p. 8.

CHAPTER FIFTEEN

1. New York *Times*, January 1, 1952, p. 6; January 2, 1952, p. 14.
2. Ibid., January 3, 1952, p. 1.
3. *Newsweek*, January 21, 1952, p. 25.
4. New York *Times*, January 4, 1952, p. 1.
5. Dean Acheson, *Present at the Creation*, p. 592.
6. *Churchill: Taken from the Diaries of Lord Moran*, pp. 376–77.
7. New York *Times*, January 6, 1952, p. 64.
8. Ibid.
9. Ibid., p. 1.
10. Ibid., p. 64.
11. Ibid., January 6, 1952, and January 8, 1952; *Time*, January 14, 1952.
12. *Present at the Creation*, p. 597.
13. *Churchill: Taken from the Diaries of Lord Moran*, p. 378.
14. New York *Times*, January 6, 1952, Section IV, p. 8.
15. *Present at the Creation*, p. 600.
16. New York *Times*, January 7, 1952, p. 1.
17. *Churchill: Taken from the Diaries of Lord Moran*, p. 379.
18. New York *Times*, January 8, 1952, p. 8.
19. *Present at the Creation*, p. 599.
20. New York *Times*, January 9, 1952, p. 1.
21. *Time*, January 21, 1952.
22. *Churchill: Taken from the Diaries of Lord Moran*, p. 386.
23. Ibid., p. 389.
24. New York *Times*, January 17, 1952, p. 5.
25. Ibid., January 18, 1952, p. 4.
26. *Present at the Creation*, pp. 601–02.
27. *Sketches from Life*, p. 66.
28. Ibid., pp. 67–69; *Present at the Creation*, pp. 602–03.
29. *Churchill: Taken from the Diaries of Lord Moran*, p. 393.
30. *Newsweek*, January 21, 1952, p. 26.
31. *Churchill: Taken from the Diaries of Lord Moran*, p. 396.

CHAPTER SIXTEEN

1. Baruch Papers.
2. New York *Times*, January 5, 1953, p. 20.
3. Ibid., January 6, 1953, p. 10.
4. Ibid.; also January 8, 1953, p. 4.
5. J. W. Wheeler-Bennett, ed., *Action This Day: Working with Churchill*, p. 130.

6. *Time*, January 19, 1953, p. 16.
7. *Action This Day*, p. 130.
8. Ralph G. Martin, *Jennie*, vol. 1, PB pp. 18–19, 324–25.
9. *The New Yorker*, January 17, 1953, pp. 20–21; New York *Times*, January 8, 1953, p. 4.
10. *Present at the Creation*, p. 715.
11. New York *Times*, January 9, 1953, p. 3.
12. *Sketches from Life*, p. 78.
13. Ibid.

CHAPTER SEVENTEEN

1. *Churchill: Taken from the Diaries of Lord Moran*, p. 540.
2. Ibid., p. 595.
3. New York *Times*, June 26, 1954, p. 1.
4. *Churchill: Taken from the Diaries of Lord Moran*, p. 596.
5. New York *Times*, June 27, 1954, p. 3.
6. *Churchill: Taken from the Diaries of Lord Moran*, pp. 599–601.
7. New York *Times*, June 29, 1954, p. 1.
8. Ibid.
9. Ibid., p. 2.
10. Ibid.
11. Ibid.
12. Ibid.
13. Ibid., p. 3.
14. *Time*, July 5, 1954, p. 9.
15. *Action This Day*, p. 132.

CHAPTER EIGHTEEN

1. *The Hinge of Fate*, PB pp. 799–800.
2. *A Thread in the Tapestry*, p. 19.
3. Baruch Papers.
4. *Churchill: Taken from the Diaries of Lord Moran*, p. 799.
5. New York *Times*, May 5, 1959, p. 1.
6. Ibid., p. 2.
7. John S. D. Eisenhower, *Strictly Personal*, p. 232.
8. *Time*, May 18, 1959, p. 19.
9. New York *Times*, May 7, 1959, p. 1.
10. Ibid., January 8, 1953, pp. 1, 4.
11. Ibid., June 26, 1954, p. 3.
12. *Churchill: Taken from the Diaries of Lord Moran*, p. 800.
13. *Time*, May 18, 1959, p. 20.
14. New York *Times*, May 8, 1959, p. 3.

15. Ibid., May 9, 1959.
16. Ibid., May 11, 1959, p. 3.

CHAPTER NINETEEN

1. *Winston S. Churchill,* companion vol. 1, part 1, p. 595.
2. New York *Times,* April 13, 1961, p. 5; New York *Herald Tribune,* April 13, 1961, p. 23.
3. *Herald Tribune,* ibid.
4. *Newsweek,* April 24, 1961, p. 33.
5. New York *Times,* April 14, 1961, p. 2.
6. *Newsweek,* April 24, 1961, p. 33.

CHAPTER TWENTY

1. Winston S. Churchill, *Marlborough: His Life and Times,* vol. 4, PB p. 919.
2. *Winston Churchill on America and Britain,* p. 42.
3. London *Times,* January 18, 1965.
4. Speech by Admiral of the Fleet Earl Mountbatten of Burma delivered at the University of Berne, Switzerland, March 4, 1970.
5. George Bernard Shaw, *Plays: Pleasant and Unpleasant,* vol. 1, p. 2.
6. *The Gathering Storm,* p. 423.
7. Winston S. Churchill, *The World Crisis,* vol. 2, p. 22.
8. *Triumph and Tragedy,* p. 341.

Bibliography

NOTE: For the reader who wishes to learn about Churchill in depth, but who does not wish to wade through the vast literature concerning his life, I venture to recommend three books which, read consecutively, will convey a very detailed picture of his accomplishments and personality. The first book is *My Early Life*, by Churchill himself, far and away the most delightful work he ever published. *My Early Life* covers the years 1874 to 1901 and serves as an admirable companion to the first volume of the official biography, which covers the same period. The second book is *Churchill: A Study in Failure*, by Robert Rhodes James. James focuses on the period from 1900 to 1939 and gives a lively and urbane, if not always meticulously accurate, account of Winston's ups and downs during those years. The final book is *Churchill: Taken from the Diaries of Lord Moran*. Moran (Sir Charles Wilson) shepherded Churchill through the war years and the final two decades of his life. His recollections give much the most intimate look at Churchill's psyche that can be found in print.

Acheson, Dean. *Present at the Creation: My Years in the State Department.* New York: W. W. Norton, 1969.
———. *Sketches from Life of Men I Have Known.* New York: Harper & Brothers, 1961.
Adamic, Louis. *Dinner at the White House.* New York: Harper & Brothers, 1946.
Adler, Bill. *The Churchill Wit.* New York: Coward McCann, 1965.
American Heritage Magazine and United Press International, comps. *Churchill: The Life Triumphant.* New York: American Heritage Publishing Company, 1965.
Berlin, Isaiah. *Mr. Churchill in 1940.* Boston: Houghton Mifflin, 1964.
Bonham-Carter, Violet. *Winston Churchill: An Intimate Portrait.* New York: Harcourt, Brace & World, 1965.

Bryant, Arthur. *The Turn of the Tide*. Garden City, N.Y.: Double-day & Company, 1957.

Churchill, John Spencer. *A Churchill Canvas*. Boston: Little, Brown, 1961.

Churchill, Randolph S. *Twenty-one Years*. Boston: Houghton Mifflin, 1965.

————. *Winston S. Churchill*. Vols. 1 and 2 and companion vols. Boston: Houghton Mifflin, 1966, 1967.

Churchill, Sarah. *A Thread in the Tapestry*. New York: Dodd, Mead, 1967.

Churchill, Winston S. *Amid These Storms*. New York: Charles Scribner's Sons, 1932.

————. *Great Contemporaries*. Chicago: University of Chicago Press, 1973.

————. *Marlborough: His Life and Times*. 4 vols. New York: Charles Scribner's Sons, 1933–38.

————. *My Early Life: A Roving Commission*. New York: Charles Scribner's Sons, 1930.

————. *The River War*. New York: Longmans, Green, 1899.

————. *Savrola*. New York: Longmans, Green, 1900.

————. *The Second World War*. 6 vols. Boston: Houghton Mifflin, 1948–54.

————. *The World Crisis*. 6 vols. Reissue. New York: Charles Scribner's Sons, 1963–64.

————. *Sir Winston Churchill: Memorial Addresses and Tributes in the Congress of the United States*. Washington: U.S. Government Printing Office, 1965.

Coit, Margaret. *Mr. Baruch*. Boston: Houghton Mifflin, 1957.

Davis, Richard Harding. *The Young Winston Churchill*. Austin, Texas: Pemberton Press, 1964.

Eade, Charles, ed. *Churchill by His Contemporaries*. New York: Simon & Schuster, 1953.

————. *The War Speeches of Winston S. Churchill*. Boston: Little, Brown, 1942–46.

Eisenhower, Dwight D. *Crusade in Europe*. Garden City, N.Y.: Doubleday & Company, 1948.

————. *General Eisenhower on the Military Churchill: A Conversation with Alistair Cooke*, New York: W. W. Norton, 1970.

Eisenhower, John S. D. *Strictly Personal*. Garden City, N.Y.: Doubleday & Company, 1974.

Fishman, Jack. *My Darling Clementine*. New York: David McKay, 1963.

Friedel, Frank. *Franklin Delano Roosevelt: The Apprenticeship.* Boston: Little, Brown, 1952.

Gilbert, Martin. *Churchill: A Photographic Portrait.* Boston: Houghton Mifflin, 1974.

——. *Winston S. Churchill.* Vol. 3 and companion vols. Boston: Houghton Mifflin, 1971.

Gilbert, Martin, ed. *Churchill.* Great Lives Observed. Englewood Cliffs, N.J.: Prentice-Hall, 1967.

Guiles, Fred L. *The Intimate Biography of Marion Davies.* New York: McGraw Hill, 1972.

Halle, Kay, ed. *Irrepressible Churchill.* Cleveland: World Publishing Company, 1966.

——. *Winston Churchill on America and Britain.* New York: Walker & Company, 1970.

Harrity, Richard, and R. G. Martin. *Man of the Century: Churchill.* New York: Duell, Sloan & Pearce, 1962.

Hassett, William D. *Off the Record with FDR, 1942–1945.* New Brunswick, N.J.: Rutgers University Press, 1958.

Hoover, Herbert C. *The Memoirs of Herbert Hoover.* Vol. 1, *Years of Adventure, 1874–1920.* New York: Macmillan, 1952.

Howells, Roy. *Churchill's Last Years.* New York: David McKay, 1966.

James, Robert Rhodes. *Churchill: A Study in Failure.* New York: World Publishing Company, 1970.

Life, eds. of. *The Unforgettable Winston Churchill.* New York: Time-Life Books, 1965.

Longford, Elizabeth. *Winston Churchill.* New York: Rand McNally, 1974.

Lowenheim, Francis, Langley, Harold D., and Jonas, Manfred, eds. *Roosevelt and Churchill: Their Secret Wartime Correspondence.* New York: Saturday Review Press/Dutton, 1975.

Macmillan, Harold. *The Blast of War.* New York: Harper & Row, 1968.

Marshall, George C. *Memoirs of My Services in the World War, 1917–18.* Boston: Houghton Mifflin, 1976.

Martin, Ralph G. *Jennie.* 2 vols. Englewood Cliffs, N.J.: Prentice-Hall, 1969, 1971.

Moir, Phyllis. *I Was Winston Churchill's Private Secretary.* New York: W. Funk, 1941.

Oxford and Asquith, Earl of. *Memories and Reflections.* 2 vols. Boston: Little, Brown, 1928.

Pawle, Gerald. *The War and Colonel Warden*. New York: Alfred A. Knopf, 1963.

Pelling, Henry. *Winston Churchill*. New York: E. P. Dutton, 1974.

Pogue, Forrest C. *George C. Marshall: Ordeal and Hope*. New York: The Viking Press, 1966.

Rigdon, William. *White House Sailor*. Garden City, N.Y.: Doubleday & Company, 1962.

Roosevelt, Anna Eleanor. *This I Remember*. New York: Harper & Brothers, 1949.

Roosevelt, Elliott, et al., eds. *F.D.R.: His Personal Letters 1905–1928*. 3 vols. New York: Duell, Sloan & Pearce, 1947–50.

Roosevelt, Franklin D. *Complete Presidential Press Conferences of Franklin Delano Roosevelt*, 12 vols. New York: Da Capo Press, 1972.

Roosevelt, Theodore. *The Letters of Theodore Roosevelt*. 8 vols. Edited by Elting E. Morison. Cambridge, Mass.: Harvard University Press, 1951–54.

Sherwood, Robert E. *Roosevelt and Hopkins*. New York: Harper & Brothers, 1948.

Shirer, William L. *The Rise and Fall of the Third Reich*. New York: Simon & Schuster, 1960; Fawcett World Library, 1972.

Sproat, Ian, and Sykes, Adam. *The Wit of Sir Winston*. London: L. Frewin, 1965.

Taylor, A. J. P., et al. *Churchill Revised*. New York: Dial Press, 1969.

Thompson, R. W. *Churchill: The Yankee Marlborough*. Garden City, N.Y.: Doubleday & Company, 1963.

Thompson, Walter H. *Assignment: Churchill*. New York: Farrar, Straus and Young, 1955.

Whalen, Grover. *Mr. New York*. New York: G. P. Putnam's Sons, 1955.

Wheeler-Bennett, J. W., ed. *Action This Day: Working with Churchill*. New York: St. Martin's Press, 1969.

Wilson, Charles. *Churchill: Taken from the Diaries of Lord Moran*. Boston: Houghton Mifflin, 1966.

NEWSPAPERS

American
Atlanta *Constitution*
Baltimore *Sun*

Boston *Evening Transcript*
Boston *Globe*
Boston *Herald*
Chicago *Tribune*
Hartford *Courant*
New Haven *Evening Register*
New Haven *Morning Journal*
New Orleans *Times-Picayune*
New York *Herald Tribune*
New York *Times*
New York *Tribune*
San Francisco *Chronicle*
Springfield *Republican*
Washington *Post*

British
London *Daily Mail*
London *Daily Telegraph*
The Times

MAGAZINES
The Atlantic Monthly
Michigan Quarterly Review
Newsweek
The New Yorker
Time

Index